ANALYTICAL PERSPECTIVES ON THE INDIAN ECONOMY

ANALYTICAL PERSPECTIVES ON THE INDIAN ECONOMY

Editors
Ankur Bhatnagar
C. Saratchand

AAKAR

Analytical Perspectives on the Indian Economy
Ankur Bhatnagar and C. Saratchand

First Published 2019

ISBN 978-93-5002-594-9

Published by
AAKAR BOOKS
28 E Pocket IV, Mayur Vihar Phase I
Delhi 110 091 India
aakarbooks@gmail.com

Laser Typeset at
Arpit Printographers, Delhi 110 032

Printed at
DK Fine Art Press, Delhi

Contents

Introduction

This book has emerged out of a National Conference on the topic 'Contemporary Challenges Before the Indian Economy' held at Satyawati College, Delhi University on March 8-9, 2017. While some papers were specially comissioned for this volume, all the authors were involved in the Conference. The papers in this volume encompass a number of themes including industry, agriculture, inequality and education.

Chapter 1 provides a brief overview of the Indian economic experience since 1947 and highlights the political economy concerns that remain relevant today including unemployment, inequality and secularism. Chapter 2 seeks to understand the macroeconomic dimensions of the impasse that the Indian economy finds itself in during the second decade of the 21st century when the growth path based on cheap labour has run aground. Chapter 3 argues that inflation in India is primarily on account of the rise in oil prices (or primary commodities) for a given share of profits in output. Inflation targeting monetary policy which squeezes the share of wages in output may temporarily reduce the rate of inflation but will also squeeze demand. Chapter 4 is a detailed examination of the short run and long run transmission of international prices on domestic prices of rice and wheat.

Chapter 5 examines the consequences of the neoliberal regime in India on agriculture and argues that agrarian distress may be overcome by state intervention whose objective is the ensuring of a stable path of income growth for small and marginal farmers.

Chapter 6 examines the role of the interaction between social oppression with class exploitation in explaining the educational and income inequality between and within different social groups. Chapter 7 explores another dimension of educational inequality between students of government schools and those of private schools. Chapter 8 reviews the experience of Turkey with neoliberal educational policies and draws lessons for India in the light of similar moves by the Indian government. Chapter 9 calls for a reappraisal of the teaching of Economics in India in the backdrop of the world economic crisis that began in the last decade and urges for the incorporation of insights from psychology and sociology. Chapter 10 probes into the gender dimension of public transport in India and argues that government policy has at best been protectionist while the need is for incorporating gender equality concerns into policy making on public transport.

The essays in this volume will be of interest to diverse segments of teachers, students, researchers and professionals in the development sector. Even when the readers may not concur with the conclusions of an author the analysis presented by each author will provide a framework for them to pose their own questions.

1

India's Economic Development: An Assessment

Pulin B. Nayak

I

The year 2017 marks the 70th year of India's independence from colonial subjugation. At the stroke of the midnight hour on August 15, 1947, Pandit Nehru had addressed the nation with the stirring words: 'Long years ago we made a tryst with destiny, and now the time comes when we shall redeem our pledge, not wholly or in full measure, but very substantially'. Seventy years are possibly a long enough time period: long enough for a human being to have lived a full life and to hope for some years of retirement and reflection. But for a country of subcontinental proportions, seven decades would perhaps constitute a minor span in her rich civilizational history that extends over several millennia. In his *Glimpses of World History*, Nehru (1934-35, 1991) wrote that at the end of 1,000 years after Christ, 'the old civilizations of India and China still continue and flourish. Indian culture spreads to Malaysia and Cambodia and brings rich fruit there...trade and learning and the arts flourish; great cities abound; and famous universities attract students from afar' (p. 179).

By the beginning of the 20th century India's condition had changed rather dramatically for the worse. After the annexation of large chunks of India by the British East India Company from the 18th century onwards and the gradual subjugation of the entire Indian subcontinent, British imperial policy had ensured greater penetration of British mill goods into the Indian market and the steady decline of Indian home grown cottage and small industry, leading to a general process of 'de-industrialization'. The grand old man of India, Dadabhai Naoroji (1901), was also able to convincingly demonstrate that there was a massive drain of wealth from India to the colonial master country, Britain.

The rate of growth of the Indian economy during the half century before her independence was under 1%. Famines occurred with regular frequency, the last major one being the great Bengal famine of 1943. Sutherland (1908) points out that during 1800-80, no less than 18 million Indians perished in various famines. In the very year 1857 when Queen Victoria assumed the title of Empress, 5 million people in Southern India were starved to death. The British left India with a very low level of per capita income and extremely poor levels of achievement in education and health. To their credit they had helped set up the rail network, the post and telegraph system, the general administration, the police system and the judiciary, among others. However, there is no denying that the average Indian lived a wretched existence.

On taking over the reins of the government in 1947 of a partitioned country the task before the new ministry under Nehru was nothing short of stupendous. For long, prior to this conjuncture, Nehru had been attracted to the idea of planning. In 1927 he had in fact visited the USSR at the invitation of the Soviet government on the occasion of the 10th anniversary of the October Revolution. The USSR was well on its path of economic development and the Soviets were to embark on their first five year plan in 1928. Nehru was impressed with what he saw and was determined to introduce planning in India as soon as it was politically feasible.

It was Nehru who was called upon by Subhas Chandra Bose, the Congress President, to Chair the National Planning Committee in 1938. It consisted of 15 members plus representatives of provincial governments and such Indian states as chose to collaborate with the Congress Party. 'It was a strange assortment of different types and it was not clear how such an odd mixture would work', Nehru (1946) was to write later in the *The Discovery of India*. Yet the group was able to come up with concrete suggestions regarding agriculture, industry, unemployment, literacy and medical services, among others. It was of course obvious that the country's independence was a prerequisite to the implementation of any of the blueprints.

II

It is of course well known that Mahatma Gandhi's ideas on development were considerably at variance from the views held by Nehru. In his *Hind Swaraj*, Gandhiji (1909) had made a case for self-sufficient village republics. He was against industrialization and machinery, especially when the latter displaced labour, because he believed that the key to India's economic resurgence lay in removing the massive burden of unemployment. Nehru, in contrast, was for modernization and industrialization. He believed that it is this which will ultimately be required to solve the problem of open and disguised unemployment both in the rural and urban areas. Gandhi had tried his best to sort out these differences with Nehru in the mid-1940s, but without any major success, and each held on to his views quite resolutely.

Gandhiji's assassination in January 1948 made Nehru the supreme arbiter of the country's economic management, and true to his long-standing conviction, the Planning Commission was set up in 1950. The First Five Year Plan was initiated in 1951 with a fairly balanced allocation of resources between agriculture, industry and the tertiary sectors. It was the Second Five Year Plan (1956-61), which, following the formulations of the Russian economist Feldman and our physicist statistician Mahalanobis, emphasized the importance of the capital goods sector, relative to the consumption goods sector, in order to bring about a faster rate of growth for the economy. Nehru, too, owned this model, and the idea soon came to be known as the Nehru-Mahalanobis model.

It was in this period that a massive inpetus was given to setting up of the heavy industries sector, and units were set up in Ranchi and Bhopal. The three steel plants in Bhilai, Rourkela and

Durgapur were also commissioned at this time. But there were other aspects too. Nehru was conscious of the importance of the building up of human capital in the development of any country and it is during this period that a massive push was given to the growth of higher and professional education by making ample allocations for new universities, the new IITs and IIMs, the AIIMS in Delhi and institutions of fundamental research like the Council of Scientific and Industrial Research (CSIR). Lest one were to conclude that agriculture was left out, it should be mentioned that during this period large allocations were also made for setting up research centres for rice, wheat and agricultural research generally and institutions like the Indian Council of Agricultural Research (ICAR) came into their own.

Despite the intense debates between Gandhi and Nehru during the mid-1940s regarding the relative importance to be attached to agriculture and industry, it is possible to say that about a decade after the introduction of centralized planning in India, Nehru became more, not less, appreciative of the importance of agriculture and therefore came closer to his mentor's essential position. The formulation of the Third Five Year Plan (1961-66) was Nehru's last intellectual engagement with the idea of planning. As the Chairman of the Commission he was known to be always careful about the drafting of the 'approach' document to the plan. At the very beginning of this document, we have:

> In the scheme of development during the Third Plan, the first priority necessarily belongs to agriculture. Experience in the first two Plans, and especially in the Second, has shown that the rate of growth of agricultural production is one of the main limiting factors in the progress of the Indian economy. Agricultural production has, therefore, to be increased to the largest extent feasible, and adequate resources have to be provided under the Third Plan for realizing the agricultural targets (Planning Commission, 1961).

III

The Indian economy grew at the 'Hindu' rate of about 3.5 to 4% during the first three decades of relatively autarkic planning. During Indira Gandhi's second stint as Prime Minister beginning in 1980, there were many pressures to free the economy as well as to open it up to the external sector. The process continued through Rajiv Gandhi's tenure as well, and the result was a step up of the GDP growth rate in the decade of the 1980s to somewhere in the region of about 5 to 5.5%. This was definitely an improvement over the earlier tepid growth over a long span of three decades. Yet, at the beginning of the last decade of the 20th century poverty was still substantial in large tracts of the country, especially in tribal and drought-prone dry areas. There was a strong point of view expressed in several quarters that opportunities had been missed in the early years of independence, and a strong course correction was needed. Indeed there has been much in the recent media, mistaken and motivated in my view, which puts the blame on all our present-day ills at Nehru's doorstep.

The course correction in economic policy that was brought about in 1991 was the result of the twin crises in the fiscal as well as the foreign trade sectors. During the decade of the 1980s the hegemony of the old Congress Party was slowly crumbling and a number of regional parties came to the fore. This led to a phase of political populism that had its counterpart in fiscal giveaways. The combined fiscal deficit of the Centre and the states had regularly been in the range of about 10% of GDP, subsidies and loan waivers were the order of the day, and the national debt was mounting. The foreign trade sector had been stressed for a long time with the annual import bill far outstripping our export earnings, and during the brief tenure of Chandra Shekhar as Prime Minister, the reserves of foreign exchange were down to barely two weeks' import bill, which naturally set alarm bells ringing.

It is in this setting that the Congress Party returned to power with a huge mandate after the assassination of Rajiv Gandhi, and the new Prime Minister Narasimha Rao took a call on 'economic reforms', an idea—as Victor Hugo had observed, and as Finance Minister Dr Manmohan Singh very appositely proclaimed in the Lok Sabha—whose time had come. Broad based reforms were introduced in fiscal, monetary and trade sectors, as well as in agriculture and industry. The omniscient role of the state was now underplayed; and the state was now to perform the role more of a facilitator than doer, and the sphere of the market and incentives had now to be widened substantially. A lot of the pent up animal spirits were raring to go in the Indian economy for quite some time, and the results were almost immediate. The growth rate of GDP touched the 6 to 6.5% range in the last decade of the 20th century.

As the country was entering the new millennium there were two nagging features of the economy that continued to vex our leaders and thinkers, and the issues remain valid concerns even today. The percentage of the population below the poverty line still continued to hover around the 30% range in 2000, too high for comfort, and there was hardly any major addition to jobs in the organized sector, giving rise to the epithet of 'jobless growth'.

It is only in the first decade of this millennium that the growth rate of India's GDP touched the 9% plus range during 2005-08, a feat that China had perfected over the previous quarter century on a sustained basis. But the realization now dawned on the Indian policy makers as well as the world media that India's achievement was not simply a one off phenomenon for a single year; it had been sustained over three consecutive years. What had clearly helped was that the gross savings and investment rates of the Indian economy had by now touched the 35% of GDP zone, and with a capital:output ratio of around 4, the crude Harrod-Domar formulation in fact predicted a 9% plus growth rate.

After the onset of the economic reforms of 1991, much of the Indian economy, especially the services sector and IT in particular, had now been operating in a globalized setting, and it was indeed IT that was the key driver of the growth figures. The international financial crisis of 2008 put a serious dampener on the Indian growth rate, and within a few years, by 2013-14, the growth rate had declined to the sub 5% level. But fortunately the Indian economy was relatively still unscathed when one noted that Europe, North America and Japan were all experiencing even lower growth, in the range of barely 2 to 3 per cent, and, in fact, some economies like those of Brazil and Russia, went through negative growth rates during 2014-15.

The past two years have placed India not only at the high table of the fastest growing major economies of the world, but what is more, India now finds itself at the head of the table. It is a matter of some interest to note that India seems to have even tipped the mighty China. Two years ago, India's growth rate was 7.6% and China was at 7.1%. Latest computations of the World Bank suggest that India's GDP is set to grow at 7.2% in 2017-18. The report goes on to say: 'India remains the fastest growing economy in the world and it will get a big boost from its approach to GST which will reduce the cost of doing business for firms, reduce logistics costs of moving goods across states, while ensuring no loss in equity' (*Indian Express*, New Delhi, May 30, 2017).

IV

It is now time for us to conclude. Even till as late as the end of the past century, few analysts anywhere in the world would have predicted that in less than two decades India would emerge as the fastest growing major economy of the world. But this has now happened for at least two years now. Our development process has a lot to answer for, and we shall briefly touch on these presently, but this is no mean achievement. It also goes to show that there must have been certain core policies adopted somewhere during our economic management which has brought us to this happy pass. It would be a no brainer to assert that a country simply does not become the fastest growing country in the world overnight. It is difficult to pinpoint what precisely has brought this about, but one could possibly hazard some hypotheses. First, the emphasis on a pivotal role of the state in promoting education at all stages, and in particular, the growth of the IITs, medical colleges and the university system from the mid 1950s onwards. Second, an extended and widely divergent industrial base, as well as a large infrastructure sector, which has received constant push from the policy makers. Third, our commitment to political democracy and a free and active media, which immediately alerts the policy makers when they go wrong. Fourth, a broad consensus that seems to have emerged in the past two decades amongst the major political parties of the country, regardless of their ideological hue, that economic reforms are here to stay and that we would not go back to a purely statist kind of mindset in the coming years.

While giving ourselves encomiums it would be wrong on our part to ignore some of the glaring problems of our political economy that stare us in the face. While in percentage terms the poverty ratio has dropped somewhat, the absolute number of poor continue to be staggeringly large. The performance in terms of job creation has been hopelessly poor. And most worryingly, there is plenty of evidence to show that inequalities of income and wealth are getting sharper by the day. The ecology is very severely degraded. Politically and socially there appear to be extraordinarily serious strains. Under the present political dispensation the secular fabric of the country is possibly going through its severest travail that the minorities have known in recent decades. These are not positive auguries. It is not enough to sit at the head of the high table of the fastest growing countries if we are not able to ensure a more humane and just world for all citizens of this great country of astounding diversity with its rich civilizational past.

(Note: A slightly longer version of this paper appeared in Uma Kapila (ed), *India's Economy: Pre-Liberalisation to GST*, Academic Foundation, New Delhi, 2017.)

REFERENCES

Gandhi, Mohandas Karamchand (1909). *Hind Swaraj* (*Indian Home Rule*), Navjivan Publishing House, Ahmedabad.

Indian Express (2017). World Bank Pegs India's Economic Growth at 7.2% This Financial Year, ENS Economic Bureau, New Delhi, May 30, 2017.

Naoroji, Dadabhai (1901). *Poverty and Un-British Rule in India*, Swan Sonnenschein & Co., London.

Nehru, Jawaharlal (1934-35, 1991). *Glimpses of World History*, Kitabistan, Allahabad, and Oxford University Press, New Delhi.

Nehru, Jawaharlal (1946, 1982). *The Discovery of India*, The Signet Press, Calcutta, and Oxford University Press, New Delhi.

Planning Commission (1961). The Third Five Year Plan, Government of India.

Sutherland, Jabez T. (1908). 'The New Nationalist Movement in India', *The Atlantic Monthly*, Washington, D.C.

2

The Indian Economy in the Second Decade of the 21st Century: Signs of a Crisis?

Surajit Mazumdar

Introduction

While there are many who may baulk at using such a strong term as 'crisis' to describe the state of the Indian economy in the second decade of the 21st century, the word crisis does fit the situation very well even if this is not obvious at first sight. If an economy is stuck in a situation where its spontaneous economic processes have put a brake on its path of economic expansion and the prospects of any self-correcting tendency emerging are remote, then one could perhaps justifiably say that such an economy confronts a crisis. There are reasons to believe that the Indian economy may currently be in precisely such a phase of its history.

The most obvious challenge to any crisis thesis would be of course India's GDP growth record. It would be argued that India has been growing at a reasonably quick clip in the last few years—not as rapidly as in the first decade of the century but much faster than almost all the other countries in the world. How can growth rates tending to be in the 6-7% per annum range reflect a crisis? The first point to note, however, is that these growth rates emerge from the controversial new GDP series with 2011-12 as the base year on which there has been extensive debate (Goldar (2015), Mazumdar (2015), Nagaraj (2015), Rajakumar (2016). There are many who hold the view that the new series overestimates the

Indian growth rate. A case for India experiencing a crisis can however be made even if it is conceded that the overall GDP growth rate is what the new series shows it to be, or would still be at a reasonable level of 5% per annum or thereabouts after adjustments are made for any overestimation. GDP is after all only an aggregate and only one indicator of the pace of economic expansion. It is when one goes behind this aggregate that the picture of crisis becomes visible.

The Slowdown and its Features

To establish the fact that the second decade of the century saw a transition to a crisis, we undertake a simple exercise of comparing the movement of some selected variables in two time-periods of equal length which we define as Periods 1 and 2. Period 1 spans the years 2002-03 to 2007-08 and Period 2 from 2011-12 to 2016-17.

There is a case for such a comparison. Period 1, which ended with the onset of the global crisis, marked a transition to unprecedentedly high GDP growth rates. Till then, the major turning point in India's post-independence growth history had been way back in 1980 when the growth rate moved up from the 'Hindu rate of growth' (3.5% per annum) to levels between 5-6% (Virmani (2004)). Indeed, the absence of any acceleration in the growth rate after 1991, when the more substantive economic 'reforms' were undertaken, had led to a debate about how much of the shift to a higher growth trajectory could be attributed to economic liberalization (Rodrik and Subramaniam (2004), Panagariya (2004), Srinivasan (2005)). The year 2011-12 on the other hand was one in which at least the older GDP series indicated the onset of a slowdown after a brief period of growth revival following the drop in the immediate aftermath of the global crisis. Whether the high growth phase in the early part of the century marked a long-term shift of India's growth trajectory, or was it a temporary phase, can be at least partially assessed by examining whether the features that went with it were sustained beyond that phase. Period 1 was also significant as the one phase in the post-1991 period in which the tax-GDP ratio improved significantly and the share of direct taxes in total taxes increased. This allowed a stepping up of public expenditure growth alongside a process of reduction in the fiscal deficit to the GDP ratio. However, the post-crisis stimulus package led to a slippage on the tax front while expenditure growth persisted for a few years, resulting in the fiscal deficit climbing sharply. The year 2011-12 then marked the reversion to fiscal consolidation in which the consistent emphasis was on curbing public expenditure while the recovery on the tax revenue side was slower and driven more by indirect taxes. Finally, the two periods also fall in different phases of the global economy —the first in the phase of the developing economy centred global boom and the second in which the global conditions are more subdued, and austerity has tended to rule everywhere.

To facilitate the comparison between Periods 1 and 2, we designate the first year of each of them as their respective Year 0, the next year as Year 1 and so on till Year 6. In other words, 2002-03 would be Year 0 of Period 1 and 2011-12 would be the Year 0 for Period 2, and 2007-08 and 2016-17 would be their respective Year 6s. Further, each of the variables for both periods are converted into indices with their respective Year 0 as the base year.

The first comparison we undertake is of the movement of output of different broad sectors of the economy in the two periods from their respective base year levels. This is summed up in Table 1 (and graphically represented in Appendix Figure 1). For Period 1 we consider GDP at Factor Cost in each sector at constant 2004-05 prices, while for Period 2 we take at GVA at Basic Prices at constant 2011-12 prices as the measure of output.

Table 1 clearly shows that every sector's growth performance in Period 2 has been below the level in Period 1. However, the degree to which this is the case varies across sectors. The services performance in the two periods are relatively similar but the gap is particularly marked for the agricultural and construction sectors. In the case of agriculture, the comparison of the movement of the separately available index of agricultural production in the two periods corroborates the story emerging from the value-added data (Table 2). However, the situation is different for the industrial sector. The index of industrial production, even the new series introduced recently with 2011-12 as the base year, indicates a much sharper slowing down of industrial and manufacturing growth in Period 2 (Table 3) than that indicated by the GDP/GVA trends. This difference in Period 2 between the GVA trend and the IIP trend in the case of manufacturing clearly is on account of the changed method of measuring manufacturing value added adopted in the new GDP series—which is obscuring the stark picture of industrial stagnation that IIP data brings out.

Table 1: Indices of GDP at Factor Cost/GVA at Basic Prices (at Constant Prices) for Periods 1 and 2 (Respective Year 0 = 100)

Sector	*Period*	*Year 0*	*Year 1*	*Year 2*	*Year 3*	*Year 4*	*Year 5*
Agriculture & Allied Activities	Period 1	100	109.0	109.2	114.9	119.6	126.6
	Period 2	100	101.5	107.1	106.9	107.7	112.9
Industry	Period 1	100	107.3	117.9	129.3	145.0	159.1
	Period 2	100	103.3	107.2	115.2	125.3	132.3
Manufacturing	Period 1	100	106.3	114.2	125.7	143.7	158.5
	Period 2	100	105.5	110.7	119.8	132.8	143.3
Construction	Period 1	100	112.4	130.8	147.5	162.8	180.3
	Period 2	100	100.3	103.0	107.8	113.2	115.1
Services	Period 1	100	108.1	116.8	129.6	142.6	157.3
	Period 2	100	108.3	116.6	127.9	140.4	151.2

Source: Reserve Bank of India, *Handbook of Statistics on the Indian Economy* [Original Source: Central Statistics Office (CSO)]

Table 2: Indices of Agricultural Production for Periods 1 and 2 (Respective Year 0 = 100)

Year	*Foodgrains*		*Non-Foodgrains*		*All Crops*	
	Period 1	*Period 2*	*Period 1*	*Period 2*	*Period 1*	*Period 2*
Year 0	100.0	100.0	100.0	100.0	100.0	100.0
Year 1	122.5	99.9	91.1	99.5	107.3	99.8
Year 2	113.9	103.2	92.5	105.5	105.6	104.4
Year 3	120.5	97.0	107.3	102.3	118.5	99.8
Year 4	125.4	96.7	128.2	94.4	135.4	95.6
Year 5	133.2	108.5	130.3	94.7	139.5	101.4

Source: Reserve Bank of India, *Handbook of Statistics on the Indian Economy* [Original Source: Ministry of Agriculture & Farmers Welfare, Government of India]

Table 3: Indices of Industrial Production for Periods 1 and 2 (Respective Year 0 = 100)

	Manufacturing			*General Index*		
	Period 1	*Period 2 (2004-05 Series)*	*Period 2 (2011-12 Series)*	*Period 1*	*Period 2 (2004-5 Series)*	*Period 2 (2011-12 Series)*
Year 0	100	100	100	100	100	100
Year 1	107.4	101.3	104.8	107.0	101.1	103.3
Year 2	121.5	100.5	108.6	119.5	101.0	106.7
Year 3	134.0	102.8	112.7	129.8	103.9	111.0
Year 4	154.1	104.9	115.9	146.6	106.4	114.7
Year 5	182.4	104.9	121.0	169.3	106.4*	120.0

*Based on April-February Average

Source: Reserve Bank of India, *Handbook of Statistics on the Indian Economy* [Original Source: Central Statistics Office (CSO)]

The upshot of this is that not only has growth in Period 2 been more subdued than in Period 1, it has also become even more concentrated in services activities, already the largest sector, with the rest of the economy showing signs of extreme sluggishness. Agriculture, the sector which still accounts for the largest share in employment, has been doing very poorly after the high achieved in 2011-12. From the employment perspective, the sharp and persistent slowdown of the construction sector that had grown quite rapidly since the mid-1990s is also extremely significant. The construction sector has been by far the largest absorber of labour shifting out of agricultural activities—it increased its share in total employment from less than 4% in the early 1990s to 11% in 2011-12, even as agriculture went down from 61% to 49%. The industrial slowdown on the other hand reinforces the story of India experiencing premature de-industrialization (Rodrik (2015)). Indeed, even the more favourable manufacturing output figures in the new GDP series have not been able to prevent the sector's share in GDP from persistently falling.

Are these all signs of a robust process of economic expansion? One should also keep in mind that 'output' of services is not constrained in the same way as that of agriculture and industry, by land and capital constraints. Further, in India unlike elsewhere in the world, the high share of services in GVA is achieved with a relatively extremely low share in employment. In such circumstances, how valid is it to claim a relatively high GDP growth as a significant achievement?

The problems of India's current growth trajectory appear even more sharply if we track the movements in the components of the demand measure of GDP in the two periods. These are presented for most of the major components in Table 4 (graphical representation in Appendix Figure 2).

Table 4: Indices of Components of GDP at Constant Market Prices for Periods 1 and 2 (Respective Year 0 = 100)

Item	*Period*	*Year 0*	*Year 1*	*Year 2*	*Year 3*	*Year 4*	*Year 5*
Private Final Consumption Expenditure	Period 1	100	105.9	111.4	121.0	131.3	143.6
	Period 2	100	105.5	113.2	120.2	127.5	138.6
Government Final Consumption Expenditure	Period 1	100	102.8	106.9	116.4	120.7	132.3
	Period 2	100	100.6	101.2	110.9	114.6	138.4
Gross Fixed Capital Formation	Period 1	100	110.6	137.1	159.3	181.3	210.7
	Period 2	100	104.9	106.6	110.2	117.4	120.2
Exports of Goods and Services	Period 1	100	109.6	139.4	175.7	211.5	224.0
	Period 2	100	106.8	115.1	117.2	110.9	116.0
Import of Goods and Services	Period 1	100	113.9	139.2	184.5	224.1	247.0
	Period 2	100	106.0	97.4	98.2	92.5	94.6

Source: Reserve Bank of India, *Handbook of Statistics on the Indian Economy* [Original Source: Central Statistics Office (CSO)]

The first noticeable fact there is that in Period 2, only consumption expenditure growth has come close to maintaining the pace of growth seen in Period 1. Moreover, it seems that the demand/expenditure growth in this period has been consumption-led. In sharp contrast to Period 1 in which both investment (GFCF) and India's trade grew rapidly and outpaced consumption growth by a wide-margin, in Period 2 they seem to have been virtually stagnant. If Period 1 saw an extremely sharp rise in India's investment ratio, Period 2 has been one of a consistent downward trend in this, and the same pattern is replicated in the case of the trade-GDP ratio (Appendix Figure 3). Investment stagnation is consistent with the poor growth of construction activities as well as manufacturing stagnation. These, along with the global economic situation, also perhaps underlie the sharply shrunken role of India's foreign trade in Period 2 while in Period 1 it was extremely important.

Thus, the growth process of the Indian economy in the second decade of this century can hardly be described as the continuation of the same process witnessed in the first at a slightly moderated pace. The high-growth phase of five years before the global crisis was in that sense temporary insofar as some of its distinctive mutually related features—rapid growth of investment, a construction boom, high levels of industrial growth and expanding trade—did not last beyond that phase. In the second decade, income growth in the Indian economy increasingly come through expansion of services activities which together employ much less than a third of India's workforce. This growth has not been so heavily dependent on capacity creation through investment nor has it induced capital formation. Clearly also the linkage effects of this growth of services on the rest of the economy have been very weak and its demand has been generated by the growth of domestic consumption of services accompanying it. How did such a transition come about and so quickly? The answer perhaps lies in the fundamental imbalance that has not only been a feature of the Indian growth process for the last two and a half decades but also got aggravated over time—this is the imbalance in the distribution of income.

Explaining the Transition: The Limits to Cheap Labour Based Growth?

One of the harsh realities of the Indian economy is that whether they are counted below or above the official poverty line, the overwhelming majority of Indians continue to sustain themselves on extremely low levels of income. Growth in the last two and a half decades has not changed that situation substantially (Government of India 2007a)—one of the reasons being that it has been accompanied by sharply increasing inequality. In the absence of data on household income distribution, gauging of inequality trends in India have been mainly based on examination of estimates of consumption expenditure levels across different segments of the population. The broad consensus based on these is that the period of economic reforms has seen a significant rise in inequality (Kapoor (2012); Radhakrishna (2015); Subramanian and Jayaraj (2015)).Recently, other sources have also been combined to arrive at a picture of trends in income distribution (Chancel and Piketty (2017)) and these indicate extreme concentration of income growth at the top of the distribution, reversing the trend observed between independence and 1980.

The Annual Survey of Industries (ASI) and National Accounts data also bring out two additional dimensions of the income distribution story since 1991. One of these is the almost complete stagnation in real wage levels in the organized factory sector (Mazumdar (2013), (2014); Muralidharan et al. (2014); Sen and Das, (2015); Sood et al. (2014)). The second is the dramatic growth of the share of the private corporate sector surplus in total income that has accompanied the increasing weight of the sector in the Indian economy (Mazumdar (2013), (2014)). What is significant is that while both reflect longer-term trends, they were particularly marked features of the high-growth phase we have termed as Period 1.

Real wage stagnation in the factory sector (Figure 1), accompanied by and also working through a process of increasing contractualization and informalization of labour (Government of India (2007a); Sood et al. (2014), reflected a larger picture of the general and persistent availability of cheap labour in the Indian economy—something that even a process of rapid growth did not change. The underlying basis for this was the agrarian crisis that set in since the mid-1990s (Patnaik (2003), (2007); Reddy and

Figure 1: Index of Real Wage Per Worker in the Factory Sector (2002-03 = 100)

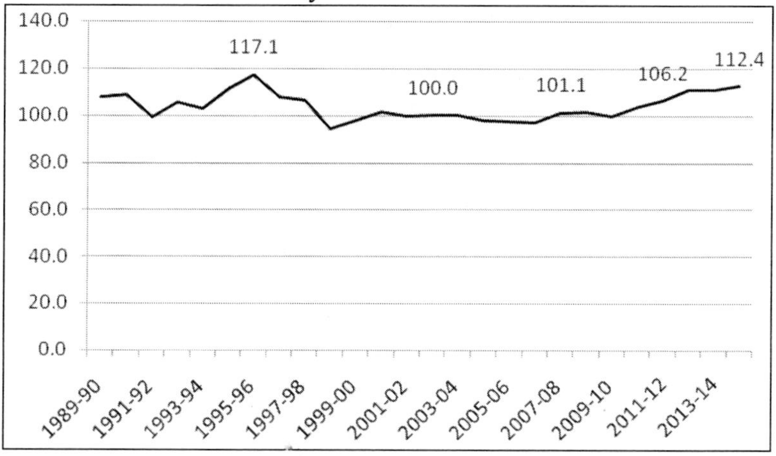

Source: CSO, Annual Survey of Industries and RBI, *Handbook of Statistics on the Indian Economy*

Mishra, (2008); Government of India (2007b); Bhattacharyya, et al. (2013); Ramakumar (2014)). The increasing inability of agrarian households to sustain themselves through economic activity in that sector swelled the ranks of those seeking work in non-agricultural activities even as rural wages tended to stagnate. This enlarged the labour reserves which expansion outside agriculture could then draw on without that process exerting any upward pressure on wage levels. The context for a polarizing growth was thus created whose principal beneficiary was the corporate sector.

The rapid and unprecedented expansion that the corporate sector in India experienced since 1991 received a further fillip in the high-growth Period 1 and it enlarged its weight in the Indian economy.This trend has ebbed after 2007-08 though it was not reversed. The level of the share of the private corporate sector appears to be considerably higher in the new GDP series than in the previous or older series. Till this new series, the value added in private corporations was not being explicitly measured. A proxy indicator, the estimated share of the private organized sector in national income, grew to a peak level that was a slightly under a quarter of NDP in 2007-08, up from under 15% in 1990-91 (Figure

2). In the new GDP series on the other hand, the share in GVA and NDP of private corporations since 2011/12 has stayed around 35% compared to 20% and 45% of the public and household sectors respectively. Whatever the actual level, however, it is clear that the relative significance of the private corporate sector in India's economy has become considerably greater than it was before liberalization. A similar story of the sharp rise up to 2007-08 can be seen in the corporate sector's share in the economy's net fixed capital stock.

Figure 2: Share of the Private Organized Sector in Net Domestic Product at Current Prices, 1990-91 to 2012-13 (%)

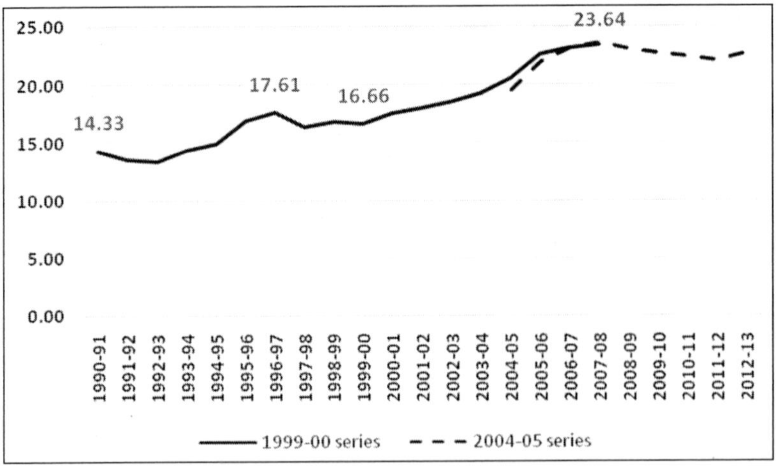

Source: CSO, National Accounts Statistics

The extremely elastic labour situation of the Indian economy characterized by a strong wage-depressing tendency underlay the growth of the corporate sector and its rapid pace in Period 1 in several ways. To the extent that this depended directly or indirectly on significant expansion of employment in certain sectors like construction (and even organized manufacturing to an extent), the growth made use of the expanding labour reserve without facing any constraint. Real wage stagnation despite that in turn facilitated a decline of the wage share in value added after 1991. This is clearly visible in the ASI data but it must have also underlain the observed decline in the share of aggregate compensation of employees in the corporate sector as a whole between 1990-91 and 2007-08 (Table 5)—which happened despite the fact that this period also produced a class of high salary white-collar workforce in the private corporate sector. As a result, corporate savings, which were generally below 2% of GDP for more than four decades after independence, climbed to reach a peak level of 9.4% of GDP by 2007/08.

Table 5: Distribution of Factor Incomes in the Private Organized/Corporate Sector

1999-00 Base Year Series (Private Organized)			
	1990-91	2002-03	2007-08
Compensation of Employees	54.85	35.58	29.08
Operating Surplus	45.15	64.42	70.92
2004-05 Base Year Series (Private Organized)			
	2004-05	2007-08	2012-13
Compensation of Employees	32.46	27.69	32.12
Operating Surplus	67.54	72.31	67.88
2010-12 Base Year Series (Private Corporations)			
	2011-12	2012-13	2015-16
Compensation of Employees	33.96	35.13	37.00
Operating Surplus	66.04	64.87	63.00

Source: CSO, National Accounts Statistics

The impact of the declining share of compensation of employees in value added on profits served as part incentive as well as a significant source of financing the investment boom in the first decade of the 2000s. The corporate sector drove this boom and a significant part of the capital formation was in organized manufacturing (Mazumdar (2014)). If this investment was the source of increasing organized manufacturing sector employment (Nagaraj, (2011)), it may have also facilitated the declining labour-intensity of the sector—taking place as it did in a background of cheapening of capital goods and an increase in the product wage-rates owing to faster rises in prices of wage-goods (Sen and Das, (2015)). The declining wage share trend thus in part reinforced itself. Apart from investment in manufacturing, the increasing demand for assets spurred by income growth at the top also played its part in the making of the real estate boom and rapid growth of the construction sector. Manufacturing investment and the real estate boom played an important part in generating the growth of demand for manufactured products.

Wage stagnation and low wages have also served to limit the potential adverse consequences of India's opening up to trade and capital flows (Mazumdar (2016)). It kept unit labour costs in check and shored up the profitability of Indian production at internationally competitive prices—in manufacturing, even in the face of increasing capital and material costs per unit of output. Cheap labour in various supporting activities also partially compensated for the Indian economy's infrastructure deficits. Indeed, by holding down the prices of non-tradeables, it has helped to maintain the Indian economy's 'national price level' (ratio of PPP conversion factor to market exchange rate) lower than that of many other Asian economies—allowing even high employee compensation sectors like the software industry to be internationally competitive by being located in a generally cheap labour economy.

India's low wages did not, however, provide her manufacturing sector any decisive competitive advantage in export markets. Testimony to this was the fact that in Period 1, even as manufactured exports grew, and the composition changed to newer products from the traditional labour-intensive exports, this was accompanied by an even more rapid growth of manufactured imports (Mazumdar (2014)). Indeed, the very dramatic widening of India's trade deficit during that period was in fact led by her manufacturing trade (Chaudhuri (2013)). Software service exports were, however, able to grow rapidly and combined with remittances from Indians abroad to moderate the consequences of the rising trade deficit on the current account. Capital flows from abroad were thus not deterred and in fact also fuelled the boom in Period 1 and pushed up the value of the rupee. In Period 1, therefore, on balance the interaction of India's low-wage economy with the international economy helped spur growth rather than to constrain it. After 2007-08, however, as both manufactured and services export growth was hit, international oil prices rose and the demand for assets partially switched towards imported items like gold, the current account deficit widened. The rupee also gradually depreciated which partially helped maintain manufacturing competitiveness as manufacturing prices increased more slowly (Mazumdar (2016)). It is only the subduing of growth and investment, and the sharp fall in international oil prices from 2014, that eventually restored some balance.

After 2007-08, not only were global demand conditions no longer the same, the growth process also started facing the adverse domestic demand consequences of the distributional processes and wage-stagnation on which it was based. Even as manufacturing capacity had grown by leaps and bounds, the demand for manufactured consumption goods could not keep pace as the market remained narrow and the consumption of higher income groups moved increasingly towards services (Mazumdar (2008)). Without fast growing consumption demand or that from exports, its self-generated demand was not sufficient to sustain the investment boom in manufacturing. A real estate boom simply dependent on the asset demand of a narrow stratum of the population was also not sustainable beyond a point. The collapse of the investment and real estate booms was thus inevitable, and this in turn reinforced the demand constraint facing the manufacturing sector. At the same time, there were also limits to combining the holding down of wages with continued extraction of 'productivity' increases (Mazumdar (2016)).

Thus, after 2007-08, the distributional imbalances that were in part the cause and in part the effect of the Indian economy's growth process in Period 1, started expressing themselves more strongly as constraints on that growth. These constraints were firmly set by the early years of the current decade even as fiscal consolidation returned as a primary objective of state economic policy. The employment consequences of the slow-down have served to keep in check whatever little tendency was there after

2008 for wages to rise—they did rise for a period of time but not by very much (this was true of both industrial as well as rural wages). On the other side, with neither demand growth from a widening of the market or its anti-thesis—the squeezing of the wage-share—being able to provide a basis for investment expansion, the growth of the corporate surplus and of corporate profits has also been checked.

Conclusion: The "Low-Income Trap"

The Indian economy seven decades after independence can scarcely be described as being caught in a low-level equilibrium trap in the classical sense of the term. Currently classified as a lower middle-income economy by the World Bank, it cannot even be said to have graduated to being in what is described as a middle-income trap. Yet, a large segment of the Indian population may be said to be caught in a low-income trap as the spontaneous growth process offers them scarcely any prospect of steady and remunerative employment. It did not do so when the consequent cheap labour regime spurred rapid growth and expansion of investment. It is not going to do so when the very same cheap labour condition has brought that kind of expansion phase to an end. The crisis of India's macroeconomy in the second decade of the 21st century—the narrowing of the elements of its expansion and the slackening of its pace—is only a generalization of the income and employment crisis that has characterized the economy for a long time. Dealing with that income and employment crisis has to be integral to addressing the macroeconomic crisis. The former cannot be left to be the spontaneous result of the latter.

REFERENCES

Bhattacharyya, S., Abraham, M., and D'Costa, A. (2013). "Political Economy of Agrarian Crisis and Slow Industrialisation in India", *Social Scientist*, Vol. 41, No. 11/12.

Chancel, L. and T. Piketty (2017). "Indian Income Inequality, 1922 to 2014: From British Raj to Billionaire Raj?", Wealth and Income Database (WID.world) *Working Paper Series No. 2017/11.*

Chaudhuri, S. (2013). "Manufacturing Trade Deficit and Industrial Policy in India", *Economic and Political Weekly,* Vol. 48, No. 8,

Goldar, B. (2015). "Growth in Gross Value Added of Indian Manufacturing 2011–12 Series vs 2004–05 Series", *Economic and Political Weekly,* Vol. L, No. 21.

Government of India (2007a). National Commission for Enterprises in the Unorganized Sector (NCEUS): *Report on Conditions of Work and Promotion of Livelihoods in the Unorganized Sector,* New Delhi.

Government of India. (2007b). *Report of the Expert Group on Agricultural Indebtedness,* Ministry of Finance, New Delhi.

Kapoor, R. (2012). "Inequality Matters", *Economic and Political Weekly,* Vol. 48, No. 2

Mazumdar, S. (2008). "Investment and Growth in India under Liberalization: Asymmetries and Instabilities", *Economic and Political Weekly,* Vol. 63, No. 49.

Mazumdar, S. (2013). 'Continuity and Change in Indian Capitalism' in *The BRICs and Emerging Economies in Comparative Perspective: Political Economy, Liberalization and Institutional Change,* Uwe Becker (ed.) London: Routledge.

Mazumdar, S. (2014). 'Globalisation and Growth: The Indian Case in Perspective' in *Market, Regulations and Finance: Global Meltdown and the Indian Economy,* Ratan Khasnabis and Indrani Chakraborty (ed.) Springer 2014, pp. 213-230.

Mazumdar, S. (2015). "Manufacturing Growth in the New GDP Series", *Economic and Political Weekly,* Vol. 50, No. 24.

Mazumdar, S. (2016). "The Interaction Between Growth and Distribution: The Low-Wage Trap of Indian Manufacturing", *Indian Journal of Economics (Special Centennial Issue),* July, XCVII (384).

Muralidharan, T., Paul, G.D., Murti, A.B. (2014). "Should Real Wages of Workers Go Up in Indian Manufacturing?", *Economic and Political Weekly* , Vol. 49, No. 30.

Nagaraj, R. (2011). "Growth in Organized Manufacturing Employment: A Comment", *Economic and Political Weekly,* Vol. 46, No. 12.

Nagaraj, R. (2015). "Seeds of Doubt on New GDP Numbers: Private Corporate Sector Overestimated?", *Economic and Political Weekly,* Vol. L, No. 13.

Panagariya, A. (2004). "Growth and Reforms During the 1980s and 1990s", *Economic and Political Weekly,* Vol. 39, No. 25, June 19.

Patnaik, U. (2003). "Food Stocks and Hunger: The Causes of Agrarian Distress", *Social Scientist,* Vol. 31, No. 7/8.

Patnaik, U. (2007). "Neoliberalism and Rural Poverty in India", *Economic and Political Weekly,* Vol. 42, No. 30.

Radhakrishna, R. (2015). "Well-being, Inequality, Poverty and Pathways Out of Poverty in India", *Economic and Political Weekly,* Vol. 50, No. 41,

Rajakumar, J.D. (2016). "Estimates of High GDP Growth for 2015–16: Not Entirely Convincing", *Economic and Political Weekly,* Vol. 51, No. 26 & 27.

Ramakumar, R. (2014). "Economic Reforms and Agricultural Policy in India", Paper presented at the Tenth Anniversary Conference of the Foundation For Agrarian Studies, Kochi, 9-12 January.

Reddy, D.N. and Mishra, S. (2008). 'Crisis in Agriculture and Rural Distress in Post-Reform India', in *India Development Report 2008,* R. Radhakrishna (ed), New Delhi, Oxford University Press, 40-53.

Rodrik, D. (2015). "Premature Deindustrialization", NBER Working Paper Series, Working Paper 20935 (http://www.nber.org/papers/w20935).

Rodrik, D. and Subramanian, A. (2005). "From 'Hindu Growth' to Productivity Surge: The Mystery of the Indian Growth Transition", *IMF Staff Papers,* Vol. 52, No. 2.

Sen, K. and Das, D.K. (2015). "Where Have All the Workers Gone? Puzzle of Declining Labour Intensity in Organised Indian Manufacturing", *Economic and Political Weekly,* Vol. 50, No. 23,

Sood, A., Nath, P. and Ghosh, S. (2014). "Deregulating Capital, Regulating Labour: The Dynamics in the Manufacturing Sector in India", *Economic and Political Weekly* , Vol. 49, Nos. 26 & 27.

Srinivasan, T.N. (2005). Comments on "From 'Hindu Growth' to Productivity Surge: The Mystery of the Indian Growth Transition", *IMF Staff Papers,* Vol. 52, No. 2.

Subramanian, S. and Jayaraj, D. (2015). "Growth and Inequality in the Distribution of India's Consumption Expenditure: 1983 to 2009–10", *Economic and Political Weekly,* Vol. 50, No. 32.

Virmani, A. (2004). "India's Economic Growth: From Socialist Rate of Growth to Bharatiya Rate of Growth", *Working Paper No. 122,* Indian Council for Research in International Economic Relations (ICRIER), New Delhi.

Appendix Figure 1 (Re: Table 1): Movement of Indices of GDP at Factor Cost/GVA at Basic Prices (at Constant Prices) for Periods 1 and 2 (Respective Year 0 = 100)

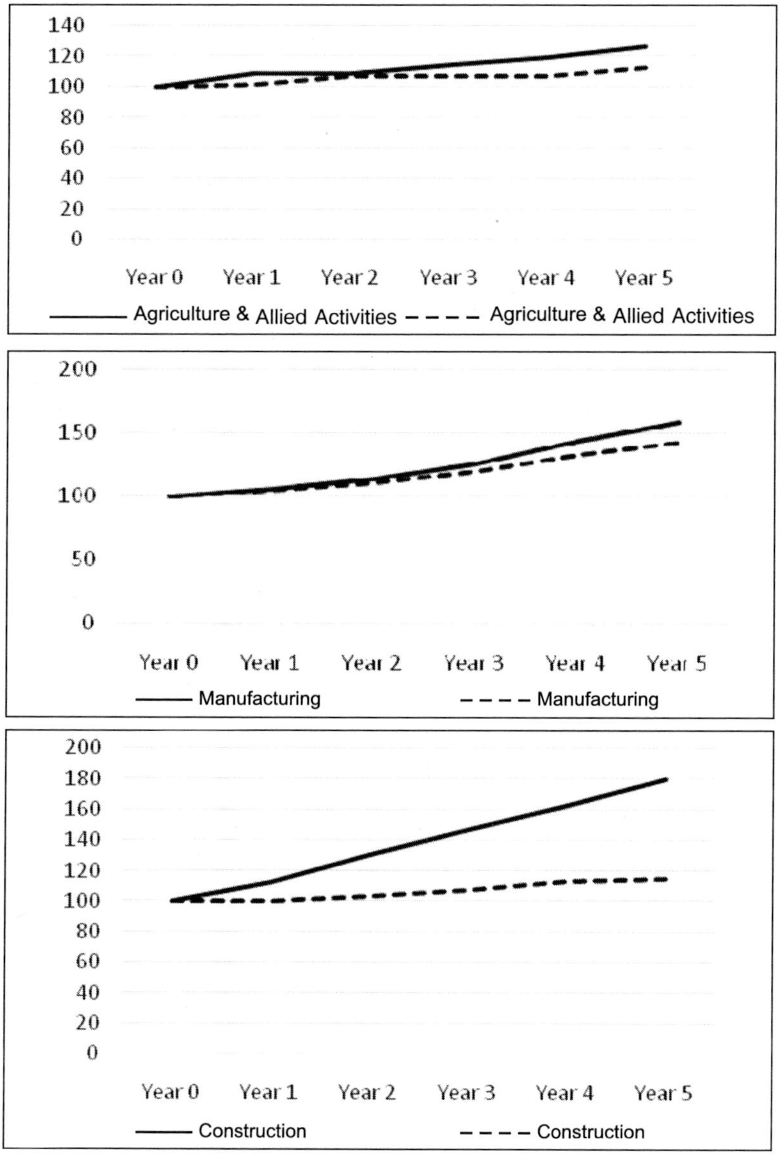

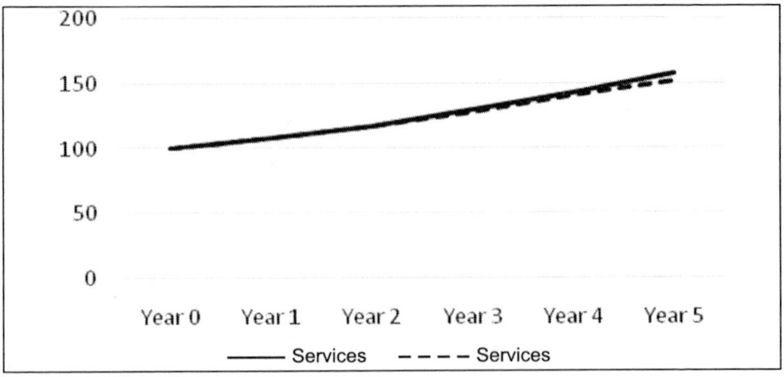

Appendix Figure 2 (Re: Table 4): Movement of Indices of Components of GDP at Constant Market Prices for Periods 1 and 2 (Respective Year 0 = 100)

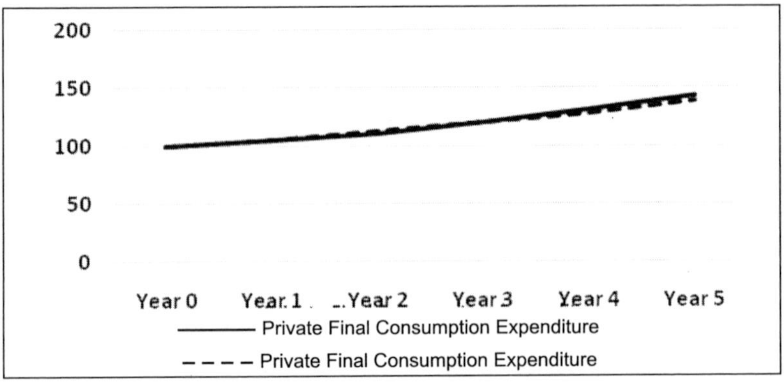

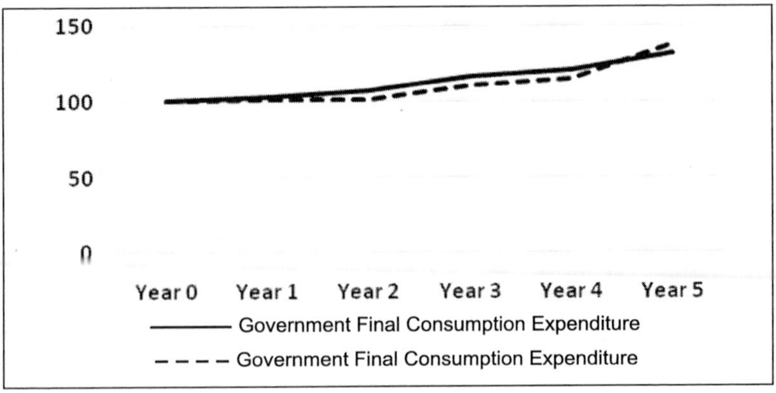

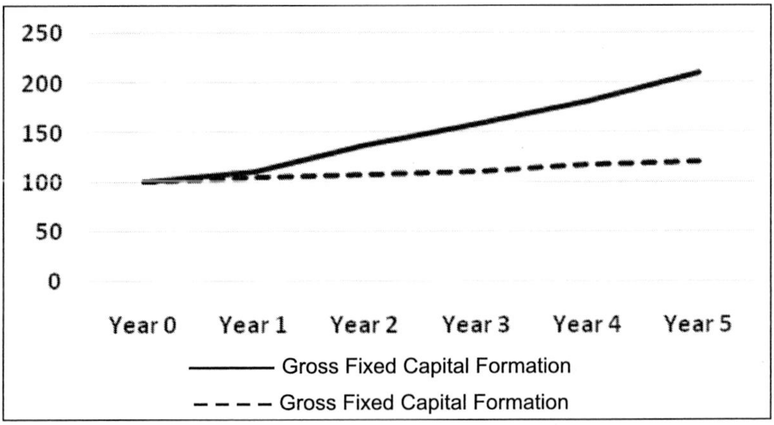
250
200
150
100
50
0
Year 0
Year 1
Year 2
Year 3
Year 4
Year 5
Gross Fixed Capital Formation
Gross Fixed Capital Formation

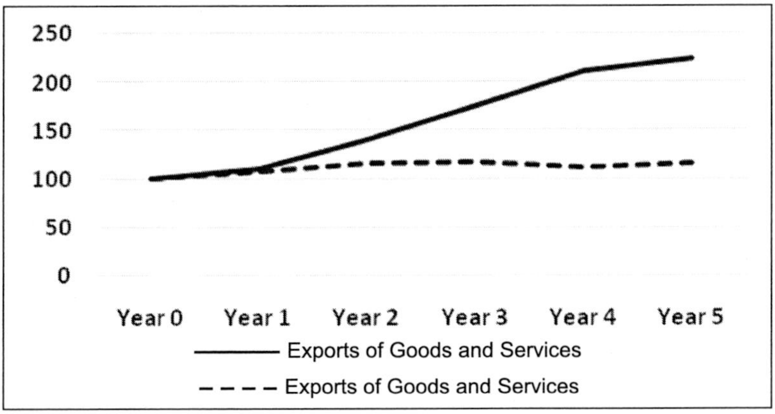
250
200
150
100
50
0
Year 0
Year 1
Year 2
Year 3
Year 4
Year 5
Exports of Goods and Services
Exports of Goods and Services

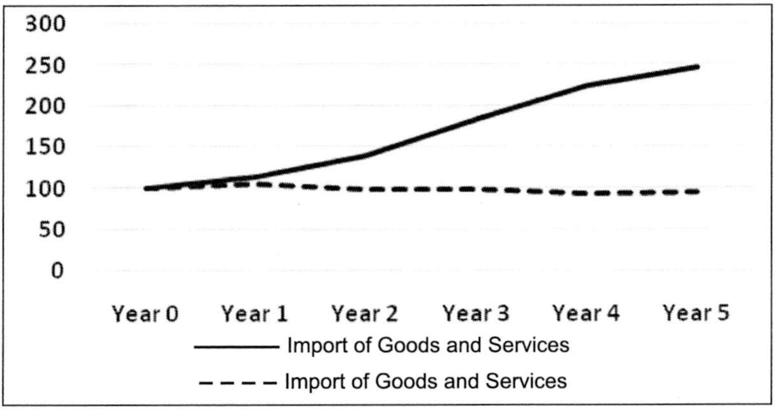
300
250
200
150
100
50
0
Year 0
Year 1
Year 2
Year 3
Year 4
Year 5
Import of Goods and Services
Import of Goods and Services

Appendix Figure 3: Investment and Trade in Goods and Services Ratios to GDP at Current Market Prices (Percentage)

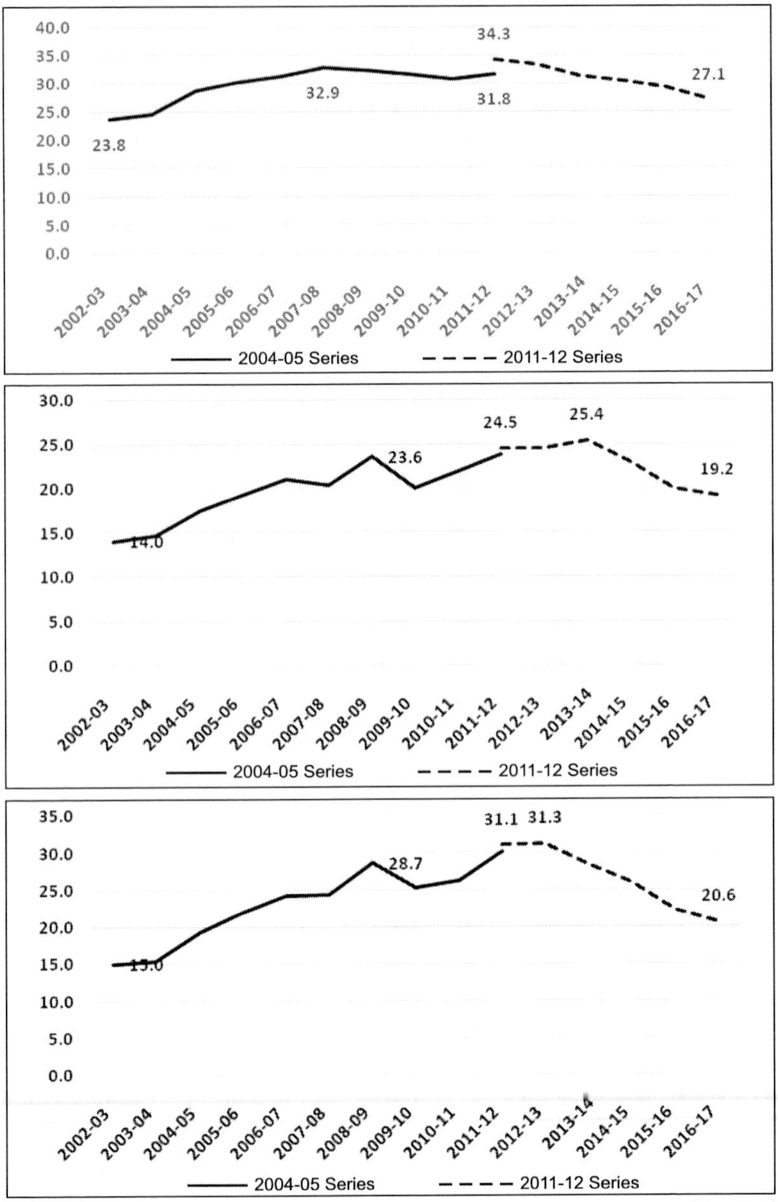

Source: Reserve Bank of India, *Handbook of Statistics on the Indian Economy* [Original Source: Central Statistics Office (CSO)]

3

Inflation in India in the Recent Past: An Explanation

Indranil Chowdhury

Introduction

There is almost unanimous agreement amongst the economists that inflation is one of the most important economic variables and sustained high inflation is not good for any economy. It has been argued that inflation affects the poor the most. Thus controlling inflation should be the main objective of monetary policy.

In the advanced countries following the experience of high rates of inflation during the 1970s, the incapability of the Keynesian demand management in combining output and price stability came to the fore. Monetarism emerged as the alternative to Keynesianism. The central tenets of monetarism comprised a revival of the quantity theory and the classical long run neutrality of money. It was argued that in the long run, changes in money supply cannot affect real variables like output and employment and its only effect would be on the level of prices. The policy prescription, which followed from this understanding, was that the Central Bank should maintain a fixed rate of growth of money supply in order to maintain a stable rate of inflation (Friedman, 1968). Although monetarism was challenged on the grounds of taking the exogeneity of money for granted and assuming velocity of circulation to be an empirical constant without any theoretical explanation (Kaldor, 1986), monetary targeting by the Central Banks in order to control inflation became the centrepiece of economic policy making.

1. Three Regimes

1. 1 *Monetary Targeting with Feedback*

The Committee to Review the Working of the Monetary System (Chakraborty Committee, 1985) formed in India in the backdrop of the policy shift that had occurred in the advanced economies vis-à-vis the role of the government and the monetary authorities came to the conclusion that the objective for which monetary policy should be properly used is price stability. 'Monetary targeting with feedback' was recommended to regulate money supply in line with the increase in output. The target for the monetary expansion can be given by the equation

$$\widehat{g_M} = \hat{\pi} + e_{M,Y}\widehat{g_Y}$$

where $\widehat{g_M}$ is the target for monetary expansion, $\hat{\pi}$ is the acceptable rise in price, $\widehat{g_Y}$ is the anticipated real output growth, and $e_{M, Y}$ is the income elasticity of the demand for money. (Shetty and Ray, 2015).

It also advocated an agreement between the Central Bank and government on the level of monetary expansion and the extent of monetization of fiscal deficit. It also opined that the interest rates could not be arbitrarily set at any level and so the rates should be set in such a way that they satisfy some important criteria. Supposed benefits from positive real rates were also highlighted. It has been by the later adherents of the same policy approach that such monetary targeting is not necessarily equivalent to rigid monetary targets and neither does it amount to being an inflexible policy rule (Rangarajan, 2009, 2001). The monetary target was said to be fixed as a range in order to control inflation, while also taking into account the expected rate of growth of the real sector. While the Chakraborty Committee regarded 4% as the acceptable level of inflation, for Rangarajan it is 5-6%.

It was claimed on the basis of empirical evidence that there was a degree of stability in the money demand function in India and therefore the inflation rate over a long period was said to be reasonably explained by the growth in money supply (Rangarajan, 2009). In keeping with that objective and to regulate the volume of the money supply, an agreement was reached between the

Reserve Bank of India and the union government to limit the credit extended to the government. In 1997 the government and the RBI signed an agreement that ended the practice of automatic monetization of fiscal deficits. This was replaced by a scheme of Ways and Means Advances (WMA). With effect from April 1, 1998, the interest rate on WMA was fixed normally at the bank rate. This is believed to have enhanced the 'autonomy' of the RBI with relation to the fiscal decisions of the government, which is deemed essential to undertake effective monetary policies to achieve the price stability.

Shetty and Ray (2015) think that despite the analytical critiques of the Chakraborty Committee Report, it could be credited with highlighting the issue of the monetary fiscal nexus in monetary policy decision-making in India. However, out of the total 13 years of monetary targeting, in only four years could the targets be achieved (Table 1).

Table 1: Performance of Monetary Targeting Regime

Year	*M_3*	*GDP*	*Inflation*
1985-86	16.0 target achieved	4.1	4.8
1986-87	18.6	4.3	5.1
1987-88	16.0 target achieved	4.3	10.7
1988-89	17.8	10.0	5.7
189-90	19.4	6.9	9.1
1990-91	15.1 target achieved	5.4	12.1
1991-92 (Oct.)	19.3	0.8	13.6
1992-93	15.7	5.3	7.0
1993-94	18.4	6.2	10.8
1994-95 (Oct.)	22.3	7.8	10.4
1995-96	13.7 target achieved	7.2	5.0
1996-97	16.2	7.5	6.9
1997-98	17.6	5.1	5.3

Source: Mohanty and Mitra (1999) as cited in Shetty and Ray (2015)

1.2. Multiple Indicators Approach

In April 1998, the monetary policy was changed from monetary targeting to a policy of multiple indicator approach. The Reserve

Bank of India announced that it was done to 'widen the range of variables that could be taken into account for monetary policy purposes rather than rely solely on a single instrument variable such as the growth in broad money (M_3)'. Thus, money supply became one of the many variables. Money market interest rates, exchange rates, foreign exchange reserves, credit to government and commercial sector, and fiscal position of the government was supposed to be closely monitored to initiate policy actions. Moreover, this approach was augmented by forward looking indicators such as RBI's industrial outlook survey, capacity utilzation survey, professional forecasters' survey and inflation expectations survey. Projection of growth and inflation were done on the basis of the assessment arrived at by these surveys.

Moreover, based on the argument that large fiscal deficits impair the ability of the Central Bank to manoeuvre with interest rate, since fiscal deficit is believed to lead to an increase in the interest rate, legislation was called for. The Fiscal Responsibility and Budget Management Bill was passed in Parliament in 2003 and the rules were notified in 2004. This was seen as an important step towards removing impediments to the effective conduct of monetary policy. Thus, the dominant view on monetary policy was that the nominal interest rate can only be brought down when the inflation rate remained and was expected to remain low. Therefore, a credible assurance to maintain a low inflation rate in the future was advocated, which is somewhat similar to the targets set by inflation targeting Central Banks (Rangarajan, 2001).

Many important financial reforms were undertaken during this period. RBI started deregulating the interest rates in the early 1990s. Also the SLR was gradually reduced from 38.5% in 1991 to 25% in 1997. Currently the SLR is pegged at 20.5%. CRR was also reduced from a very high level of 14.5% in 1993 to 10% in 1997 and subsequently to 5% in 2002. At present the CRR is 4% (See Appendix 1, Fig. 2). It is argued that the moderation of the SLR and CRR resulted in the improvement of the lendable resources to the banking sector. The call money market was also developed in the early 2000s. It is primarily an overnight market among commercial banks, cooperative banks and primary dealers, i.e. financial institutions who exclusively deal in government securities. Liquidity adjustment facility (LAF) corridor was also set up during this period. This mechanism is used for sucking or injecting temporary liquidity by the RBI to the commercial banks. This is done by operating repo and reverse repo rates. From the beginning of 2001, repo and reverse repo rates[1] started to provide a corridor for market interest rates to evolve. Moreover, Ray (2013) notes that the call money market rate is the rate at which one bank lends to another at the end of the day and this rate is expected to lie between the repo and reverse repo rates. This has emerged as the RBI's operating target of monetary policy. Repo and reverse repo could be termed as price base instruments and CRR and SLR

Figure 1

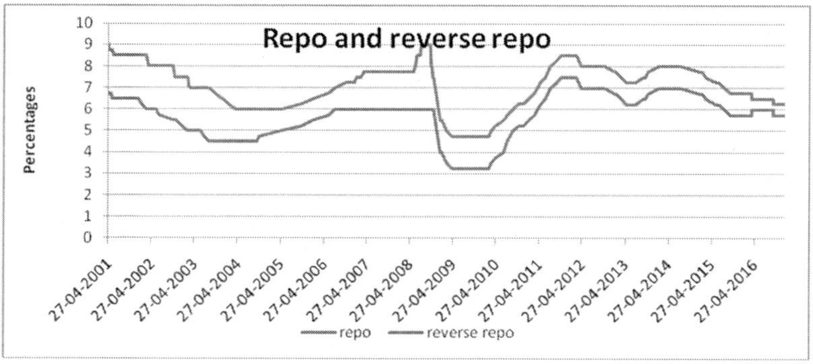

Source: Database on Indian Economy, RBI, 2017

Figure 2

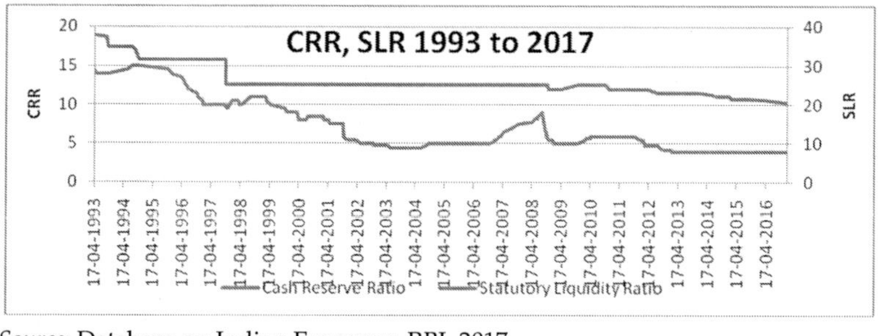

Source: Database on Indian Economy, RBI, 2017

as quantity-based instruments. The repo rate has been changed 50 times from 2001 till date (Fig. 1). During the period of very high inflation in 2009-10 to 2013-14, the repo rate was changed 21 times to control the inflation as measured by the WPI.

1.3. Flexible Inflation Targeting

In the backdrop of the global financial crisis and its aftermath, along with persistent high inflation and low growth rate experienced in India, an expert committee with Urjit Patel as the chairperson was set up by the Reserve Bank of India in 2013. The main objective of the Committee (UPC) was to recommend 'what needs to be done to revise and strengthen the current monetary policy framework with a view to, inter alia, making it transparent and predictable'. The Committee noted that though monetary aggregates have served as nominal anchors but they have been undermined by instability and loss of predictability of the demand for money. This supposedly reduces the accountability of the monetary authority when targets are missed. It also highlighted that since the 1980s many countries have adopted inflation as the nominal anchor for the monetary policy. That supposedly has strong theoretical and empirical support. So, inflation targeting regimes, the report claims, have yielded significant benefits in terms of reduced volatility. Inflation targeting as a monetary framework, it noted, has been adopted, starting with Chile in 1991, by many emerging market economies. Thus on the basis of experiences of other inflation targeting countries and recommendations of the previous committees, UPC recommends, that "inflation should be the nominal anchor for the monetary policy framework. This nominal anchor should be set by the RBI as its predominant objective of monetary policy in its policy statements. The nominal anchor should be communicated without ambiguity, so as to ensure a monetary policy regime shift away from the current approach to one that is centred on the nominal anchor. Subject to the establishment and achievement of the nominal anchor, monetary policy conduct should be consistent with a sustainable growth trajectory and financial stability."

New Keynesian Macroeconomics (NKM) provides the theoretical foundation for inflation targeting, monetary policy rules, and central bank credibility. According to Clarida et al. (1999), it is 'new' as it incorporates the recent methodological advances in macroeconomics modelling and it is 'Keynesian' because it adopts the Keynesian approach of stressing nominal price rigidities. Within this approach the short-term interest rate is the instrument of monetary policy. How the interest should adjust to the current state of the economy is, therefore, a policy design problem (Clarida et al., 1999). With the interest rate as the instrument and inflation as the target, it is a one instrument-one target framework. Here, we will use the BMW model from Bofinger et al. (2006) to summarize the NKM.

There are three main building blocks in the model. They are an IS curve, a Phillips curve and a monetary policy rule. The first block, IS curve, is given as

$$y = a - br + e_1 \tag{1}$$

where y is the output gap. It is defined as the deviation of (the log)aggregate output from its potential or full capacity level. r is the real interest rate. a is the autonomous demand component. e_1 is a demand shock. Now, y will be zero in the absence of shocks and thus it will depend on the real interest rate r--$_0$ = a/b. This r_0 is called the neutral short-term interest rate. Phillips curve is the second building block.

$$\pi = \pi^6 + dy + e_2 \tag{2}$$

Where π is the inflation, π^6 is expectation about inflation, d is a non-zero positive parameter and e_2 is a supply shock. Thus, inflation is determined by the expectations about inflation, output gap and a supply shock. Credibility of the Central Bank is assumed and so, $\pi^6 = \pi_0$, where π_0 is the Central Bank's inflation target. So, (2) becomes

$$2\pi = \pi_0 + dy + e_2 \tag{3}$$

It is argued that (3) is not a short-term supply curve but simply a device for calculating the inflation rate that is associated with an output gap. The third building block is the monetary policy rule,

$$r = r_0 + e\,(\pi - \pi_0) + fy, \text{ with } e, f > 0 \qquad (4)$$

Where r_0 is the equilibrium real rate of interest, and e and f are the weights attached to inflation and output gap respectively. The Diagram 1 below is the graphical representation of NKM.

Diagram 1

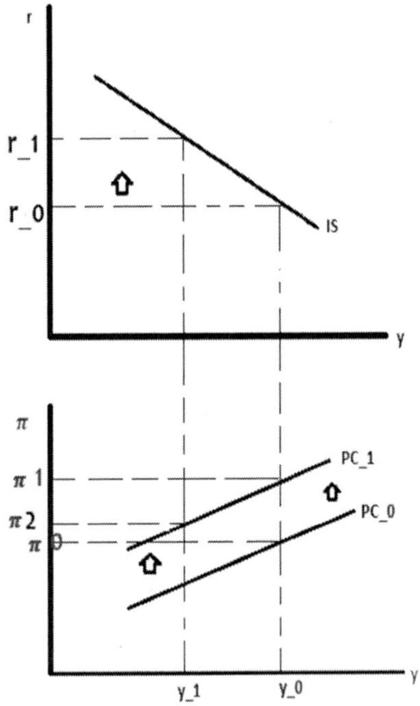

From the figure it is obvious that if there is a supply shock and as a result if the Phillips curve moves to the left then that will result in inflation. If the Central Bank decides not to intervene then the inflation will increase from π_0 to π_1 and the output gap will remain unchanged at this higher inflation. However, an increase in the nominal interest rate increases the real interest rate due to nominal rigidities. This would result in the gap between the actual and real interest rate to increase. In the process, the output gap is reduced which in turn would reduce the inflation via the Phillips curve. In other words, an increase in the policy rate will result in opening up of the output gap and a fall in inflation from π_1 to π_2.

A number of important features of NKM have been criticized by heterodox economists. It has been pointed out that inflation targeting by the use of interest rate would depend on whether the price index includes items that are directly sensitive to the interest rates. Some components of prices might be demand related and others might be more driven by costs (Arestis and Sawyer, 2008). Also, one for one relationship between the short-term interest rate set by the Central Bank and investment has been questioned. It has been argued that the quantity of credit rather than its price which influences investment. However, it has been acknowledged that contractionary monetary policy, through increased short-term interest rate, can have some effect on aggregate demand. But in times of recessions reductions in interest rates are unlikely to stimulate investment.

Also, the notion of a 'neutral', 'equilibrium', or 'natural' real rate of interest is rejected by the critics of NKM. It has been pointed out that an unchanging equilibrium rate of interest would require a in the equation (1) was not shifted through fiscal policy or through 'animal spirits'. Moreover, wide ranges of different results have been obtained by using different methods while estimating the natural rate of interest (Weber et al., 2008). Further, it has been argued that inflation need not rise with increased capacity utilization. For large ranges of output there seems to be little impact on inflation. It has been pointed out that changes in capacity utilization need only be inflationary at levels of capacity near full utilization. Thus, the inflation rate should remain constant for levels of large intermediate levels of capacity. This assertion is based on the post-Keynesian pricing models of mature economies. It is claimed that price is determined as mark-up overcosts. So, cost pressures will remain constant over a long-range of capacity utilization. From it follows, the Phillips curve will be horizontal for large ranges of output and employment. There could be a vertical shift of the horizontal segment of the Phillips curve owing to the increase in prices of the primary commodities.

The UPC also recommended that the combined consumer price index (CPI) should be adopted as the measure of the nominal anchor for the policy communication as it supposedly reflects the cost of living and influences inflation expectations. Also, the target for inflation, according to the committee, should be set at 4% with a band of +/–2% around it.[2] The target should be set in the frame of a two-year horizon was also proposed. The committee recognized the fact that food and fuel account for more than 57% of the CPI on which the direct influence of monetary policy is limited. Nevertheless, it recommended that 'commitment to the nominal anchor would need to be demonstrated by timely monetary policy response'. However, it has been argued that using CPI as the indicator for monetary policy might lead to a more restrictive monetary policy. Also, it has been pointed out that the evidence from other countries shows that the impact of interest rate on changes on inflation is weak. So, with high interest rates also there could be high inflation. This would happen if the inflation is essentially due to cost-push factors like rise in the international prices of oil, reduction of subsidies, etc. Moreover, the theoretical model of the UPC is based on a closed economy. In a world of cross-border capital flows and relatively open financial borders, Central Banks supposedly have to focus on exchange rate more than inflation. Thus, it can be concluded that this whole report is like a defence of the RBI's policy of maintaining very high interest rate (Chandrashekhar, 2014).

2. Inflation in the Recent Past

For our analysis we will mainly consider the inflation as measured by the WPI. This is due to the fact that till very recently, i.e. December 2014, RBI had been targeting the WPI inflation. As we have already discussed, though the formal inflation targeting regime has been set in motion from January 2015 onwards, the RBI had been trying to control the inflation by using its policy rate, i.e. repo since 2001. Some would argue that during that phase the monetary policy framework might be lacking credibility as inflation targeting was not formally acknowledged by the Central Bank. Nonetheless, RBI's operating principle since 2001 has been of inflation targeting in nature.

At present the inflation as measured by WPI (base 2004-05) or new CPI (base 2012) are both below 5%. However, there was persistent high inflation in the recent past. Let us first look at the annual variation of inflation as measured by WPI and its components[3] (Figure 3). The average annual WPI inflation of all commodities combined in 2001-01 was 3.2% it increased to 6.5% in 2004-05. In 2006-07 it became 6.6% and then in 2008-09 it was 8.1%. From 2010-11 to the next four years it was 9.6%, 8.9%, 7.4% and 6.0%. Only in the last two years it had come down below 3%. It was 2% and 2.5% in the last two years. WPI inflation of primary articles also followed almost the same trend. It reached its highest value of 17.7% in 2010-11. It remained consistently above 9% from 2006-7 to 2013-14 with an exception of only one year in 2007-08. For fuel and power the annual inflation had been 12.3%, 14.0%, 10.3%, 10.2% in 2010-11to 2013-14 and thereafter it fell sharply to –0.9% and –11.7% in the last two years. Manufactured goods sector also experienced high inflation of 7.3% in 2011-12 and after that it had gradually decreased to –1.1% in the last year.

Figure 3: WPI Inflation Annual Variation

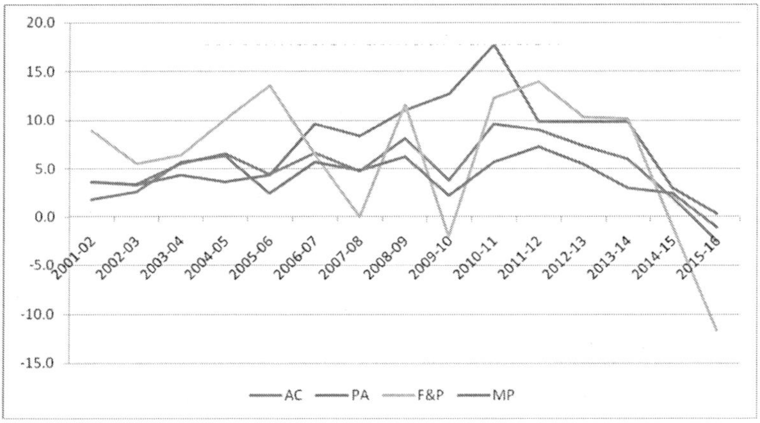

Source: Database of Indian Economy, RBI. 2001 April to 2005 March Base 1993-94, 2005 April to 2016 December Base 2004-05.

Let us now look at the data of WPI inflation and crude prices at the monthly level. From June 2006 to April 2007 WPI inflation was more than 6%. There was a brief phase when inflation tapered off but it picked up again from March 2008 and reached 11.1% in August 2009. The next inflationary phase started from December 2009 and continued till November 2013. In 2010 the inflation was more than 9% in almost all the months. It was more than 9% throughout the year in 2011 also. In 2012 the inflation remained more than 7.5% throughout. After that WPI inflation started to fall from the middle of 2014 which coincided with the sharp fall in international oil prices. As evident from the following figures 4, 5, 6 and 7, the year-on-year growth rate of WPI has been closely associated with similar movements in the growth rate of crude oil prices. Oil prices rose from $30 per bbl in January 2004 to $49 per bbl in March 2005. Similarly, in 2007-09 also it increased from $65 per bbl in April 2007 to $113 per bbl in August 2009. The price was more than $100 per bbl from February 2011 to August 2014. Then it started to fall from November 2014 which most probably led to a fall in the WPI inflation.

The RBI continuously increased the repo rates during this inflationary phase. However it was unsuccessful in controlling inflation (see Figure 7). It could be argued that inflation during this phase might be due to the supply shock emanating from the rise in crude prices. Moreover, if the economy is in a flat section of the new Keyenesian Phillips curve then inflation cannot be controlled by increasing the policy rate as it is graphically shown in the following diagram 2.

Diagram 2

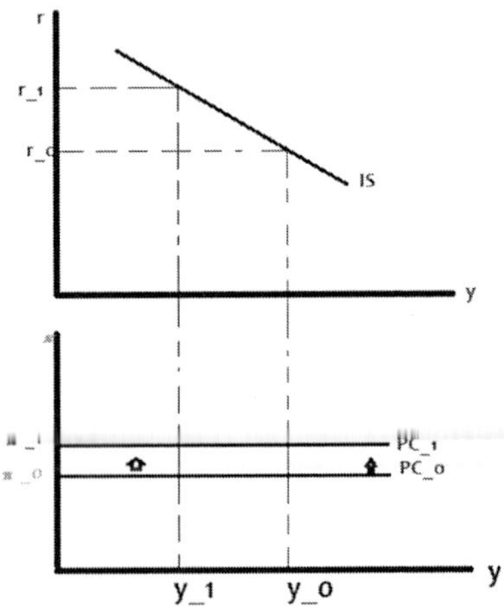

The supply shock has moved the Phillips curve upwards and as a result the inflation has increased. To reduce that inflation if the policy rate is increased then it might only worsen the situation by opening up the output gap by contracting demand. In the empirical section we will try to see whether this was what happened to the Indian economy during that phase.

But some of the explanations which have been put forward to explain persistent high inflation in India in the recent past are: Robust economic growth resulted in the change in consumption. Demand for consumption goods increased which led to inflation. It was also argued that rural wages were pushed up without raising the productivity. Rural incomes increased though the supply did not keep pace with rural consumption. Thus, wage inflation led to inflation in food prices. Increase in minimum support price was also cited as one of the reasons. Some have also pointed out that MGNREGA wages were formally indexed to inflation and thus too much buying power chased too few goods and services. Similarly growing prosperity and dietary shifts, increase in rural liquidity and credit were also noted as causing inflation. It was argued that inflation expectations have always spiked due to these factors resulting in further inflation.[4] Two important objections could be raised against such views. Firstly, if had been the case that the wages are increasing more than the prices then it would have no adverse impact on the workers or poor people. Their real wages would have increased and they would have been protected from the increasing prices. A country like ours, where most of the workers were not indexed to the prices, a rise in general level of prices may not be attributed to the wage price spiral. Secondly, it is argued that the expectations of high future inflation lead to higher inflation at the present. However, if all agents can perfectly foresee the future then they would have also anticipated the anti-inflationary measures adopted by the Central Bank and accordingly moderate their expectations about future inflation. Since that apparently does not happen it leads us to question this whole hypothesis of expectations of the future deciding the actual inflation.

Needless to say that in all these views inflation is seen almost exclusive in demand pull in nature. And it seems that there is some reluctance to accept the role of oil prices in determining the inflation rate. Now we will try to develop an alternative explanation to the phenomenon of inflation by looking at the cost push factors, mainly international oil prices. We will look at the inflation data of WPI (base 2004-05) and the new CPI (base 2012). Till now descriptive data analysis shows that there is definitely a pattern in which inflation has moved contemporaneously with the international oil prices. We will try to find out whether there is any econometrically significant relation between the two.

Figure 4: WPI Inflation y-o-y*

Year/ Month	Apr.	May	Jun.	Jul.	Aug.	Sep.	Oct.	Nov.	Dec.	Jan.	Feb.	Mar.
2001-02	5.5	5.6	5.3	5.3	5.4	4.5	2.9	2.6	2.1	1.5	1.4	1.6
2002-03	1.5	1.5	2.4	2.8	3.3	3.5	3.1	3.4	3.3	4.2	5.3	6.0
2003-04	6.6	6.5	5.4	4.6	3.9	4.9	5.1	5.4	5.8	6.5	6.1	4.8
2004-05	4.5	5.0	6.7	7.6	8.5	7.9	7.3	7.5	6.7	5.5	5.0	5.4
2005-06	5.3	4.6	4.7	4.8	3.5	4.4	4.7	3.9	4.4	4.4	4.5	4.2
2006-07	5.0	6.0	6.8	6.5	7.1	7.0	6.9	6.7	7.0	6.6	6.6	6.7
2007-08	6.2	5.5	4.5	4.4	4.0	3.4	3.2	3.7	4.0	4.5	5.7	7.7
2008-09	7.9	8.2	10.9	11.1	11.1	10.8	10.7	8.6	6.7	5.9	3.6	1.6
2009-10	1.2	1.5	-0.4	-0.3	0.5	1.4	1.8	4.7	7.1	8.7	9.7	10.4
2010-11	10.9	10.5	10.3	10.0	8.9	9.0	9.1	8.2	9.4	9.5	9.5	9.7
2011-12	9.7	9.6	9.5	9.4	9.8	10.0	9.9	9.5	7.7	7.2	7.6	7.7
2012-13	7.5	7.5	7.6	7.5	8.0	8.1	7.3	7.2	7.3	7.3	7.3	5.7
2013-14	4.8	4.6	5.2	5.9	7.0	7.0	7.2	7.5	6.4	5.1	5.0	6.0
2014-15	5.5	6.2	5.7	5.4	3.9	2.4	1.7	-0.2	-0.5	-0.9	-2.2	-2.3
2015-16	-2.4	-2.2	-2.1	-4.0	-5.1	-4.6	-3.7	-2.0	-1.1	-1.1	-0.9	-0.5
2016-17	0.8	1.2	2.1	3.7	3.9	3.8	3.4	3.2	3.4	-	-	-

Source: Database of Indian Economy, RBI. 2001 April to 2005 March Base 1993-94, 2005 April to 2016 December Base 2004-05.

Figure 5: Crude Oil Prices, Indian Basket, ($/bbl)*[5]

Year	April	May	June	July	August	September	October	November	December	January	February	March
2000-01	22.51	26.60	28.49	27.26	28.46	31.34	30.50	30.92	23.25	24.02	25.92	23.82
2001-02	24.82	26.95	26.63	23.99	25.01	24.79	20.05	18.24	18.24	18.92	19.55	23.31
2002-03	25.03	25.00	24.05	25.18	25.86	27.49	26.90	23.68	27.11	29.59	31.26	28.83
2003-04	24.21	25.00	26.42	27.46	28.66	26.27	28.45	28.20	28.97	30.01	29.61	32.21
2004-05	32.36	36.09	34.22	36.35	40.53	39.15	43.37	38.82	36.85	41.00	42.58	49.27
2005-06	49.43	47.02	52.72	55.01	60.03	59.74	56.28	53.31	55.05	60.61	58.95	60.01
2006-07	67.06	67.33	66.90	71.29	70.87	60.94	57.26	57.80	60.34	52.62	56.49	60.26
2007-08	65.48	65.76	68.10	72.58	68.97	74.78	79.33	89.15	87.92	89.52	92.16	99.76
2008-09	105.77	120.91	129.72	132.47	113.05	96.81	69.12	50.91	40.61	43.99	43.22	46.02
2009-10	50.14	58.00	69.12	64.82	71.98	67.70	73.06	77.39	75.02	76.61	73.69	78.02
2010-11	84.08	76.16	74.33	73.54	75.13	76.09	81.11	84.26	89.77	93.87	101.62	110.71
2011-12	118.64	110.80	109.99	112.53	106.94	108.79	106.11	109.62	107.19	110.47	117.67	123.61
2012-13	117.97	108.05	94.51	100.34	110.07	111.77	109.79	107.87	107.28	109.55	112.68	106.45
2013-14	101.57	101.10	101.11	104.86	108.45	109.47	107.37	106.55	108.72	105.29	106.19	105.30
2014-15	105.56	106.85	109.05	106.30	101.89	96.96	86.83	77.58	61.21	46.59	56.43	55.18
2015-16	59.07	63.82	61.75	56.30	47.33	46.10	46.68	42.50	35.68	28.08	30.53	36.42
2016-17	39.88	45.01	46.96	43.52	44.38	44.48	49.25	44.46	52.74			

Source: Petroleum Planning and Analysis Cell (PPAC), GoI.

Figure 6: Y-o-Y Change in Crude Prices

Year/ Month	Apr.	May	Jun.	Jul.	Aug.	Sep.	Oct.	Nov.	Dec.	Jan.	Feb.	Mar.
2001-02	10.3	1.3	-6.5	-12.0	-12.1	-20.9	-34.3	-41.0	-21.5	-21.2	-24.6	-2.1
2002-03	0.8	-7.2	-9.7	5.0	3.4	10.9	34.2	29.8	48.6	56.4	59.9	23.7
2003-04	-3.3	0.0	9.9	9.1	10.8	-4.4	5.8	19.1	6.9	1.4	-5.3	11.7
2004-05	33.7	44.4	29.5	32.4	41.4	49.0	52.4	37.7	27.2	36.6	43.8	53.0
2005-06	52.8	30.3	54.1	51.3	48.1	52.6	29.8	37.3	49.4	47.8	38.4	21.8
2006-07	35.7	43.2	26.9	29.6	18.1	2.0	1.7	8.4	9.6	-13.2	-4.2	0.4
2007-08	-2.4	-2.3	1.8	1.8	-2.7	22.7	38.5	54.2	45.7	70.1	63.1	65.5
2008-09	61.5	83.9	90.5	82.5	63.9	29.5	-12.9	-42.9	-53.8	-50.9	-53.1	-53.9
2009-10	-52.6	-52.0	-46.7	-51.1	-36.3	-30.1	5.7	52.0	84.7	74.2	70.5	69.5
2010-11	67.7	31.3	7.5	13.5	4.4	12.4	11.0	8.9	19.7	22.5	37.9	41.9
2011-12	41.1	45.5	48.0	53.0	42.3	43.0	30.8	30.1	19.4	17.7	15.8	11.7
2012-13	-0.6	-2.5	-14.1	-10.8	2.9	2.7	3.5	-1.6	0.1	-0.8	-4.2	-13.9
2013-14	-13.9	-6.4	7.0	4.5	-1.5	-2.1	-2.2	-1.2	1.3	-3.9	-5.8	-1.1
2014-15	3.9	5.7	7.9	1.4	-6.1	-11.4	-19.1	-27.2	-43.7	-55.8	-46.9	-47.6
2015-16	-44.0	-40.3	-43.4	-47.0	-53.6	-52.5	-46.2	-45.2	-41.7	-39.7	-45.9	-34.0
2016-17	-32.5	-29.5	-23.9	-22.7	-6.2	-3.5	5.5	4.6	47.8			

Source: Author's calculations from data given in Petroleum Planning and Analysis Cell (PPAC), GoI.

Figure 7: WPI y-o-y, Repo, % Change in Crude Prices

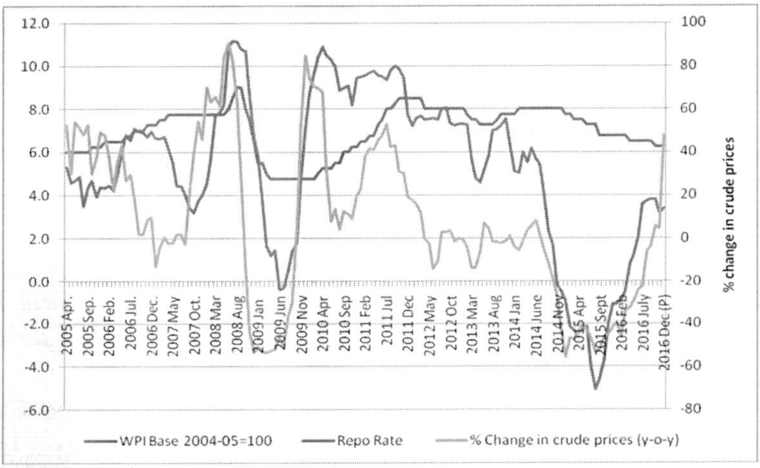

3. Empirical Results[6]

In order to examine the trend in the inflation rate and its plausible causes, we consider the following indicators: for measuring the inflation rate, we take monthly data of WPI (base 2004-05) and the new CPI (base 2012) from RBI. Since, the WPI series for the base 2004-05 starts from April 2004, it is linked with the WPI series for the base 1993-94 through the conventional splicing method in order to get a longer series. To examine the impact of cost-push factors, we take the monthly data of the international crude oil price (Indian basket) from 2000 onwards from the Petroleum Planning and Analysis Cell (PPAC). The repo rate is taken as the indicator of RBI's policy rate. The quarterly data of GDP at constant prices for the base 2004-05 and base 2011-12 are taken as the indicators of output. Since we are interested in examining the relationship among these variables for a given period and the data for GDP is only available on a quarterly basis, we convert the data for WPI, CPI, crude oil price and repo rate into quarterly series by taking their respective mean values at every quarter.

To check for the existence of seasonal unit roots, we conduct the HEGY test for all the quarterly series mentioned above[7]. The HEGY test rejects the possibility of the existence of seasonal unit roots in the four variables, namely, the WPI, the CPI, crude oil price and the repo rate at 5% significance level. In the absence of any seasonality factor, we calculate the inflation rates as quarter-to-quarter growth rates in WPI and CPI[8]. Similarly, in order to examine the impact of cost-push factors on inflation rate, we calculate the quarter-to-quarter growth rate of crude oil prices. However, it is only for the two quarterly GDP series, one for the base 2004-05 and the other for the base 2012-12, that the HEGY test indicates the possibility of existence of seasonal unit roots. Thus, X-12 ARIMA is used to de-seasonalize the quarterly GDP series for the base 2004-05 and 2011-12[9]. The trend output for these two seasonally adjusted GDP series is then calculated by using the standard two-sided Hodrick-Prescott (HP) filter, whereas the output gap is calculated as a difference between the seasonally adjusted GDP and the trend GDP[10]. It is in this backdrop, that we try to examine the relationship between the inflation rate, output gap and the growth rate of crude oil prices.

The very proposition of controlling the rate of inflation through adjustments in the policy rate, as evident from the above discussion, is based on the following two assumptions: a) that the rate of inflation is positively related with the output gap and b) that there exists a negative relationship between the policy rate and the output gap, such that any rise in the policy rate reduces the rate of inflation by reducing the level of output gap. But, if the fluctuations in the rate of inflation are primarily driven by cost-push factors at a given level of output gap, then independent of the impact of adjustments in the interest rate on output, the policy rate itself becomes an ineffective policy instrument in controlling the inflation rate. Whether the changes in the inflation rate in India are driven by a demand pull (output gap) or cost-push factors (growth rate of crude oil prices) is a matter of empirical investigation, which is precisely what we do now.

Since, the fluctuations in the inflation rate can be caused both by the demand pull and cost-push factors, we first consider a simple price equation of the following form, where 'π' is the rate of inflation, 'C' is an exogenously given constant, 'y' is the output gap, 'z' is the growth rate of crude oil prices (capturing the cost-push factor) and 'A' and 'B' are the coefficients for 'y' and 'z' respectively:

$$\pi = C + Ay + Bz \tag{5}$$

The above equation would capture the essence of an upward sloping New Keynesian Phillips Curve (NKPC) in the inflation-output space as described in equation (4), if A>0. However, if 'A' turns out to be zero after taking into account the impact of cost-push factors on the inflation rate, then the NKPC can be argued to be flat (with slope zero) for any given level of output gap. Since, we are examining time-series quarterly data, for the purpose of estimation, we modify equation (5) to include various time lags of output gap and growth rate of crude oil prices. Though we start by taking four lags for each of the independent variables, we would drop some of the lags in the wake of the multicollinearity problem. We do a simple OLS time series regression, where the inflation rate is taken as the dependent variable while the output gap, the growth rate of crude oil price and their various lags are taken as independent variables. We do this exercise for both the WPI (base 2004-05) and the CPI (base 2012). For WPI, we use the output gap calculated with GDP base 2004-05, whereas for the CPI, we take the output gap as calculated with GDP base 2011-12.

Let us first consider the case of WPI, where the quarter-to quarter growth rate of WPI is taken as a dependent variable while the output gap, the growth rate of crude oil prices and their respective four lags are taken as independent variables. An intercept term is also included in this regression. The period of analysis is from 2001Q1 to 2014Q2. The Breusch-Godfrey Lagrange multiplier test for the residuals is statistically significant at 5% level indicating the existence of serial correlation. Thus, we use the Heteroskedasticity and Autocorrelation Consistent Covariance (HAC) or Newey-West estimator to estimate the standard errors. However, the Variance Inflation Factor (VIF) for the second, third and the fourth lag of crude oil prices is greater than 5, indicating a problem of multicollinearity. Accordingly, we drop these variables from the regression analysis and re-estimate the standard errors for the remaining independent variables by using the Newey-West estimator, as reported in Table 2. The Augmented Dickey Fuller test rejects the null hypothesis of the existence of the unit root in the residuals at 1% significance level.

As evident from Table 1, the coefficients for the output gap and its various lags are statistically insignificant even at 10% significance level. However, the coefficient for the growth rate of crude oil prices, both at the level and lag1, are positive and statistically significant at 1% level. The VIF for all the variables, as evident from Table 2, are well under 5 which rules out the multicollinearity problem.

Table 2: Regression Result for WPI

Variable	*Coefficient*	*Std. Error*	*t-Statistic*	*Prob.*	*VIF*
CRUDE OIL	0.032625	0.011417	2.857626	0.0064	1.861503
OUTPUT GAP	0.017650	0.012698	1.389923	0.1712	4.174210
LAG1_CRUDE OIL	0.044523	0.007267	6.126798	0.0000	1.465324
LAG1_OUTPUT GAP	-0.006110	0.014729	-0.414801	0.6802	3.075640
LAG2_OUTPUT GAP	0.018007	0.013041	1.380794	0.1740	2.086475
LAG3_OUTPUT GAP	0.003331	0.012127	0.274664	0.7848	2.104218
LAG4_OUTPUT GAP	-0.010110	0.010179	-0.993252	0.3258	2.633684
C	0.011976	0.001166	10.27330	0.0000	

R-squared	0.533650	Mean dependent var	0.014476
Adjusted R-squared	0.462683	S.D. dependent var	0.012170
S.E. of regression	0.008921	Akaike info criterion	-6.464919
Sum squared resid	0.003661	Schwarz criterion	-6.170255
Log likelihood	182.5528	Hannan-Quinn criter.	-6.351278
F-statistic	7.519755	Durbin-Watson stat	1.556209
Prob(F-statistic)	0.000005	Wald F-statistic	14.62144
Prob(Wald F-statistic)	0.000000		

Let us now consider the case of new CPI. Similar to the regression done in the case of WPI, the quarter-to quarter growth rate of CPI is taken as a dependent variable while the output gap, the growth rate of crude oil prices and their respective four lags are taken as independent variables. The period of analysis is from 2012Q1 to 2016Q2. Again, the Breusch-Godfrey Lagrange multiplier test for the residuals is statistically significant at 5% level indicating the existence of serial correlation. After making appropriate adjustments in the standard errors by using the Newey-West estimator, we find the VIF to be greater than 5 for the second, third and the fourth lag of crude oil prices along with the third lag of output gap. Accordingly, we drop these variables from the regression analysis and re-estimate the standard errors for the remaining independent variables by using the Newey-West estimator, as reported in Table 2. The Augmented Dickey Fuller test rejects the null hypothesis of the existence of unit root in the residuals at 5% significance level.

Similar to the case in WPI, the coefficients for the output gap and its various lags are statistically insignificant even at 10% significance level. Again, the coefficient for the growth rate of crude oil prices at the level is positive and statistically significant at 1% level while that for lag1 is statistically significant only at 10% level. The VIF for all the variables, as evident from Table 3, are less than 5. However, a note of caution in interpreting this result is added here- that the low R^2 (0.38) and high p-value of F-statistic in the regression reflects the fact that the model fails to adequately capture the trend of the CPI inflation rate during this period, which in turn, indicates the need to include additional explanatory variables. Nonetheless, since the objective of the present exercise is not the general modelling of inflation rates per se, but rather to examine its relationship with demand pull and cost-push factors specifically , the above mentioned problem does not deter us here from drawing adequate inference on the value of coefficients unless the described model has specification errors. The fact that the estimators would be biased and inconsistent in the wake of such specification errors indicates the need for a standard Regression Specification Error Test (RESET) in this case. However, after including two fitted terms in the test regression, the p-value of the RESET test is 0.58 and accordingly, indicates the absence of any specification error in the model. Thus, we continue with our inference on the value of coefficients in the given regression, as described earlier.

Table 3: Regression Results for CPI

Variable	*Coefficient*	*Std. Error*	*t-Statistic*	*Prob.*	*VIF*
CRUDE OIL	0.053343	0.015263	3.494864	0.0050	2.599122
LAG1_CRUDE OIL	0.036440	0.016857	2.161754	0.0535	1.968701
OUTPUT GAP	-0.008314	0.025801	-0.322239	0.7533	4.040905
LAG1_OUTPUT GAP	0.010637	0.009059	1.174238	0.2651	1.459471
LAG2_OUTPUT GAP	0.010264	0.013924	0.737096	0.4765	2.753244
LAG4_OUTPUT GAP	-0.013098	0.012821	-1.021583	0.3289	2.927626
C	0.021295	0.003886	5.480396	0.0002	

R-squared	0.375516	Mean dependent var	0.017723
Adjusted R-squared	0.034888	S.D. dependent var	0.014096
S.E. of regression	0.013848	Akaike info criterion	-5.436039
Sum squared resid	0.002109	Schwarz criterion	-5.089783
Log likelihood	55.92435	Hannan-Quinn criter.	-5.388295
F-statistic	1.102422	Durbin-Watson stat	1.790766
Prob (F-statistic)	0.419241	Wald F-statistic	2.749419
Prob (Wald F-statistic)	0.069563		

For reasons discussed earlier, the above exercise indicates a flat Phillips Curve for any given level of output gap during the given period. Rather, the positive relationship of the inflation rate with the crude oil prices indicates the fact that inflation in the

Indian economy has been particularly driven by cost-push factors. However, in case the level of output gap is sensitive to the interest rate as described in equation (1), then it follows, *ceteris paribus*, that any monetary policy rule to increase the policy rate in the wake of rising inflation would reduce the output by keeping the inflation rate unchanged. This leads us to address the following question: has the output gap been sensitive to the changes in the policy rate?

In order to examine the relationship between output gap and the policy rate, we consider two distinct periods: first, the period between 2002Q1 to 2014Q2 where we use the GDP base 2004-05 to estimate the output gap and second, the period between 2012Q1 to 2016Q2 where we use the GDP base 2011-12 to estimate the output gap. In both the periods, the output gap is taken as a dependent variable, whereas the repo rate along with its various lags is taken as independent variables. To capture the impact of demand side factors on the output gap, we further include various lags of output gap in the regression analysis. Similar to the methodology adopted in the case of previous exercises, we start by taking four lags and later drop some of the lags in the wake of the multicollinearity problem.

In the case of the first period, we drop the lags with VIF greater than 5 and only keep the first lag of output gap and the fourth lag of repo rate in the regression analysis. Though the Breusch-Godfrey Lagrange multiplier test does not indicate the existence of autocorrelation in the residuals at 5% significance level, the Breusch-Pagan-Godfrey test does indicate the possibility of heteroscadasticity at 5% significance level. Accordingly, we use the White's correction to estimate the standard errors as reported in Table 4. As evident from Table 4, the coefficient for the fourth lag of repo rate is negative and statistically significant. The low VIF, indicated in Table 4, rules out any possibility of multicollinearity. The Augmented Dickey Fuller test rejects the null hypothesis of the existence of the unit root in the residuals at 1% significance level.

Table 4: Regression Results for Output Gap, 2002Q1–2014Q2

Variable	*Coefficient*	*Std. Error*	*t-Statistic*	*Prob.*	*VIF*
LAG1_OUTPUT GAP	0.579890	0.120561	4.809934	0.0000	1.06
LAG4_REPO	-0.026007	0.009249	-2.811790	0.0072	1.06
C	0.175643	0.060659	2.895570	0.0057	

R-squared	0.516741	Mean dependent var	-0.016808
Adjusted R-squared	0.496176	S.D. dependent var	0.111804
S.E. of regression	0.079359	Akaike info criterion	-2.171545
Sum squared resid	0.295999	Schwarz criterion	-2.056824
Log likelihood	57.28862	Hannan-Quinn criter.	-2.127858
F-statistic	25.12813	Durbin-Watson stat	2.045499
Prob (F-statistic)	0.000000	Wald F-statistic	19.81740
Prob (Wald F-statistic)	0.000001		

Following precisely the same methodology and exactly for the same reason as before , for the second period we consider the first and the fourth lag of output gap, the repo rate at the level and its fourth lag as the independent variable. The Breusch-Godfrey Lagrange multiplier test and the Breusch-Pagan-Godfrey test respectively reject the possibility of autocorrelation and heteroscadasticity at 5% significance level. As evident from Table 5, the coefficients for the repo rate at the level and the fourth lag are negative and statistically significant at 5% significance level. The Augmented Dickey Fuller test rejects the null hypothesis of the existence of the unit root in the residuals at 1% significance level.

Table 5: Regression Results for Output Gap, 2012Q1–2016Q2

Variable	*Coefficient*	*Std. Error*	*t-Statistic*	*Prob.*
Variable	Coefficient	Std. Error	t-Statistic	Prob.
LAG1_OUTPUT GAP	-0.265158	0.164627	-1.610659	0.1313
LAG4_OUTPUT GAP	0.460851	0.119971	3.841359	0.0020
REPO	-0.281891	0.060276	-4.676657	0.0004
LAG4_REPO	-0.242362	0.089037	-2.722032	0.0174
C	3.941508	0.822437	4.792477	0.0004

R-squared	0.757952	Mean dependent var	-0.062659
Adjusted R-squared	0.683476	S.D. dependent var	0.229205
S.E. of regression	0.128952	Akaike info criterion	-1.028624
Sum squared resid	0.216171	Schwarz criterion	-0.781299
Log likelihood	14.25762	Hannan-Quinn criter.	-0.994521
F-statistic	10.17709	Durbin-Watson stat	1.676266
Prob(F-statistic)	0.000586		

The above exercises indicate that the output gap has been sensitive to the fluctuations in the policy rate during the recent period. However, for reasons discussed earlier, such a phenomenon of a negative relationship between policy rate and the output gap along with the insensitivity of the inflation rate vis-à-vis the output gap, implies the following: firstly, it makes the present monetary policy rule ineffective in combating inflation and secondly, in the wake of rising inflation, any rise in the policy rate becomes counter-productive as it reduces the output by keeping the inflation rate unchanged. Ironically, this has precisely been the case for the Indian economy during the period mid-2009 to mid-2014 when the policy rate was kept at a higher level in the wake of the persistent high inflation rate compared to that during the pre-crisis period.

4. An Alternative Model

The price level that would prevail if there is a fixed mark-up over unit prime cost

$$p_t = [\, lwt + \lambda\Phi_t] \,(1 + \mu) \tag{7}$$

Where, p_t is the price at 't',

w_t is money wage at 't',

l is the labour coefficient, i.e. the reciprocal of the labour productivity. It is assumed to be a constant,

λ is the non-labour input coefficient, i.e. the reciprocal of the non-labour input productivity,

Φ_t is the cost of the non-labour input,

$(1 + \mu)$ is the mark up over the unit prime cost.

Workers' wages are assumed to be adjusted after a time lag. Thus,

$$w_t = \omega p_{t-\theta} \tag{8}$$

Where ω is the desired real wage rate that workers are supposed to be compensated for

And θ is the time lag and we assume θ > 0.

$$\phi_t = \phi p_t \tag{9}$$

Where ϕ is the real cost of the non-labour input.

From equations 1, 2, 3 we get

$$\frac{p_t}{p_{t-\theta}} = \frac{\omega l(1+\mu)}{1-(1+\mu)\lambda\Phi} \tag{10}$$

Let $p_t = (1 + r)p_{t-1}$ where *r* is the inflation rate.[11]

For continuous time we get

$$e^{r\theta} = \frac{\omega l(1+\mu)}{1-(1+\mu)\lambda\Phi} \tag{11}$$

ω, l, μ are all constants.

So, if ϕ increases then the right hand side increases. Therefore, the left hand side should increase for that *r* should also increase. Or to keep the inflation at check the è should increase. Therefore the condition for inflation in the economy will be

$$[\omega l + \lambda\Phi]\ [1 + \mu) : 1 \tag{12}$$

Suppose there is an increase in the oil prices in the international market, it will lead to an increase in inflation. Now to reduce the inflation to its original level or to even zero or should fall assuming *l* and Φ as constant at the given technology.

But workers will be unwilling to accept a lower ω and capitalists will also be reluctant to reduce the mark up. In that case the only way inflation can be checked is by increasing θ, the time lag.

5. Conclusion

Price stability remained as the main objective of monetary policy. Here we have critically discussed the framework of monetary policy. We have empirically tested the validity of arguments which are put forward to explain the phenomenon of inflation in India in the recent past. We have done the empirical exercise for the period in which inflation was tried to be controlled by using the policy rate, i.e. repo. Our results suggest that inflation most probably can be better explained by the cost-push factor like crude oil price and we have not found any evidence to conclude that the interest rate affects inflation. Our study suggests that a rise in the policy rate compresses the demand without affecting the inflation. Moreover, it seems that the Indian economy was most probably operating at the horizontal section of the Phillips curve. Lastly, through our cost-plus model of determining prices we have shown that the inflation due to the increase in the oil prices could be checked only when the oil prices come down or by squeezing the workers by lengthening the time lag of the wage adjustment.

NOTES

1. Till May 2011, repo and reverse repo were announced separately. The difference between them varied between 1% to 3%. In April 2016, RBI narrowed the difference from 1% to 0.5%.
2. The Government of India and RBI made an agreement on monetary policy framework on February 20, 2015. In it they agreed that the price stability, while keeping in mind the objective of growth, is the primary objective of the monetary policy and monetary policy framework, in India, will be operated by RBI. It is also agreed that RBI will aim to bring inflation below 6% by January, 2016. Thereafter, the target inflation for subsequent years shall be 4% with a band of +/- 2% around it (Government of India, 2015)
3. WPI (base 2004-05) weightages: 1. All commodities: 100, I. Primary Articles: 20.11815, A. Food articles: 14.33709, B. Non-food articles: 4.25756, C. Minerals: 1.52350, II. Fuel and power: 14.91021, III. Manufactured products: 64.97164. Source: Office of the Economic Advisor, Ministry of Commerce & Industry, Government of India.
4. See Gokarn (2011), Rajan (2014), Subbarao (2016).
5. * These are heat charts to show the rise in WPI and oil prices. The shade of the colour represents the value in the cell. Red and green signifies high and low values respectively.
6. These empirical results have been used in another paper by the authors, Chowdhury and Dasgupta (2017)
7. Following Hylleberg et al. (1990), the seasonal unit root test is implemented using constant, trend and seasonal dummies as deterministic components in the test regression. The lag length is chosen using the AIC. The critical values and p-values for the test are obtained using 1,000 Monte Carlo simulations.
8. Though the inflation rate is generally calculated as a year-on-year growth rate of price indices, here we use the quarter-to-quarter growth rate of price indices to make the empirical investigation

consistent with the theoretical discussion made earlier. Since, the rate of inflation in the NKM is linked with the level of output gap at any given period, and this level of output gap itself changes here on quarter-to-quarter basis, we define the inflation rate as the growth rate of price indices during the same period. The alternative way in which the time period for year-on-year growth rate of prices can be made comparable vis-à-vis the output gap, as done in various studies, is by taking the year-on-year growth rate of output gap. However, we avoid this latter route since the theoretical framework discussed earlier argues for a positive relationship between the inflation rate and the level of output gap instead of its growth rate.

9. The X-12 Arima, developed by the US Census Bureau, has been widely used in the published official statistics in India including the RBI.
10. Instead of using the one-sided HP filter, here we use the two-sided HP filter due to the limited size of the sample in this study.
11. We assume that inflation is not demand pull in nature. Here, inflation is essentially cost-push.

REFERENCES

Arestis, P. and M. Sawyer (2008). "A Critical Reconsideration of the Foundations of Monetary Policy in the New Consensus Macroeconomics Framework". *Cambridge Journal of Economics*, No. 32.

Bofinger, P., E. Mayer, and T. Wollmershauser (2006). "The BMW Model: A New Framework for Teaching Monetary Economics". *The Journal of Economic Education*, Vol. 37, No. 1.

Chandrashekhar, C.P. (2014). "Off-Target on Monetary Policy". *Economic and Political Weekly*, Vol. XLIX, No. 9.

Chowdhury, I. and Z. Dasgupta (2017). "A Study of the Monetary Policy in the Post Liberalisation Period". *Mimeo*, University of Delhi.

Clarida, R., J. Gali, and M. Gertler, (1999). "The Science of Monetary Policy: A New Keynesian Perspective". *Journal of Economic Literature*, Vol. 37, No. 4.

Friedman, M. (1968). "The Role of the Monetary Policy". *American Economic Review*, Vol. 58.

Gokarn, S. (2011). "This Time it is Different", *Kale Memorial Lecture*, Gokhale Institute of Politics and Economics, Pune.

Government of India (1998). Report of the Committee on Banking Sector Reforms (Narasimham Committee II).

Kaldor, N. (1986). *The Scourge of Monetarism*. Oxford University Press.

Mohanty, D. and A.K. Mitra, (1999). Experience with Monetary Targeting in India, *Economic and Political Weekly*, 34(3/4):123-32.

Patnaik, P. (1986). "Public Debt as a Mode of Financing Public Expenditure". *Economic and Political Weekly*, Vol. XXI, No. 35.

Rajan, R. (2014). "Fighting Inflation", *Inaugural Speech* at FIMMDA-PDAI Annual Conference, Mumbai.

Rangarajan, C. (1998). *Indian Economy: Essays on Money and Finance*. UBSPD, New Delhi.

Rangarajan, C. (2001). "Some Critical Issues in Monetary Policy". *Economic and Political Weekly*, pp. 2139-2146.

Rangarajan, C. (2009). *India Monetary Policy Financial Stability and Other Essays*. Academic Foundation, New Delhi.

Ray, P. (2013). *Monetary Policy*. Oxford University Press, New Delhi.

Reserve Bank of India (1985). *The Committee to Review the Working of the Monetary System*.

Reserve Bank of India (1991). The Report of the Committee on Financial System (Narasimham Committee I).

Reserve Bank of India (2014). Report of the Expert Committee to Revise and Strengthen the Monetary Policy Framework. Technical Report.

Shetty, S.L. and P. Ray, (2015)." The evolving contours of monetary policy and Commercial Nanking in India", *ICSSR Research Surveys and Explorations, Economics, Macroeconomics*, Vol. 3.

Subbarao, D. (2016). *Who Moved My Interest Rate?* Penguin, New Delhi

Vasudevan, A. (2002). "Evolving Monetary Policy in India Some Perspectives". *Economic and Political Weekly*, Vol. 37, No. 11, 1055-1061.

Weber, A., W. Lemke, and A. Worms (2008). "How Useful is the Concept of the Natural Real Rate of Interest for Monetary Policy?" *Cambridge Journal of Economics*, No. 32.

4

An Analysis of Transmission of International Price on Domestic Price of Rice and Wheat in India

Madhvi Moni K.

Introduction

In India, close to 47% of the workforce are engaged in agriculture, out of which most of them are small, marginal, and landless farmers. Therefore, understanding the price policy and the marketing structure of the commodity becomes crucial as it directly affects the farmer. In addition, world prices also affect farmers. Many extant literatures have claimed that price variability in the world markets influences price variability in the local market or domestic market. However, the extent of influence depends on the structure of agriculture the market in a country. High degree of government intervention characterizes the structure of the Indian agricultural market. This is particularly true in the case of rice and wheat. The government is involved in agriculture price policy, production, minimum support prices, procurement, storage, public distribution system, trade, regulatory measures, etc. The effect of government intervention in agricultural/food markets can also be evaluated by analysing the extent of market integration. Market integration is defined as the degree to which price change/shock in one market leads to a price change/shock in another market. Integration can be categorized into two, as price channelizes both horizontally and vertically.

- Horizontal Integration–It is defined as the interrelationship of prices in two or more spatially separated markets. This is also known as Spatial Integration. Spatial market integration occurs when prices of a homogeneous commodity in two or more separated markets move together, and prices are transmitted fully and timely.
- Vertical Integration–This is defined as the interrelationship of prices between different stages of marketing during a marketing season in a given region or area.

This study of agricultural market integration is fundamental to policy discourse on trade, prices, and overhaul of government trading agencies. The extent of integration regulates the behaviour of a market and as a result, regulates their market efficiency too. The study of market integration is of utmost importance in the scenario of rising prices and falling growth in most of the economies, as integration could be a key to price stability. Analysis of the price transmission is of extreme importance for understanding the markets and policy formulation. The study of market integration is similar to studying price efficiency in the marketing system. Acharya and Chaudhuri (2001) note that efficiency of prices takes place when the market or the marketing system is able to allocate commodities optimally across time, space, trade, etc., so that both producers and consumers are better off. In our study, we only assess the extent of market integration as the co-movement of prices between markets. We find that the overall degree of integration to be less in the short run than in the long run analysis. This can happen due to various reasons like flow of market information, availability of transport facilities and other supporting infrastructures, number of buyers and sellers and the most important extent of government intervention. The main goal of the study is to evaluate the size of spatial market integration of rice and wheat in India. The market integration ascertains the speed of price adjustment to any policy reforms.

With market competition, spatial arbitrage should bring down the price differences between markets to the extent of transaction costs. However, certain features of agricultural marketing and distribution such as inadequate infrastructure, market entry barriers, and price information may inflate the costs beyond the transport costs. The law of one price states that given perfectly competitive and spatially integrated markets, the price difference between two similar commodities should only reflect the transportation and processing costs (Bathla, 2011). In fact, Conforti et al. (2004) in their study trace some of the factors affecting the extent of integration, for example, transportation costs, returns to scale, market power, degree of homogeneity, trade policies, exchange rates, internal policies etc. Sekhar (2012) also points to the lack of integration, risk, infrastructural bottlenecks, etc. to be partially the basis of arguments for state intervention and against liberalization. Rather, both of them in return exacerbate the lack of integration. Any effect on the commodity, whether supply or a price shock has severe implications on the demand and supply. Both, producers and consumers are worst affected. As far as the Indian economy is concerned, not all domestic price changes are the result of international price change. Dasgupta et al (2011) in their study of domestic wheat price estimation and the World Bank paper on commodity markets[1] support the fact. Generally, countries with large infrastructure bottlenecks or countries that follow protectionist policies largely suffer from complacent policymaking. Poor rural connectivity or infrastructure bottlenecks increase the transaction costs and slacken the transmission of higher consumer prices to farmers, which is necessary for timely agricultural supply response.

Bathla and Srinivasulu (2011) also noted in their article that the magnitude of transmission is a signal for efficient resource allocation, a fundamental requirement of market efficiency. The study of integration counts in understanding the nuances of the rice and wheat market and the consequent diligent policymaking as it plays a fundamental role in policy formulation at the regional level. Therefore, the study expects to give a better understanding of correlation or mutuality between the markets, whether between domestic markets in a particular economy or between a domestic market and an international market. Efficient markets facilitate farmers to increase production levels.

Literature Review

As mentioned, this study proposes to evaluate empirically, the spatial/horizontal integration of rice and wheat market in India. Unlike most of the studies, especially in the Indian context, this study also evaluates if the estimated transmission is symmetric or asymmetric in nature. Although the literature below, does trace the reasons for no or less market integration, however the main reasons identified for less than complete integration in the case of the Indian economy has been government intervention and lack of knowledge of the various commodities analysed. For example, Chand (2009) revisits the basic rationale for government intervention, especially in the wheat market and argues that despite the excessive presence of the government in the food market, the fluctuations in these imbalances have gone up since the late 1990s. He highlights the asymmetric nature of government intervention in the food management as the reason for the volatile nature of buffer stocks, especially in the wheat market. This, the author claims, in turn affects the price variation. Similarly, Sekhar (2004) discusses price volatility by calculating inter and intra year variability. Perfect integration between markets is an example of efficient functioning markets (Conforti, 2004). One of the main aims of evaluating the extent of integration is to assess the structure of the market and draft agricultural policies accordingly. Conforti (2004) measures the extent of transmission by evaluating both spatial and vertical integration in several agricultural markets such as Asia, Africa, and Latin America and for several commodities such as wheat, soyabeans, meat, maize, etc. As mentioned earlier, the current study measures only spatial integration, which is believed to give suggestions regarding the agricultural price policy and the current policy implications on the agricultural market. However, one of the limitations of our study is that we do not consider transaction costs to measure the extent of price transmission. Sekhar (2012) acknowledged the inclusion and then analysed the extent of transmission.

Several studies generally define domestic markets at the state level and thus, we also follow suit in our study for rice and wheat.

Jha et al. (2005) test the level of rice market integration in India, They evaluate the extent of integration for 55 rice markets for the monthly period spanning from January 1970 to December 1999. As expected, the results indicate absence of any such integration across many markets. Bathla (2011) in her book on *Trade Liberalization and Indian Agriculture* devotes a chapter (Chapter 4) to assess price transmission between the world and domestic markets. The author runs a sub-sample analysis and finds the results to be better in the case of the post-liberalization period, i.e. existence of long and short run relationship between domestic and world markets.

After establishing the presence of integration, it is also important to test for the nature of that transmission, i.e. whether it is symmetric or asymmetric. Most literatures on price transmission assume symmetric transmission, i.e. international prices affect domestic prices in the same manner irrespective of price increase or decrease. Although enough literature exists on Asymmetric Price Transmission (APT), it has not been sufficiently explored in the Indian setting. This study intends to fill that gap to some extent. In a paper published in 1977, Houck attempts to bring in more operational clarity and extends the work of Wolffram (1971) in the empirical testing of non-reversibility hypothesis or asymmetric changes. Although the first observation is important to asymmetric analysis, however, it does not have an impact on the overall analysis, as the effects measured depends on the previous observation rather than the level. This was the key point of departure from Wolffram. He formulated the test for asymmetric price transmission, in which, he suggested bifurcating the independent variable into rising and falling stages, using a dummy variable. Nevertheless, the technique's limitation lies in its inconsistency in dealing with the non-stationary series, i.e. the paper disregarded the important attributes of a time series and hence the method is not advisable to apply when using the time series. Presence of asymmetry is a reflection of market failure and inefficiency (Bathla and Srinivasulu, 2011). Ward (1982), in his paper, looks at the extent of asymmetric price transmission in the case of a vertical market structure, i.e. among wholesale, retail, and shipping point. The study offers several reasons for asymmetry, perishability being a major reason in this case.

The paper by Von Cramon-Taubadel (1998) is a groundbreaker, as it develops formal tests for asymmetric price transmission for a cointegrated series. As mentioned above, one limitation of Houck's (1977) paper was disregarding of the time series properties. Von Cramom-Taubadel (1998) recognized this drawback and developed formal tests for asymmetry. A precursor for testing asymmetry is testing for transmission; and this transmission can be asymmetric as well as lagged. In addition, both magnitude and speed of the price transmission can be asymmetric. Abdulai (2000) studies the spatial price transmission and asymmetry in the three Ghanian maize markets, by employing the procedure developed by Enders and Granger. Serra and Goodwin (2003) measure the vertical price transmission in the Spanish Dairy Market for the 1990s. The results indicate no asymmetries in the price transmission of highly perishable products. As mentioned earlier, Von Cramon-Taubadel (1998) developed a technique for testing asymmetric transmission for the cointegrated series. In this paper, Meyer and Von Cramon-Taubadel (2004) study the existing literature on Asymmetric Price Transmission (APT) and assess their strengths and weaknesses. The survey of literature on APT informs the reader about the technique in detail, as not many extant literatures have explained it comprehensively. They start with distinguishing different types of APT and their causes; and explain the difference between pre-cointegration and the cointegration process of testing APT.

Speaking of comprehensive explanation, one cannot disregard Bathla and Srinivasulu (2011). Their study is an important addition to the existing literature on APT, especially in the Indian context. They test the asymmetry in a vertical market by considering groundnut seed and oil prices in three wholesale markets. The authors test the APT by employing both the Houck and Von-Taubdel (2004) approach, the latter involving the cointegration analysis. Their study rejects the null hypothesis of price symmetry, in case of all the selected markets. The paper definitely encourages further research in APT, especially in other commodities and markets. Such studies will definitely throw some light on the nexus between market power and APT. Another well-explained study on both price transmission and price asymmetry is by Weldesenbet (2013). The aim of the paper is to establish for vertical price transmission between the Slovakian liquid milk prices at the producer, wholesale and retail levels, and to check for Granger Causality and Price Asymmetry. The paper employs both the Houck and Error correction approach to check for asymmetry. The test confirms asymmetry with transmission of increase in prices to be higher transmission of decrease in prices.

Data Description

As discussed above, the objective of the study is to analyse wheat and rice markets in India, and to study the extent of price transmissions from a global market to domestic markets in India. The implicit assumption in the price transmission model is that the nature of that transmission is symmetric. However, it may not be so and hence, we also intend to determine the nature of the price transmission, i.e. whether it is asymmetric or symmetric; as the speed of transmission usually depends on whether the adjustment of the variable is submitted to a negative or a positive shock (Acharya et al., 2012). The first step towards accomplishing the tasks above is to extract the wheat and rice price time series. In this study, we work with two datasets; one, for a short run analysis and second, for a long run analysis. The dataset used for a short run analysis is the annual wholesale price indices from 1970 to 2013. However, considering the number of observations of an annual series[2], to analyse price transmission and to ascertain long run relationship, we also work with monthly actual domestic and international price series for wheat and rice. The data for the domestic wholesale price index is from the *Office of the Economic Advisor*, while the monthly wholesale price data is from *Agricultural Prices in India, Ministry of Agriculture.* The source for the international wheat and rice price index data is *IFS* data source, whereas the data for actual international prices is from the *World Bank Pink Sheet*. All price indices for international commodities are according to the base year 2005. Therefore, to make it comparable to the international series, we converted the domestic price index base for both rice and wheat to 2005. For that purpose, we derived the linking factor. The linking factor is important for maintaining continuity, in order to merge the old series with the new one. Figure (1) represents the comparison for rice from the period 1970-2013.

Figure (1): Domestic Rice Price Index vs. International Rice Price Index

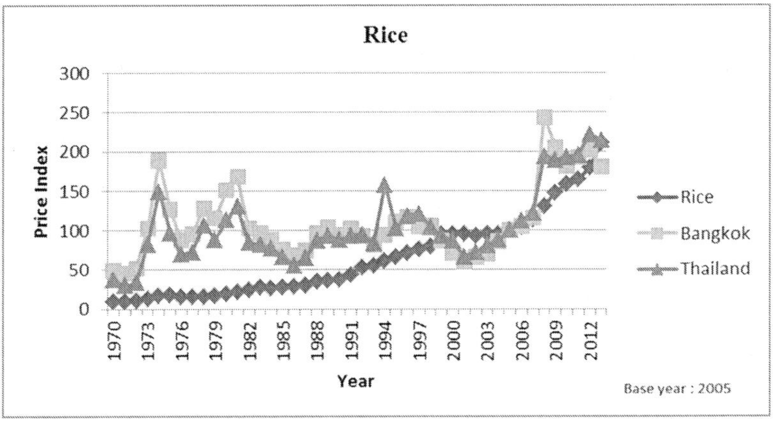

Source: *Office of Economic Advisor* and *IFS*

The global price index has been well above the domestic wholesale price index till the late 1990s. There is a clear rising trend. The domestic price index remains above the global prices series only for a short period. The series does seem to meet but that does not imply that they move together. However, all of them definitely have a rising trend. This comparison confirms one key point, i.e. the global agricultural rice market is less stable than the domestic rice market.

A similar comparison for wheat is shown in Figure (2) below. The global market in this case is the United States. It is clear that both the series have an increasing trend with a rather smooth one for Indian wheat. Compared to rice, the Indian wheat market seems to be more stable than the global wheat market. The prices have diverged till the late 1990s, and since then have moved together with a few intervals of spurts. In fact, looking at both the figures above, in case of both rice and wheat, domestic prices have diverged from international prices in the 1980s and in most of the 1990s. It is only around 1998 that we see a diverging trend. Prices in the US experience a steep increase in price in 2008, followed by a sudden drop in the following year.

Figure (2): Domestic Wheat Price Index vs. International Wheat Price Index

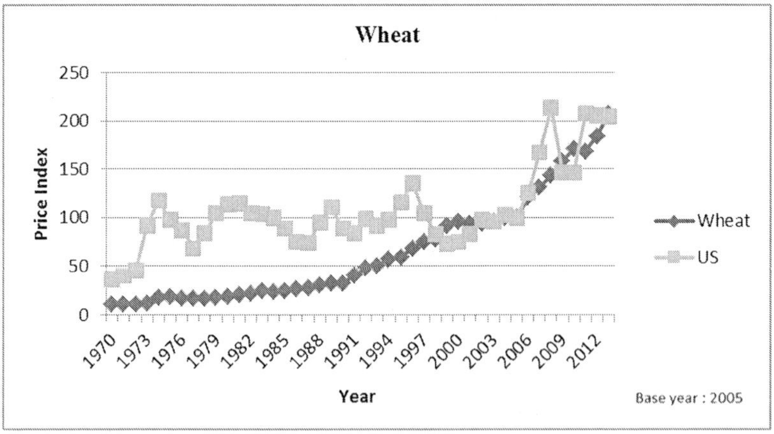

Source: *Office of Economic Advisor* and *IFS*

The international market had more than 30% fall in 2009. In contrast, there was an 11% increase in the case of Indian wheat. Nayyar and Sen (1994) suggest such increases in domestic prices could be due to price support policies that lead to faster increase in domestic prices than global prices. If we closely watch the figures above, we see that, in case of both wheat and rice, domestic prices series were almost flat till 1990. The series changes its slope after 1990 and remains well below the international price series till 1997-98. It is only beyond 1998 that the domestic price index merges or moves together with the international price index. Important policy changes occurred during these two periods.

Along with the chief economic reforms of 1991, we also saw revamping of the PDS, done to ensure effective distribution of food grains especially to backward, drought-prone, hilly, tribal areas and to its people. This distribution system was made targeted, known as the TPDS, in 1997, with the objective to reach all the poor in every area; leaving the identification of beneficiaries to the state government. These policy changes may or may not have an effect on the domestic price changes. Therefore, it is important that we control for these periods, otherwise our results may be biased. However, accounting for these period dummies, we find the dummy to be insignificant in most cases. Having said above, it will be rather more rational to look at the comparison of absolute prices rather than indices, as indices present relative changes rather than absolute changes. The period of analysis is from March 1992–July 2015. Unit for domestic prices were Rs/Qtl while for international prices were $/MT. Data for the rupee-dollar exchange rate was downloaded from RBI, *Handbook of Statistics on Indian Economy*. Since, the monthly exchange rate data was available only from March 1992; thus, we begin our analysis period from there. Therefore, after necessary conversions, all domestic price series were converted to $/MT for comparative analysis. As mentioned above, we collected monthly actual prices for rice and wheat from the Ministry of Agriculture, Government of India. Several markets according to their variety were considered. In the case of rice, wholesale markets in Amritsar, Mumbai, Delhi, Nagpur, Nizamabad, Patna and Rajkot were considered. Most of the varieties had an incomplete series and many missing values. Markets were chosen according to a particular variety, with data till 2015[3]. The period of analysis for the Delhi and Mumbai market for basmati variety starts from January 2002 and January 2006 respectively. This is so due to non-availability of data for previous years. Three markets, according to their variety, were considered for international markets, i.e. Thailand (25% broken), Thailand (100% broken), and Vietnam (5% broken). The World Bank pink sheet dataset was used to extract data for international markets. In the case of wheat, wholesale markets in Bengaluru, Delhi,

Hyderabad, Karnal, Mumbai, and Patna for domestic and US as the international market was studied. It is also important to state that missing data were adjusted using interpolation and seasonally adjusted with the help of Eviews software.

Looking at the individual markets[4], we find that prices of domestic regional markets are however well above the international market. Not only does there appear to be co-movement of prices, there also seems to be co-movement of volatility. It would be rather interesting to check for transmission of volatility from international to domestic markets too for both rice and wheat. This could be an interesting area of further research.

Methodology

As mentioned in the previous sections, the objective of the study is to analyse the short run as well as the long run relationship between the domestic agricultural prices and global agricultural prices. Although not fully, Indian agricultural markets have always been exposed to international markets. Thus, it may be the case that the price trend in international markets may be an important cause for a price change in domestic markets. However, domestic agricultural markets also depend on various factors apart from international prices like weather, output, stocks, trade, input prices, price of related goods, minimum support prices, transport costs, government/state taxes, etc. Therefore, to test the significance of some of the factors stated above, we analyse a regression using the OLS method. The analysis will also indicate of the significance and the magnitude of the international price on the domestic price. However, to check the robustness of the significance of the international price, we estimate an alternative model called the long run model using the Johansen co-integration method. As mentioned in Section 3, we use the price index data to carry out the short run analysis and the actual price data to find the long run relationship between the domestic and global price of a particular commodity.

Most time-series data fail to meet the requirements of OLS, i.e. to be the best linear unbiased estimators, for which the series must be stationary. A non-stationary series violates one or more of the above conditions. We label a stationary time series as I (0) and a non-stationary time series as I (1). Usually, a time series data is non-stationary in nature. Non-stationary data contain stochastic trends[5], which can lead to spurious regression problems. If not corrected for, standard t tests can misidentify about a long run relationship between two series by indicating statistically significant long run relationships in the model, which demonstrates contemporaneous correlations rather than meaningful causal relations (Harris and Sollis, 2003). Therefore, any regression between two series will mislead about an existence of a relationship even if the variables are independent. Granger and Newbold (1974) coined the term *spurious regression* in 1974. They showed that even if y_t and x_t are independent of each other, a simple OLS analysis leads to statistical significance of t values.

Testing for Co-integration

The unit root test helps us to distinguish true regression from spurious regression. Ideally, a linear combination of two non-stationary variables should be non-stationary. Nevertheless, in some special cases, it may not be the case, e.g. in the case of a long run relationship between the two variables. It could be possible that a linear combination of two non-stationary variables be stationary. If such an association between the two variables exists, then they are said to be co-integrated[6]. Co-integration constructs a meaningful relationship between two non-stationary or I (1) variables (Wooldridge, 2009). Co-integration implies the presence of a long run equilibrium to which an economic system converges over time. If the variables do not exhibit a co-integrating relationship, then a linear combination of them will be non-stationary as well, i.e. the stochastic trend demonstrated by the predicted error term, i.e. $\hat{e}_t$ would simply represent the difference between the two separate stochastic trends in y and x.

The starting point of the Johansen procedure is defining a vector autoregressive (VAR) model z_t upto k lags for potentially n endogenous variables:

$$z_t = A_1 z_{t-1} + ... + A_k z_{t-k} + u_t \quad (11)$$

Where, z_t is (n × 1) each A_i is a (n × n) matrix of parameters and u_t ~IN (0, Σ); Σ is a (n × n) variance-covariance matrix. This estimates the dynamic relationship with endogenous variables without any restrictions. The above equation can be written in the form Error Correction representation or ECM:

$$\Delta z_t = \Pi_p z_{t-p} + \Sigma_{i=1}^{p-1} \Pi_i \Delta x_{t-i} + e_t \quad (12)$$

where $\Pi_i = -I_k + \Sigma_{j=1}^{i} A_j$, i = 1, ..., p. The matrix is the matrix of long run responses. The eigenvalues of Π_p are demonstrated as $1 > \lambda_1 \geq \lambda_2 \geq ... \geq \lambda_k \geq 0$. The eigenvectors associated with the non-zero eigenvalues of Π_p are the co-integrating vectors. When the rank(r) of Π_p is between 0<r<k; there are (k-r) common stochastic trends in the system and r independent linear co-integrated combinations of the elements of z_t. In this case, $\lambda_1 .... \lambda_r \neq 0$, $\lambda_{r+1} .... \lambda_k = 0$, Π_p can be factorized into $\gamma\alpha'$ where γ and α are both (k × r) matrices of rank r. The linearly independent columns of α, the co-integrating matrix, are the co-integrating vectors, such that $\alpha' x_t \sim I(0)$. After normalization to the ith element of x_t, they may be interpreted as the long run parameters of the ith equation in the system. The corresponding elements of γ, the adjustment matrix, measure the speed of adjustment of the error correction mechanisms involved i.e. they are ECM coefficients. With normalization to the ith element of x_t, we would expect the ith row of γ to contain only negative elements, facilitating negative feedback.

The existence of co-integration is tested by trace statistic and maximum eigenvalue. Johansen indicates a likelihood ratio trace statistic of the null hypothesis that there are at most r co-integrating vectors, against the alternative that there are k co-integrating vectors:

$$J(r) = -T\,\Sigma_{i=r+1}^{k} \ln(1-\bar{\lambda}_t), (0 \leq r \leq k-1) \quad (13)$$

The null hypothesis is that there are no co-integrating vectors against the alternative that there is k. If the null fails to be rejected, we conclude that there is no co-integration. If not, then, we test the next null that there is one co-integrating vector against k and keep repeating till the null that there are 's' co-integrating vectors cannot be rejected.

He also suggests a maximum eigenvalue statistic,

$\lambda_{max(r)} = -T\ln(1-\bar{\lambda}_{r+1}), (0 \leq r \leq k-1)$. The test starts by testing the null $H_0 : r = 0$ against $H_1 : r = 1$. If the null fails to be rejected, then there is no co-integration. Otherwise, we test the next null $H_1 : r = 1$ against $H_2 : r = 2$ and keep repeating till the null $H_b : r = b$ is accepted, concluding that the co-integrating is b.

However, there are some problems with this approach like, for different statistics, the procedure produces different results in small samples. Second, results are based on the lag length. Third, more variables mean less power for the tests. Finally, the errors are not always normal.

Error Correction Model

We learnt that co-integration exhibits a long run relationship between the variables. Logically, if a long run relationship exists, there should be a short run relationship too. As Dougherty (2011) states, "There must be some short run forces that are responsible for keeping the relationship intact." Therefore, for an intensive examination of the relationship, we construct an error correction model that combines both long run and short run dynamics. Consider the equation,

$$y_t = \beta_0 + \beta_1 x_t + \beta_2 y_{t-1} + \beta_3 x_{t-1} + \varepsilon_t \tag{14}$$

It is an autoregressive distributed lag (ARDL) model. Subtracting y_{t-1} from both sides,

$$\Delta y_t = \beta_0 + \beta_1 x_t + (\beta_2 - 1)y_{t-1} + \beta_3 x_{t-1} + \varepsilon_t \tag{15}$$

Now adding and subtracting $(\beta_1 - 1)x_{t-1}$ from the RHS,

$$\Delta y_t = \beta_0 + (\beta_2 - 1)y_{t-1} + \beta_1 x_t + \beta_1 x_{t-1} - x_{t-1} - \beta_1 x_{t-1} + x_{t-1} + \beta_3 x_{t-1} + \varepsilon_t$$

$$\Delta y_t = \beta_0 + (\beta_2 - 1)y_{t-1} + \beta_1 \Delta x_t + (\beta_1 + \beta_3)x_{t-1} + \varepsilon_t \tag{16}$$

Rearranging the above equation,

$$\Delta y_t = \beta_1 \Delta x_t - \lambda\,(y_{t-1} - \beta x_{t-1} - \alpha) + \varepsilon_t \tag{17}$$

where $\lambda = (1-\beta_2), \beta = \dfrac{\beta_1 + \beta_3}{1-\beta_2}, \alpha = \dfrac{\beta_0}{1-\beta_2}$

The above equation (17) is the error correction model. The term $\lambda(y_{t-1} - \beta x_{t-1} - \alpha)$ is called the error correction term. The model specifies that a change in y at any time t be influenced by a change in x, the variance between, y_{t-1} and the predicted value by regressing the co-integration equation. Observe that the error correction equation is similar to the ARDL equation above. They have the same error term too. However, re-parametrization of the equation (14) is superior to the ARDL model:

- Even though working with non-stationary variables, all terms in the error correction model are stationary. Therefore, the model can be regressed using OLS and standard hypothesis testing holds.
- Economic interpretation behind the error correction mechanism is clear. β_1 demonstrates the short run impact showing that the current change in y_t is proportional to a current change in x_t. β demonstrates the long run impact and the long run adjustment factor is given by λ. One-to-one price transmission in the long run requires β to be 1 (Greb et al., 2012). The negative sign ensures that any disequilibrium will corrected gradually as $\beta_2 < 1$. However, if $\lambda > 0$, then any disequilibrium would get compounded, getting larger and larger through time.

In our study, the ADF test confirms non-stationarity property of agricultural price series. The Johansen Co-integration method establishes whether the price is transmitted from the international market to the domestic market. Therefore, if the co-integration relation is established, it signifies market integration. The extent of integration is established by the error correction model, which demonstrates the speed and magnitude of the adjustment parameter. Finally, the study checks for price asymmetry, and hence, below is the methodology to test the same.

Testing for Asymmetric Price Transmission (APT)

After establishing that transmission exists, it is equally crucial to establish whether the price transmission between the two markets is symmetric or asymmetric. As already discussed, it denotes that the extent and speed of transmission changes according to price increase or decrease. There are several approaches to test for asymmetry; however, we sill discuss the one we employed in our study.

Co-integration Approach

As discussed, the time series are usually non-stationary implying that Houck's approach may actually give rise to spurious regressions and may not be unbiased and consistent. Under this approach, first a co-integrating relationship is found and derive the lagged residuals from the error correction term and then split that error term into positive and negative parts. Von Cramon-Taubadel and Fahlbusch initially developed the method in 1994. The error correction model is as below:

$$\Delta y_t = \alpha + \Sigma_{j=1}^{K}\beta_j \Delta x_{t-j+1} + \theta^{+}ECT_{t-1}^{+} + \theta \; ECT_{t-1} + \mu_t \qquad (20)$$

Von Cramon-Taubadel and Loy extended this in 1996. They proposed to allow for effects that are more dynamic and suggested to split Δx_t into positive and negative parts with lags,

$$\Delta y_t = \alpha + \Sigma_{j=1}^{K}\beta_j^{+} D^{+} \Delta x_{t-j+1} + \Sigma_{j=1}^{L} \beta_j^{-} \; D \; \Delta x_{t-j+1} + \theta^{+}ECT_{t-1}^{+} + \theta^{-}ECT_{t-1}^{-} + \mu_t \qquad (21)$$

The above equation is the final model for asymmetric price testing. It is also called the asymmetric error correction model. Coefficient θ measures the extent of adjustment to equilibrium while β depicts the short run parameter. An implicit assumption in the model is that the error corrections or the adjustment parameters are constant. Hypothesis testing, through an F test, on β and θ will establish whether the transmission process is symmetric or asymmetric. Thus, the null is, and $H_0 : \Sigma_{j=1}^{K}\beta_j^{+} = \Sigma_{j=1}^{L}\beta_j$ and $\theta^{+} = \theta^{-}$. Rejection of the null will imply that the process of price transmission is indeed asymmetric.

The following is a short summary of the methodology and steps that the current study has followed:

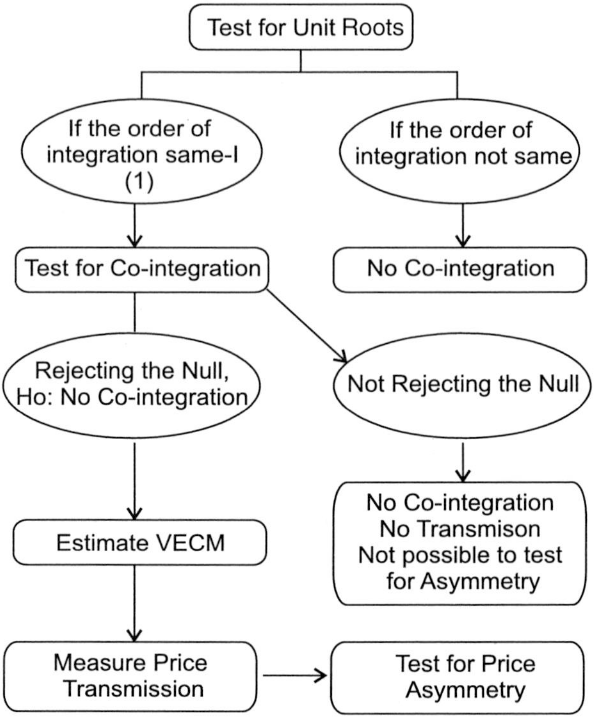

Empirical Results

Short Run Analysis for Rice

A short run model of domestic rice price formation is estimated by OLS. The international market in the case of rice is Thailand. We use the annual price index data for both the domestic and global market. The annual price index is regressed upon some of the factors as listed in the table. However, only those results with significant world price are reported. Regression results for rice clearly shows domestic factors like fertilizer price, public stocks, playing a larger role in influencing the domestic price rather than the world price. After testing for unit roots[7], we find the domestic price, world price and fertilizer price to be non-stationary at the levels and stationary at their first difference. All variables are in logarithmic form and in the first difference, the dependent variable being the domestic price. The regression results are as below:

Table (1): Regression Results for Rice

Independent Variables	*Model (1) (1972-2013)*	*Model (2) (1972-2013)*	*Model (3) (1970-2013)*
World Price	0.07**	0.08*	0.10*
	(1.95)	(4.94)	(5.00)
Fertilizer Price	0.35*	0.31*	0.31*
	(3.78)	(7.68)	(6.12)
Rice Stocks	-0.01	-0.01*	
	(-0.81)	(-2.50)	
Per Capita Availability			-0.15*
			(-2.44)
Dummy		0.09*	0.10*
		(12.53)	(9.57)
Constant	0.07**	0.07*	0.68*
	(2.09)	(4.45)	(2.58)
N	42	42	43
R^2	0.34	0.87	0.80
DW stat	1.97	1.82	1.52

t values are in parenthesis. *, ** denote significance level at 1% and 5% respectively

In model (1), we regress the domestic price with the world price, fertilizer price, and stocks. The variable of interest, i.e. world price is significant at 5%. The price transmission elasticity is quite low at 7%. Although, rice stocks have expected sign, as increase in stocks should ideally reduce the domestic price, it is not statistically significant.

We introduce dummy variable in model (2), to deal with the outliers as in the residual graph (1) in the appendix[8]. The dummy is highly significant. Therefore, incorporating the dummy into the model helps in accounting for the outliers caused by factors not explained in the model and improves the model. The extent of world price transmission on domestic price increases marginally but becomes significant at 1%; the fertilizer price seems to be robust with the significance level while the effect of rice stocks, although less in magnitude becomes highly significant with the expected negative sign.

Next, we add per capita availability of rice instead of rice stocks and observe the changes. This is defined as the net availability divided by population in a particular year. Therefore, this includes total stocks available in the economy. Adding the outlier dummy increase the price transmission elasticity to 10%, fertilizer elasticity is more or less the same at around 31%. However, our per capita availability variable becomes highly significant at 1% with an expected sign.

Short Run Analysis for Wheat

The international market in this case is the USA. Unit root results[9] confirm the variables to be non-stationary at the levels and stationary at their first difference. We start with the regressing world price and fertilizer price on the domestic wheat price. We present the results below after accounting for outliers[10]. In model (1), we find the transmission elasticity in this case to be 5% at 1% level of significance. Coefficient on fertilizer price also seems to be highly significant. It implies that an increase in fertilizer price by 1% leads to 52% increase in the domestic price of wheat.

Table (2): Regression Results for Wheat

Independent Variables	*Model (1) (1972-2013)*	*Model (2) (1970-2013)*
World Price	0.05*	0.03**
	(2.57)	(2.02)
Fertilizer Price	0.52*	0.55*
	(14.13)	(15.47)
Per Capita Availability		0.09*
		(4.02)
Dummy	0.08*	0.09*
	(15.56)	(15.56)
Constant	0.03*	-0.33*
	(5.51)	(-3.63)
N	43	43
R^2	0.90	0.91
DW stat	1.82	1.64

t values are in parenthesis. *, ** denote significance level at 1% and 5% respectively

In model (2), we add per capita availability of wheat and analyse whether it affects the domestic price of wheat significantly, along with fertilizer price and world price. After adding dummy to control for unobserved factors, the model improves. The fit of the model also increases significantly[11]. The world price transmission elasticity is significant at 5%. However, the transmission elasticity is less. This implies that the domestic factor plays a larger role in affecting both rice and wheat price than global factors. Although per capita availability becomes significant, we do not find the expected sign on the coefficient. However, if both per capita availability of wheat and domestic price of wheat seem to have an increasing trend, it is possible to expect the result as in model (2).

Therefore, the short run analysis of rice and wheat clearly shows that the domestic factors have a larger role in influencing the domestic prices than the world prices. Although the world prices have a significant effect on the domestic price of both rice and wheat, the magnitude of the effect is relatively small, as compared to other factors like fertilizer price, production levels, and stocks. In addition, looking at regression models above, we see that the magnitude of transmission elasticity of rice is higher than of wheat. This indicates a lower level of market integration between the domestic market and international market in case of wheat compared to rice. However, these results may not be robust with a larger number of observations and more explanatory variables. We shall now check the robustness of this result through a long run analysis using Johansen co-integration tests in our next section.

Long Run Analysis for Rice

We applied the ADF test, to the logarithmically transformed and seasonally adjusted monthly price series of rice[12], both at the level and the first differenced series. As seen clearly, price series of every market in the study are I (1). After conducting the unit root analysis, the next step is to find a long run relationship between the domestic market and an international market by employing

Johansen's co-integration test. Co-integration means that two variables may be non-stationary and wander through time but a linear combination of them makes them converge to a stationary process. If this happens, it implies that a long run relationship exists between those variables, i.e. they will not wander apart in the long-run, as the market forces will bring them back to equilibrium. The table below summarizes the results of the Johansen co-integration analysis. It is important to mention that co-integration results are sensitive to lag length selection. We have paired each domestic market with each international market[13]. Out of 24 pairs, only 7 show the presence of a long run relationship. Weldesenbet (2013) in his paper states that, "The absence of co-integration could be interpreted as some evidence against market competition". This stands true in our study given the intensity of government intervention in our food markets. Hence, the study only reports the results of those markets that exhibit co-integration.

Table (3): Co-integration of Rice Markets

Variables	*Null*	*Max Eigenvalue*	*5% Critical Value*	*Trace*	*5% Critical Value*
Amrtisar-Thai100	r=0	21.2	14.2	24.2	15.4
	rd≤1	63.00	63.84	63.00	93.84
Amritsar-Thai25	r=0	19.97	14.26	22.67	15.49
	rd≤1	2.70	3.84	2.7	3.84
Amritsar-Viet5	r=0	18.71	14.26	19.08	15.49
	rd≤1	0.36	3.84	0.36	3.84
Delhi-Viet5	r=0	15.48	14.26	17.41	15.49
	rd≤1	1.92	3.84	1.92	3.84
Mumbai-Thai100	r=0	15.4	14.2	20.1	15.4
	rd≤1	54.71	63.84	64.71	93.84
Nagpur-Thai100	r=0	14.0	14.2	15.5	15.4
	rd≤1	81.43	63.84	21.43	93.84
Nagpur-Viet5	r=0	15.7	14.2	17.5	15.4
	rd≤1	81.73	63.84	11.73	93.84

Source: Own calculations

Both the trace and eigenvalue statistic reject the null of no co-integration for the pairs listed above[14]. Therefore, there are co-movements in these pairs for a long time. Once we establish co-integration, the next step is to estimate a vector error correction (VECM)[15] model for short run estimates. This helps us to differentiate between the long run dynamics and the short run dynamics. It is approximated by taking the variables in the first differences, their lagged value[16] and the lagged residual estimated from the co-integrating equation. The long run price transmission elasticity in case of Amritsar and Thailand100 is 60%. This is also known as the long run coefficient, which implies that reaction of domestic price to changes in price of Thailand. The coefficient of the error term reflects the speed of adjustment, which should be negative and significant. For Amritsar and Thailand100, the speed of adjustment is 6% i.e. only 6% of adjustment towards equilibrium every month. The adjustment process is quite slow in this case. Results are similar in the case of integration between Amritsar and Thailand25. The long run price elasticity is around 64% while the adjustment parameter is only 6%. The transmission elasticity increases in case of Vietnam5% rice, around 69%. However, the speed of adjustment is even slower, at around 3% every month. As required, the adjustment parameters are negative and significant at 1%. The long run coefficient of the co-integrating equation is 63% between Delhi and Vietnam5. Although the sign of the coefficient of the error correction term is negative, it is insignificant. A negative and statistically insignificant coefficient implies that prices in these two markets may or may not return to the equilibrium path (Bathla 2011). As far as integration between Mumbai and Thailand100 is concerned, the magnitude of integration is 65% but speed of adjustment is still slow at 7%. In the case of Nagpur, with both Thailand100 and Vietnam5, the coefficient of the error term is negative but insignificant. However, the extent of transmission is 69% with Thailand100 and 62% with Vietnam5.

Asymmetric Price Transmission Test

We keep our model simple and follow the technique developed by Stephen Von Cramon-Taubadel and Fahlbusch (1994). To allow for dynamic effects Von Cramon-Taubadel and Loy (1996) suggest splitting the international price into positive and negative components. However, for simplicity, we follow the former technique, where the authors suggest splitting the ECT into positive and negative components and test for APT. The results are presented in the appendix, and in the table below, we present the summary of the results.

Table (4): APT Results – ECM Approach

Markets	*ECT⁺*	*ECT⁻*	*F-Test Statistic*	*P Value*	*Analysis*
Amritsar-Thailand100	-0.07*	-0.04	0.78	0.37	Symmetric
Amritsar-Thailand25	-0.06*	-0.05	0.07	0.78	Symmetric
Amrtisar-Thailand5	-0.07*	-0.01	2.12	0.14	Symmetric
Delhi-Thailand5	-0.06	-0.02	0.30	0.58	Symmetric
Mumbai-Thailand100	-0.12	-0.06	0.18	0.66	Symmetric
Nagpur-Thailand100	-0.04	-0.04	0.003	0.95	Symmetric
Nagpur-Thailand5	-0.04	0.006	0.64	0.42	Symmetric

Source: Own calculations

As seen above, for all the concerned markets, the joint F test is not able to reject the null of symmetric price transmission. While all the coefficients of error correction term have a negative sign, not all of them are significant. Only rising prices in case of Amritsar is significant at 1% level, which implies that positive deviations of price from the long-run market equilibrium adjust faster every month than negative deviations (Bathla, 2011). This also implies that domestic prices are above their equilibrium with respect to global prices, so we would expect to adjust downwards in the following month. Therefore, price transmission is symmetric between the domestic and international markets in our study. Acharya et al. (2012) also estimated similar results in their study of the Rice and Wheat Market Integration and Transmission in India.

Long Run Analysis for Wheat

The formal ADF test is applied to determine the existence of the unit root in different markets. The results in appendix 6(a) clearly show that the markets have different orders of integration unlike in the case of rice. All the price series are integrated of order (1) except Patna and Bengaluru. However, Bengaluru is I(0) at 5% level of significance as the ADF t statistic is 3.72 while the 1% critical value is 3.99. Therefore, we do not include Patna in our long-run analysis.

Johansen Co-integration Tests

Out of 5 domestic markets, only two of them show the presence of co-integration, i.e. Bengaluru and Mumbai. Therefore, Bengaluru and Mumbai exhibit a long-run relationship with the international market-US. Such results are highly likely as the integration of market depends on not only the location but also the type and quality of the commodity in question. Below are the results for the tests:

Table (5): Co-integration of Wheat Markets

Variables	*Null*	*Max Eigenvalue*	*5% Critical Value*	*Trace*	*5% Critical Value*
Bengaluru-US	r=0	13.9	14.2	16.2	15.4
	rd≤1	02.31	63.84	22.31	93.84
Mumbai-US	r=0	15.94	14.26	18.32	15.49
	rd≤1	2.37	3.84	2.37	3.84

Source: Own calculations

Both the trace statistics reject the null of no co-integration for both Bengaluru and Mumbai. However, the max eigenvalue test is unable to reject the null hypothesis for Bengaluru. Since, the trace test rejects the null hypothesis and confirms the presence of a long run relationship, we follow suit. Vector Error Correction Model[17] gives us the long run coefficient or the extent of transmission between Bengaluru and the global market, which is estimated to be 83%. Since both the variables are in logs, this is the long run transmission elasticity. The coefficient on the error correction model is -0.04, which is negative and significant. This implies that every month 4% of disequilibrium is corrected towards equilibrium. However, in the case of Mumbai, although the coefficient on error term is significant, the sign of the coefficient is positive. This implies that instead of correcting towards the equilibrium, the series only drifts apart in the long run. Therefore, wheat markets in these regional markets seem to be well integrated with the global market; however, the markets do not correct the disequilibrium in the case of Mumbai.

Asymmetric Price Transmission Test

Table (6): APT Results – ECM Approach

Markets	*ECT^+*	*ECT^-*	*F-Test Statistic*	*P Value*	*Analysis*
Bengaluru-US	–0.05	–0.04	0.001	0.96	Symmetric
Mumbai-US	0.009	0.001	0.07	0.78	Symmetric

Source: Own calculations

None of the error correction terms is significant, whether positive or negative error correction. It is impossible to say whether domestic prices are above or below with respect to the global price. Nevertheless, we conduct the Wald test on the error correction coefficients. It is evident from the table that we were not able to reject the null hypothesis of price symmetry. The results above are similar to those found by Conforti et al. (2004). Although, they find a substantial level of co-integration between world price and producer price, co-integration does not seem to exist between the world price and wholesale price of wheat and rice. As mentioned before, Acharya et al. (2012) also fail to reject the null hypothesis of price symmetry in case of wholesale prices of rice and wheat. Therefore, the present study affirms the existing literature with the latest and larger sample data.

Conclusion

This study attempted to evaluate the spatial price transmission between the domestic and international price of rice and wheat. The study also undertook the price asymmetry test to understand the nature of transmission. We divide the study into short run and long run analysis. The short run results indicate some extent of integration despite excessive intervention, state taxes, infrastructural bottlenecks, etc. Agricultural price policy on a national basis would be meaningless if the markets remain fragmented. All India price policy would be more appropriate and effective if a national market exists and formulation of such a policy depends on a profound knowledge of the food grain markets. Countries with better infrastructure and advancing policies experience nearly complete market integration as indicated by the given literature.

Results in this study demonstrate transmission between the international and domestic price for both the commodities. Short and long run results clearly indicate the presence. However, the result holds true for some of the regional markets in our sample. The chief reason for the presence of integration, especially in case of the Amritsar rice market is the fact that basmati rice is more highly traded than non-basmati variety. Most of our exports of basmati variety went to Saudi Arabia and non-basmati variety to Bangladesh, Sri Lanka, and Senegal in 2014-15. While there is evidence of transmission, the rate at which the disequilibrium between the markets corrects in the long run is reasonably low. Greb et al. (2012) claim the reason to be increased imports with respect to consumption, trade restrictedness, and political interference. They argue positive correlation between openness to trade and the speed of transmission. International prices are generally influenced by taxes/subsidies, income, market crisis, etc. while domestic prices are influenced by tariff/non-tariff barriers, exchange rates, infrastructure, government presence, demand and supply conditions, etc. Therefore, owing to the above factors, prices may not necessarily converge. Price transmission is also consequent upon the characteristic/quality of the goods involved. There are divergent varieties of a commodity in India of both rice and wheat.

Nevertheless, we need to deal with the empirical findings with some precautions. Presence of no co-integration does not imply absence of transmission. Greb et al. (2012) note in their paper that ignoring the breaks/phases in the sample period may lead to no co-integration. Thus, they suggest incorporating Threshold Vector

Error Correction Model (TVECM), which accounts for any specific phases for checking the robustness of the results. Structural breaks in the data may lead to mistakes in interpreting the results. Therefore, we suggest accounting for these breaks in future research work.

At last, we tested for asymmetric price transmission between those markets with co-integration using the methodology given by Von Cramon-Taubadel and Fahlbusch (1994) in Meyer and Von Cramon-Taubadel (2004). We were not able to reject the null hypothesis of price symmetry, in case of both rice and wheat. The results affirm the findings in the existing literature. Acharya et al. (2012) also find no price asymmetry in case of wholesale prices; although their study finds it in the case of retail prices. It would be interesting to see the robustness of the results using the methodology adopted by Von Cramon-Taubadel and Loy (1996) and allow for higher order polynomials, which will take into account the non-linearity in price transmission. However, the model used by this study, considers the asymmetry with respect to speed and not with respect to the magnitude. Asymmetry in the magnitude implies that the price increase and decrease phase will move apart in the long run. In addition, the model by Von Cramon-Taubadel and Fahlbusch (1996) is based on the assumption that the parameters of the error correction terms are constant, i.e. the deviation from the equilibrium remains constant.

There is a need to research further on the structure of the agricultural market; not only to understand the nuances of it but also for policy recommendations. There is a need to buttress the above study with employing better models like by Von Cramon-Taubadel and Loy using the polynomial distributed lag model; which will also account for multicollinearity unlike the distributed lag model. Alternate models will help check the robustness of the above results and give us a better understanding of the commodity market.

REFERENCES

Abdulai, A. (2000). "Spatial Price Transmission and Asymmetry in the Ghanian Maize Market". *Journal of Development Economics*, Vol. 63.

Acharya, S., Chand, R., Birthal, P.S., Kumar, S., and Negi, D.S. (2012). "Market Integration and Price Transmission in India: A Case of Rice and Wheat with Special Reference to the World Food Crisis of 2007-08". FAO.

Acharya, S.S. and Chaudhri, D.P. (eds.) (2001). *Indian Agricultural Policy at Crossroads.* Jaipur: Rawat Publications.

Barrett, B.C. (2005). 'Spatial Market Integration', in Lawrence E. Blume and Steven N. Durlauf (eds.), *The New Palgrave Dictionary of Economics*, 2nd Edition, London: Palgrave Macmillan.

Bathla, S. and Srinivasulu, R. (2011). Price Transmission and Asymmetry: An Empirical Analysis of Indian Groundnut Seed and Oil Markets. *Indian Journal of Agricultural Economics*, Vol. 66, No. 4.

Bathla, S. (2011). *Trade Liberalization and Indian Agriculture*. New Delhi: Rawat Publications.

Capps, O. and Sherwell, P. (2005). Spatial Asymmetry in Farm-Retail Price Transmission Associated with Fluid Milk Products. Paper prepared for presentation at the American Agricultural Economics Association Annual Meeting, Providence, Rhode Island.

Ceballos, F., Hernandez, M.A., Minot, N. and Robles, M. (2015). IFPRI Discussion Paper, No. 01472.

Chand, Ramesh. (2007). "Wheat Supply, Price Prospects, and Food Security". *Economic and Political Weekly*, Vol. 42, No. 19.

Chand, Ramesh. (2009). "The Wheat Market: Distortions Caused by Government Interventions." *Economic and Political Weekly*, Vol. XLIV, No. 12.

Conforti, P. (2004). Price Transmission in Selected Agricultural Markets. FAO Commodity and Trade Policy Research Working Paper No. 7.

Dasgupta, D., Dubey, R.N., and Satish, R. (2011). Domestic Wheat Price Formation and Food Inflation in India: International Prices, Domestic Drivers (Stocks, Weather, Public Policy), and the Efficacy of Public Policy Interventions in Wheat Markets. Working Paper No. 2/2011 DEA, Ministry of Finance, Government of India, http://finmin.nic.in/WorkingPaper/Domestic_Wheat_Price_Formation_Food_ Inflation_India.pdf. accessed on August 20, 2013.

Dougherty, C. (2011). *Introduction to Econometrics*, 4 ed. New Delhi: Oxford University Press.

Ghosh, M. (2003). "Spatial Integration of Wheat Markets in India: Evidence from Co-integration Tests." *Oxford Development Studies*, Vol. 31, No. 2.

Goodwin, B.K. and Holt, M.T. (1999). "Price Transmission and Asymmetric Adjustment in the US Beef Sector". *American Journal of Agricultural Economics*, Vol. 81, No. 3.

Goodwin, B.K. and Piggott, N.E. (2001). "Spatial Market Integration in the Presence of Threshold Effects". *American Journal of Agricultural Economics,* Vol. 83, No. 2.

Granger, C.W.J. and Newbold, P. (1974) "Spurious Regressions in Econometrics", *Journal of Econometrics,* Vol. 2.

Greb, F., Jamora, N., Mengel, C., Cramon-Taubadel, S., and Wuriehausen, N. (2012, October-November). Cereal Price Transmission from International to Domestic Markets in Africa. Paper Presented at the African Economic Conference, Kigali, Rwanda.

Gulati, A. and Sharma, P.K. (1990). "Prices, Procurement and Production: An Analysis of Wheat and Rice". *Economic and Political Weekly,* Vol. 25, No. 13.

Harris, R. and Sollis, R. (2003). *Applied Time Series Modelling and Forecasting.* England: Wiley.

Houck, J.P. (1977). "An Approach to Specifying and Estimating Nonreversible Functions" *American Journal of Agricultural Economics,* Vol. 59, No. 3.

Jha, R., Bhanumurthy, K.V., and Sharma, A. (2005). "Market Integration in Wholesale Rice Markets in India". ASARC Working Paper 2005/03.

Lemma, H.R. and Singh, R. (2015). "Testing for Price Co-integration Between Producers and Retailers: Evidence from Ethiopian Milk Market" *iBusiness,* http://dx.doi.org/10.4236/ib.2015.71001.

McLaren, A. (2013). "Asymmetry in Price Transmission in Agricultural Markets". Working Paper Series, WPS 13-10-2, October, Departement des sciences economiques, Universite De Geneve.

Meyer, J. and Von Cramon-Taubadel, S. (2004). "Asymmetric Price Transmission: A Survey". *Journal of Agricultural Economics,* Vol. 55, No. 3.

Ministry of Finance, GOI. (2015-16). *Economic Survey,* Vol. 1, Ch. 4.

Minot, N. (2011). "Transmission of World Food Price Changes to Markets in Sub-Saharan Africa". IFPRI Discussion Paper.

Mukim, M., Singh, K., and Kanakaraj, A. (2009). "Market Integration, Transaction Costs and the Indian Wheat Market: A Systematic Study". *Economic and Political Weekly,* Vol. XLIV, No. 22.

Nayyar, D. and Sen, A. (1994). "International Trade and the Agricultural Sector in India". *Economic and Political Weekly,* Vol. 29, No. 24, May.

Resende, M. and Alves, M.B. (2012). "Asymmetric Price Transmission in Local Fuel Markets in Brazil: An Empirical Study". IE-UFRJ Discussion Paper, TD 005, Universidade Federal do Rio de Janeiro.

Sekhar, C.S.C. (2003). "Price formation in World Wheat Markets-Implications for Policy". *Journal of Policy Modelling,* Vol. 25.

Sekhar, C.S.C. (2004). "Agricultural Price Volatility in International and Indian Markets". *Economic and Political Weekly*, Vol. 39, No. 43.

Sekhar, C.S.C. (2008). "World Rice Crisis: Issues and Options", *Economic and Political Weekly*, Vol. 43, No. 26/27.

Sekhar, C.S.C. (2012). "Agricultural Market Integration in India: An Analysis of Select Commodities". *Food Policy*, Vol. 37, June.

Serra, T. and Goodwin, B.K. (2003). "Price Transmission and Asymmetric Adjustment in the Spanish Dairy Sector". *Applied Economics*, Vol. 35, No. 18.

Vavra, P. and Goodwin, B.K. (2005). "Analysis of Price Transmission Along the Food Chain", *OECD Food, Agriculture and Fisheries Papers*, No. 3, OECD Publishing. http://dx.doi.org/10.1787/752335872456.

Von Cramon-Taubadel, S. and Fahlbusch, S. (1994). "Identifying Asymmetric Price Transmission with Error Correction Models". Poster Session EAAE European Seminar in Reading.

Von Cramon-Taubadel, S. and Loy, J.P. (1996). "Price Asymmetry in the International Wheat Market: Comment". *Canadian Journal of Agricultural Economics*, Vol. 44.

Von Cramon-Taubadel, S. (1998). "Estimating Asymmetric Price Transmission with Error Correction Representation: An Application to the German Pork Market". *European Review of Agricultural Economics*, Vol. 25.

Ward, R. (1982). "Asymmetry in Retail, Wholesale, and Shipping Point Pricing for Fresh Vegetables". *American Journal of Agricultural Economics*, Vol. 64, No. 2.

Weldesenbet, T. (2013). "Asymmetric Price Transmission in the Slovak Liquid Milk Market". *Agricultural Economics-Czech*, Vol. 59, No. 11.

Wolffram, R. (1971). "Positivistic Measures of Aggregate Supply Elasticities: Some New Approaches, Some Critical Notes". *American Journal of Agricultural Economics*, Vol. 53, Issue 2.

APPENDIX

Appendix (1)

Table (1): Rice

Markets	*Variety*
Amritsar	Basmati
Delhi	Parmal & Basmati
Mumbai	Basmati
Nagpur	Coarse
Nizamabad	Coarse
Patna	Coarse
Rajkot	Desi
Thailand	100% broken
Thailand	25% broken
Vietnam	5% broken

Source: Ministry of Agriculture, GOI and IFS

Table (2): Wheat

Market	*Variety*
Bengaluru	Bansi
Delhi	Kalyan
Hyderabad	Bansi
Karnal	Mexican/Dara
Mumbai	Not Available
Patna	White
USA	No. 2 Soft Red Winter

Source: Ministry of Agriculture, GOI and IFS

Appendix (2)

Figure (1): Amritsar Rice Market

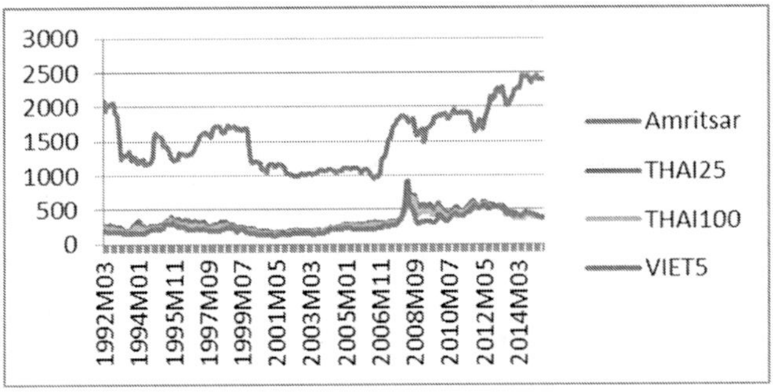

Source: Ministry of Agriculture, GOI

Figure (2): Delhi Rice Market

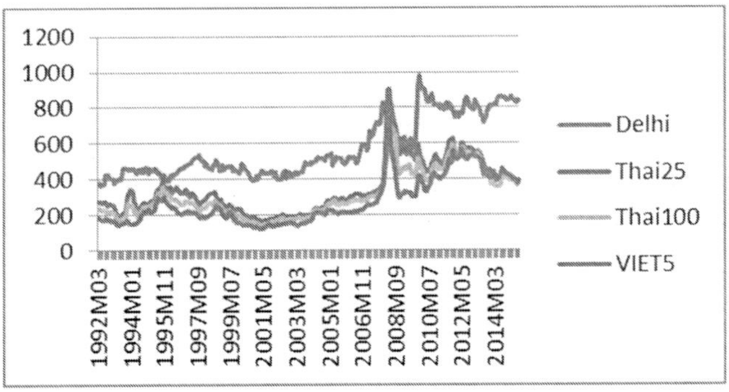

Source: Ministry of Agriculture, GOI

Figure (3): Nagpur Rice Market

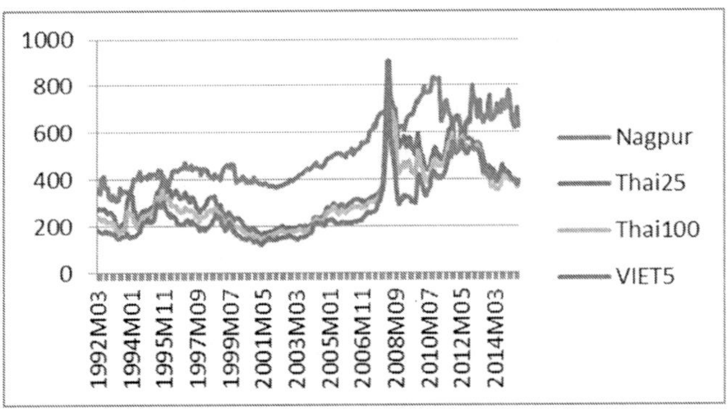

Source: Ministry of Agriculture, GOI

Figure (4): Patna Rice Market

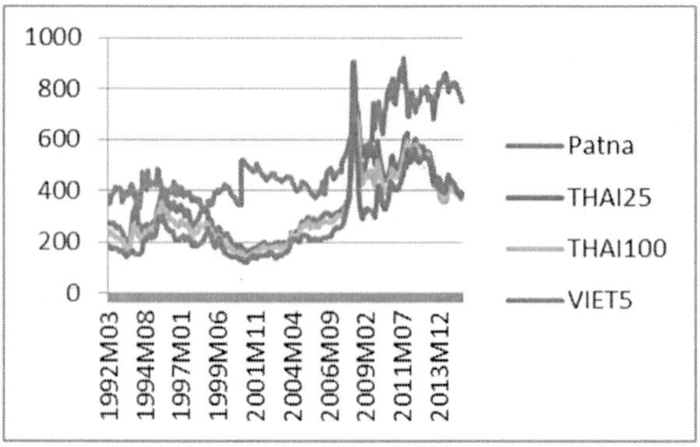

Source: Ministry of Agriculture, GOI

Figure (5): Rajkot Rice Market

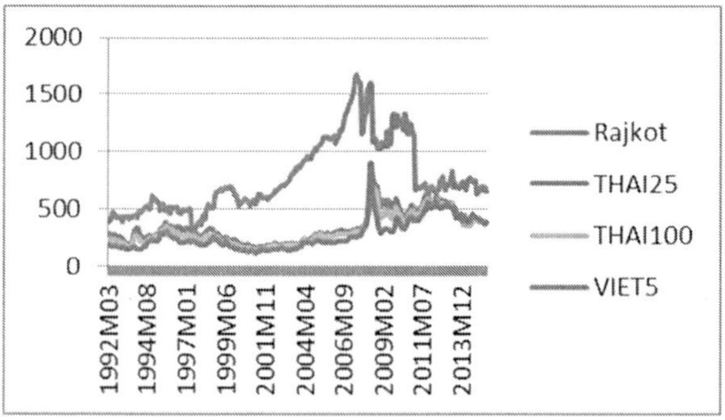

Source: Ministry of Agriculture, GOI

Figure (6): Nizamabad Rice Market

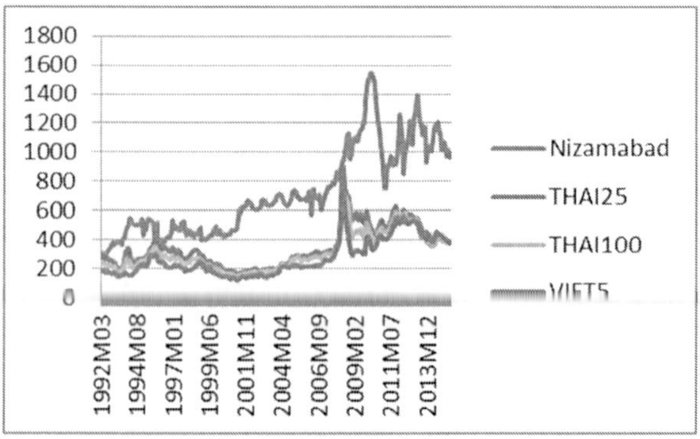

Source: Ministry of Agriculture, GOI

Figure (7): Bengaluru Wheat Market

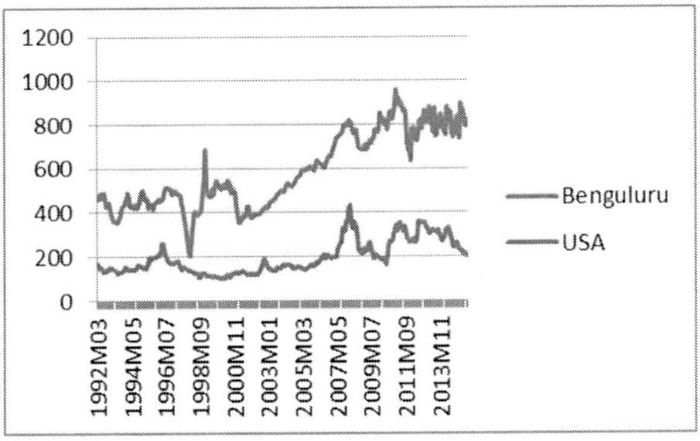

Source: Ministry of Agriculture, GOI

Figure (8): Delhi Wheat Market

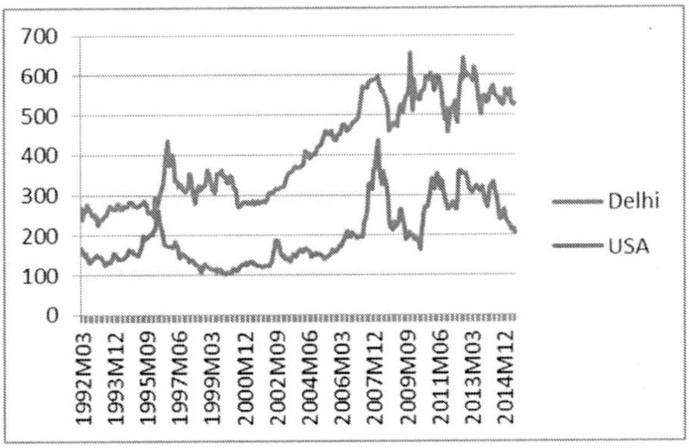

Source: Ministry of Agriculture, GOI

Figure (9): Hyderabad Wheat Market

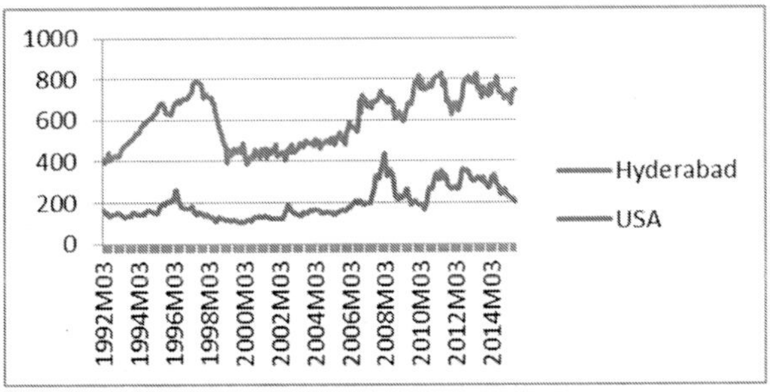

Source: Ministry of Agriculture, GOI

Figure (10): Karnal Wheat Market

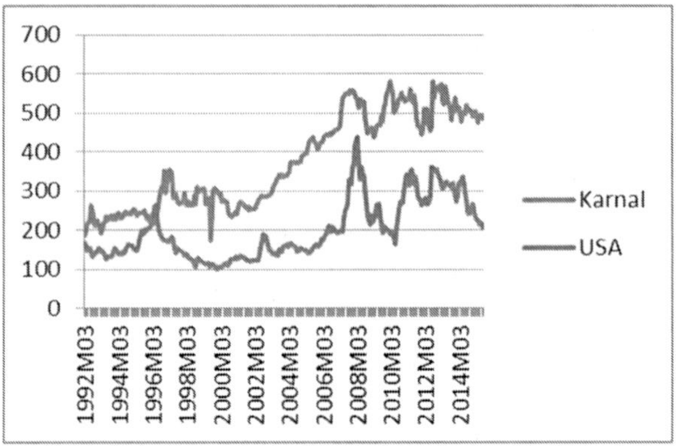

Source: Ministry of Agriculture, GOI

Figure (11): Mumbai Wheat Market

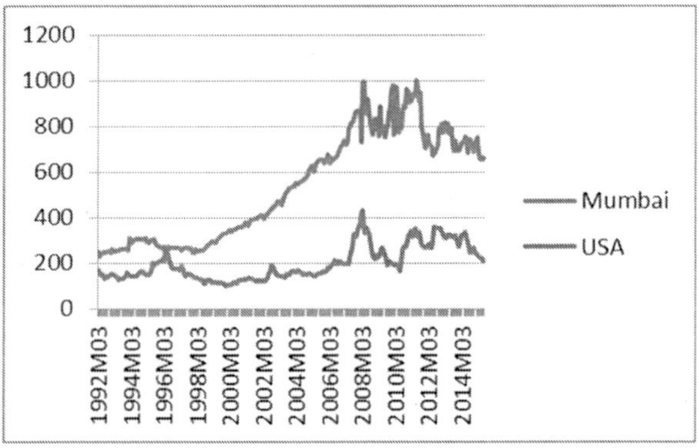

Source: Ministry of Agriculture, GOI

Figure (12): Patna Wheat Market

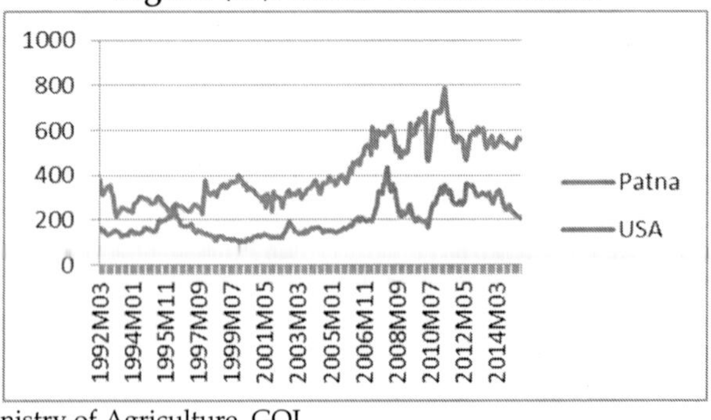

Source: Ministry of Agriculture, GOI

Appendix (3a): Unit Root Results—Rice

Series	*ADF Statistic*	*P value*	*Inference*
ldpr	-2.41	0.36	I(1)
	-5.16	0.00	I(0)
lthai	-2.87	0.18	I(1)
	-6.29	0.00	I(0)
lfertilizer price	-3.77	0.02	I(1)
	-5.13	0.00	I(0)

Appendix (3b): Residual Graphs

Figure (1): Rice Model 1

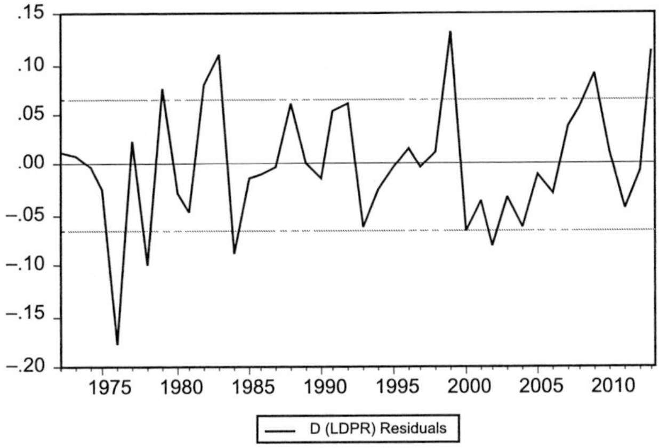

Figure (2): Rice Model 2

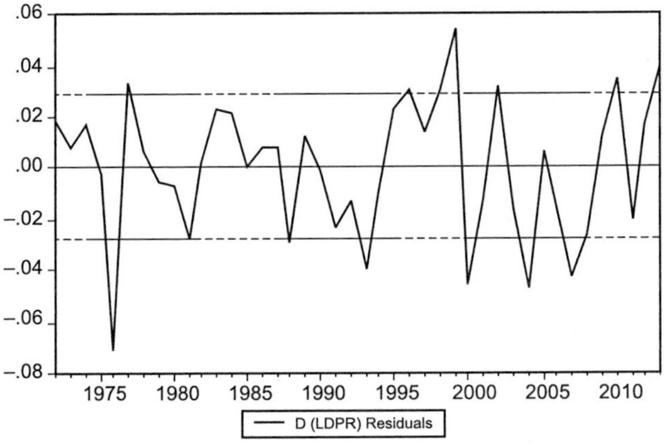

Figure (3): Rice Model 3

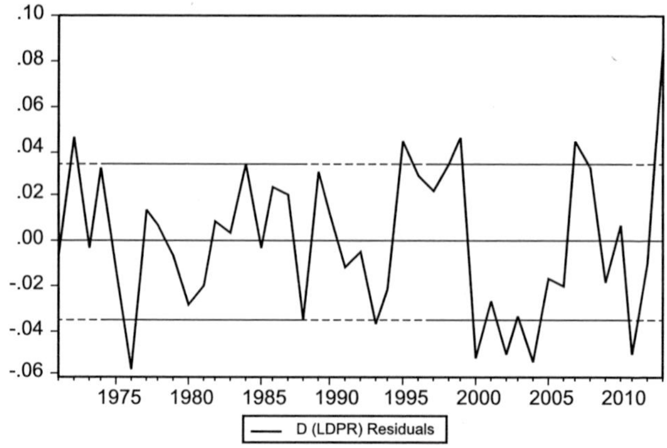

Appendix (4a): Unit Root Results – Wheat

Series	*ADF Statistic*	*P value*	*Inference*
ldpw	-2.65	0.25	I(1)
	-6.35	0.00	I(0)
lus	-2.90	0.17	I(1)
	-5.64	0.00	I(0)

Appendix (4b): Residual Graphs

Figure (4): Wheat Model 1

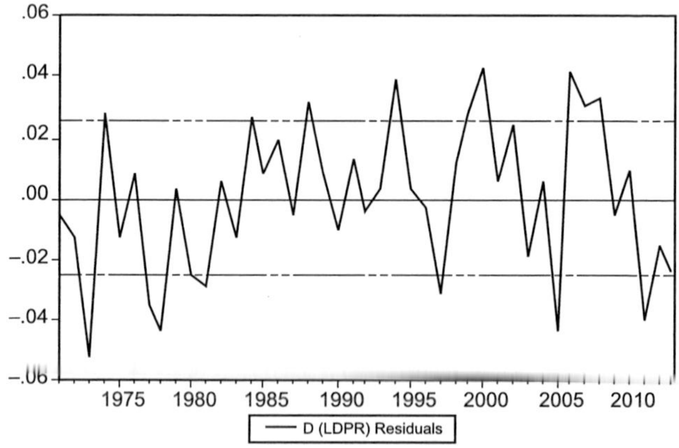

Figure (5): Wheat Model 2

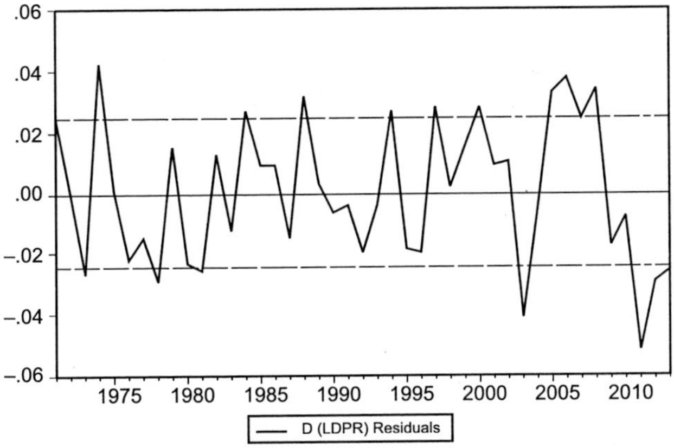

Appendix 5(a) Rice - Unit Root Results

Series	*ADF Statistic*	*P-value*	*Inference*
lnamritsar	-2.27	0.44	I(1)
	-12.4	0.00	I(0)
lndelhi	-2.88	0.17	I(1)
	-16.7	0.00	I(0)
lndelbas	-2.03	0.57	I(1)
	-10.3	0.00	I(0)
lnmumbai	-1.67	0.75	I(1)
	-14.01	0.00	I(0)
lnnagpur	-2.47	0.34	I(1)
	-19.5	0.00	I(0)
lnnizamabad	-3.27	0.07	I(1)
	-17.9	0.00	I(0)
lnpatna	-3.12	0.10	I(1)
	-18.8	0.00	I(0)
lnrajkot	-1.89	0.65	I(1)
	-18.7	0.00	I(0)
lnthai100	-2.33	0.41	I(1)
	-11.6	0.00	I(0)
lnthai25	-2.64	0.26	I(1)
	-11.6	0.00	I(0)
lnthai5	-2.8	0.19	I(1)
	-10.9	0.00	I(0)

Appendix 5(b): VECM Results

Amritsar – Thai100

Vector Error Correction Estimates
Date: 04/26/16 Time: 20:16
Sample (adjusted): 1992M12 2015M07
Included observations: 272 after adjustments
Standard errors in ( ) & t-statistics in [ ]

Cointegrating Eq:	CointEq1	
LOGAMT(-1)	1.000000	
LOGTHAI100(-1)	-0.607561	
	(0.09569)	
	[-6.34950]	
C	-3.846908	
Error Correction:	D(LOGAMT)	D(LOGTHAI100)
CointEq1	-0.062224	-0.002315
	(0.01370)	(0.01678)
	[-4.54057]	[-0.13797]
D(LOGAMT(-1))	0.336549	0.049190
	(0.06040)	(0.07395)
	[5.57240]	[0.66518]
D(LOGAMT(-2))	-0.090270	-0.021369
	(0.06329)	(0.07749)
	[-1.42630]	[-0.27575]
D(LOGAMT(-3))	0.140704	0.071732
	(0.06147)	(0.07527)
	[2.28886]	[0.95301]
D(LOGAMT(-4))	0.049620	0.081428
	(0.06198)	(0.07589)
	[0.80052]	[1.07290]
D(LOGAMT(-5))	0.015767	-0.004147
	(0.06220)	(0.07616)
	[0.25348]	[-0.05445]
D(LOGAMT(-6))	-0.055727	0.033962
	(0.06116)	(0.07488)
	[-0.91122]	[0.45354]
D(LOGAMT(-7))	0.104873	0.178754
	(0.06061)	(0.07422)
	[1.73017]	[2.40852]
D(LOGAMT(-8))	0.086352	-0.095673
	(0.05828)	(0.07136)
	[1.48162]	[1.34071]
D(LOGTHAI100(-1))	-0.117232	0.375507
	(0.05180)	(0.06343)
	[-2.26311]	[5.92036]

D(LOGTHAI100(-2))	-0.092482	0.011448
	(0.05404)	(0.06617)
	[-1.71137]	[0.17301]
D(LOGTHAI100(-3))	0.059687	-0.060467
	(0.05420)	(0.06637)
	[1.10115]	[-0.91108]
D(LOGTHAI100(-4))	-0.041232	-0.030136
	(0.05418)	(0.06634)
	[-0.76099]	[-0.45426]
D(LOGTHAI100(-5))	0.045821	-0.050865
	(0.05375)	(0.06581)
	[0.85255]	[-0.77293]
D(LOGTHAI100(-6))	-0.246263	0.015955
	(0.05370)	(0.06576)
	[-4.58560]	[0.24264]
D(LOGTHAI100(-7))	-0.019492	-0.190779
	(0.05589)	(0.06843)
	[-0.34876]	[-2.78793]
D(LOGTHAI100(-8))	-0.052479	0.064576
	(0.05334)	(0.06531)
	[-0.98380]	[0.98870]
C	0.001297	0.001429
	(0.00221)	(0.00271)
	[0.58595]	[0.52723]
R-squared	0.265265	0.229837
Adj. R-squared	0.216090	0.178290
Sum sq. resids	0.334976	0.502191
S.E. equation	0.036315	0.044465
F-statistic	5.394280	4.458838
Log likelihood	525.1806	470.1111
Akaike AIC	-3.729269	-3.324346
Schwarz SC	-3.490650	-3.085727
Mean dependent	0.000838	0.001931
S.D. dependent	0.041016	0.049052
Determinant resid covariance (dof adj.)		2.59E-06
Determinant resid covariance		2.26E-06
Log likelihood		995.9989
Akaike information criterion		-7.044110
Schwarz criterion		-6.540358

ECM

Dependent Variable: D(LOGAMT)
Method: Least Squares
Date: 07/11/16 Time: 16:40

Sample (adjusted): 1992M12 2015M07
Included observations: 272 after adjustments
D(LOGAMT) = C(1)*(LOGAMT(-1) - 0.607561496956*LOGTHAI100(-1) - 3.84690761108) + C(2)*D(LOGAMT(-1)) + C(3)*D(LOGAMT(-2)) + C(4) *D(LOGAMT(-3)) + C(5)*D(LOGAMT(-4)) + C(6)*D(LOGAMT(-5)) + C(7) *D(LOGAMT(-6)) + C(8)*D(LOGAMT(-7)) + C(9)*D(LOGAMT(-8)) + C(10) *D(LOGTHAI100(-1)) + C(11)*D(LOGTHAI100(-2)) + C(12) *D(LOGTHAI100(-3)) + C(13)*D(LOGTHAI100(-4)) + C(14) *D(LOGTHAI100(-5)) + C(15)*D(LOGTHAI100(-6)) + C(16) *D(LOGTHAI100(-7)) + C(17)*D(LOGTHAI100(-8)) + C(18)

	Coefficient	*Std. Error*	*t-Statistic*	*Prob.*
C(1)	-0.062224	0.013704	-4.540567	0.0000
C(2)	0.336549	0.060396	5.572397	0.0000
C(3)	-0.090270	0.063289	-1.426304	0.1550
C(4)	0.140704	0.061474	2.288855	0.0229
C(5)	0.049620	0.061984	0.800521	0.4242
C(6)	0.015767	0.062204	0.253476	0.8001
C(7)	-0.055727	0.061157	-0.911225	0.3630
C(8)	0.104873	0.060614	1.730166	0.0848
C(9)	0.086352	0.058281	1.481633	0.1397
C(10)	-0.117232	0.051801	-2.263109	0.0245
C(11)	-0.092482	0.054040	-1.711371	0.0882
C(12)	0.059687	0.054204	1.101152	0.2719
C(13)	-0.041232	0.054182	-0.760986	0.4474
C(14)	0.045821	0.053746	0.852547	0.3947
C(15)	-0.246263	0.053704	-4.585596	0.0000
C(16)	-0.019492	0.055888	-0.348761	0.7276
C(17)	-0.052479	0.053343	-0.983800	0.3262
C(18)	0.001297	0.002214	0.585953	0.5584

R-squared	0.265265	Mean dependent var	0.000838
Adjusted R-squared	0.216090	S.D. dependent var	0.041016
S.E. of regression	0.036315	Akaike info criterion	-3.729269
Sum squared resid	0.334976	Schwarz criterion	-3.490650
Log likelihood	525.1806	Hannan-Quinn criter.	-3.633472
F-statistic	5.394280	Durbin-Watson stat	1.997934
Prob(F-statistic)	0.000000		

Amritsar- Thailand25

Vector Error Correction Estimates
Date: 04/26/16 Time: 20:22
Sample (adjusted): 1993M01 2015M07
Included observations: 271 after adjustments
Standard errors in ( ) & t-statistics in [ ]

Cointegrating Eq:	CointEq1
LOGAMT(-1)	1.000000
LOGTHAI25(-1)	-0.641949

	(0.09579)	
	[-6.70156]	
C	-3.578632	
Error Correction:	D(LOGAMT)	D(LOGTHAI25)
CointEq1	-0.061820	0.019736
	(0.01451)	(0.02102)
	[-4.25961]	[0.93912]
D(LOGAMT(-1))	0.308254	0.046022
	(0.06069)	(0.08789)
	[5.07886]	[0.52365]
D(LOGAMT(-2))	-0.062021	-0.010367
	(0.06346)	(0.09190)
	[-0.97727]	[-0.11281]
D(LOGAMT(-3))	0.138441	0.132648
	(0.06285)	(0.09102)
	[2.20256]	[1.45740]
D(LOGAMT(-4))	0.065256	0.083111
	(0.06242)	(0.09038)
	[1.04551]	[0.91956]
D(LOGAMT(-5))	0.010433	-0.084866
	(0.06263)	(0.09069)
	[0.16659]	[-0.93583]
D(LOGAMT(-6))	-0.074219	0.065884
	(0.06247)	(0.09046)
	[-1.18809]	[0.72833]
D(LOGAMT(-7))	0.088248	0.179240
	(0.06200)	(0.08978)
	[1.42327]	[1.99634]
D(LOGAMT(-8))	0.110000	-0.133366
	(0.06218)	(0.09004)
	[1.76910]	[-1.48123]
D(LOGAMT(-9))	0.000508	-0.029507
	(0.05945)	(0.08608)
	[0.00855]	[-0.34279]
D(LOGTHAI25(-1))	-0.112751	0.427675
	(0.04402)	(0.06374)
	[-2.56132]	[6.70922]
D(LOGTHAI25(-2))	-0.073320	-0.066984
	(0.04815)	(0.06972)
	[-1.52277]	[-0.96073]
D(LOGTHAI25(-3))	0.032867	-0.036724
	(0.04685)	(0.06784)
	[0.70158]	[-0.54136]

D(LOGTHAI25(-4))	0.007138	-0.018698
	(0.04667)	(0.06758)
	[0.15294]	[-0.27669]
D(LOGTHAI25(-5))	-0.043449	-0.013231
	(0.04652)	(0.06736)
	[-0.93406]	[-0.19643]
D(LOGTHAI25(-6))	-0.172064	0.010909
	(0.04626)	(0.06698)
	[-3.71978]	[0.16286]
D(LOGTHAI25(-7))	-0.010306	-0.170129
	(0.04735)	(0.06856)
	[-0.21766]	[-2.48140]
D(LOGTHAI25(-8))	-0.070426	-0.001183
	(0.04766)	(0.06902)
	[-1.47761]	[-0.01714]
D(LOGTHAI25(-9))	0.026119	0.130771
	(0.04498)	(0.06513)
	[0.58070]	[2.00781]
C	0.001092	0.001040
	(0.00223)	(0.00323)
	[0.48899]	[0.32147]
R-squared	0.261012	0.258528
Adj. R-squared	0.205073	0.202400
Sum sq. resids	0.336707	0.706027
S.E. equation	0.036626	0.053036
F-statistic	4.665989	4.606092
Log likelihood	522.0521	421.7225
Akaike AIC	-3.705182	-2.964742
Schwarz SC	-3.439343	-2.698903
Mean dependent	0.000899	0.001531
S.D. dependent	0.041080	0.059386
Determinant resid covariance (dof adj.)		3.77E-06
Determinant resid covariance		3.24E-06
Log likelihood		943.8295
Akaike information criterion		-6.655568
Schwarz criterion		-6.097306

Amritsar- Thailand25

Vector Error Correction Estimates
Date: 04/26/16 Time: 20:22
Sample (adjusted): 1993M01 2015M07
Included observations: 271 after adjustments
Standard errors in ( ) & t-statistics in [ ]

Cointegrating Eq:	CointEq1	
LOGAMT(-1)	1.000000	
LOGTHAI25(-1)	-0.641949	
	(0.09579)	
	[-6.70156]	
C	-3.578632	
Error Correction:	*D(LOGAMT)*	*D(LOGTHAI25)*
CointEq1	-0.061820	0.019736
	(0.01451)	(0.02102)
	[-4.25961]	[0.93912]
D(LOGAMT(-1))	0.308254	0.046022
	(0.06069)	(0.08789)
	[5.07886]	[0.52365]
D(LOGAMT(-2))	-0.062021	-0.010367
	(0.06346)	(0.09190)
	[-0.97727]	[-0.11281]
D(LOGAMT(-3))	0.138441	0.132648
	(0.06285)	(0.09102)
	[2.20256]	[1.45740]
D(LOGAMT(-4))	0.065256	0.083111
	(0.06242)	(0.09038)
	[1.04551]	[0.91956]
D(LOGAMT(-5))	0.010433	-0.084866
	(0.06263)	(0.09069)
	[0.16659]	[-0.93583]
D(LOGAMT(-6))	-0.074219	0.065884
	(0.06247)	(0.09046)
	[-1.18809]	[0.72833]
D(LOGAMT(-7))	0.088248	0.179240
	(0.06200)	(0.08978)
	[1.42327]	[1.99634]
D(LOGAMT(-8))	0.110000	-0.133366
	(0.06218)	(0.09004)
	[1.76910]	[-1.48123]
D(LOGAMT(-9))	0.000508	-0.029507
	(0.05945)	(0.08608)
	[0.00855]	[-0.34279]
D(LOGTHAI25(-1))	-0.112751	0.427675
	(0.04402)	(0.06374)
	[-2.56132]	[6.70922]
D(LOGTHAI25(-2))	-0.073320	-0.066984
	(0.04815)	(0.06972)
	[-1.52277]	[-0.96073]

D(LOGTHAI25(-3))	0.032867	-0.036724
	(0.04685)	(0.06784)
	[0.70158]	[-0.54136]
D(LOGTHAI25(-4))	0.007138	-0.018698
	(0.04667)	(0.06758)
	[0.15294]	[-0.27669]
D(LOGTHAI25(-5))	-0.043449	-0.013231
	(0.04652)	(0.06736)
	[-0.93406]	[-0.19643]
D(LOGTHAI25(-6))	-0.172064	0.010909
	(0.04626)	(0.06698)
	[-3.71978]	[0.16286]
D(LOGTHAI25(-7))	-0.010306	-0.170129
	(0.04735)	(0.06856)
	[-0.21766]	[-2.48140]
D(LOGTHAI25(-8))	-0.070426	-0.001183
	(0.04766)	(0.06902)
	[-1.47761]	[-0.01714]
D(LOGTHAI25(-9))	0.026119	0.130771
	(0.04498)	(0.06513)
	[0.58070]	[2.00781]
C	0.001092	0.001040
	(0.00223)	(0.00323)
	[0.48899]	[0.32147]
R-squared	0.261012	0.258528
Adj. R-squared	0.205073	0.202400
Sum sq. resids	0.336707	0.706027
S.E. equation	0.036626	0.053036
F-statistic	4.665989	4.606092
Log likelihood	522.0521	421.7225
Akaike AIC	-3.705182	-2.964742
Schwarz SC	-3.439343	-2.698903
Mean dependent	0.000899	0.001531
S.D. dependent	0.041080	0.059386
Determinant resid covariance (dof adj.)		3.77E-06
Determinant resid covariance		3.24E-06
Log likelihood		943.8295
Akaike information criterion		-6.655568
Schwarz criterion		-6.097306

ECM

Dependent Variable: D(LOGAMT)
Method: Least Squares
Date: 07/11/16 Time: 17:46
Sample (adjusted): 1993M01 2015M07

Included observations: 271 after adjustments
D(LOGAMT) = C(1)*(LOGAMT(-1) - 0.64194894392*LOGTHAI25(-1) - 3.5786323469) + C(2)*D(LOGAMT(-1)) + C(3)*D(LOGAMT(-2)) + C(4) *D(LOGAMT(-3)) + C(5)*D(LOGAMT(-4)) + C(6)*D(LOGAMT(-5)) + C(7) *D(LOGAMT(-6)) + C(8)*D(LOGAMT(-7)) + C(9)*D(LOGAMT(-8)) + C(10) *D(LOGAMT(-9)) + C(11)*D(LOGTHAI25(-1)) + C(12)*D(LOGTHAI25(-2)) + C(13)*D(LOGTHAI25(-3)) + C(14)*D(LOGTHAI25(-4)) + C(15) *D(LOGTHAI25(-5)) + C(16)*D(LOGTHAI25(-6)) + C(17)*D(LOGTHAI25(-7)) + C(18)*D(LOGTHAI25(-8)) + C(19)*D(LOGTHAI25(-9)) + C(20)

	Coefficient	*Std. Error*	*t-Statistic*	*Prob.*
C(1)	-0.061820	0.014513	-4.259609	0.0000
C(2)	0.308254	0.060694	5.078858	0.0000
C(3)	-0.062021	0.063464	-0.977270	0.3294
C(4)	0.138441	0.062855	2.202559	0.0285
C(5)	0.065256	0.062415	1.045509	0.2968
C(6)	0.010433	0.062626	0.166587	0.8678
C(7)	-0.074219	0.062469	-1.188087	0.2359
C(8)	0.088248	0.062004	1.423269	0.1559
C(9)	0.110000	0.062178	1.769103	0.0781
C(10)	0.000508	0.059445	0.008552	0.9932
C(11)	-0.112751	0.044021	-2.561319	0.0110
C(12)	-0.073320	0.048149	-1.522771	0.1291
C(13)	0.032867	0.046846	0.701584	0.4836
C(14)	0.007138	0.046669	0.152940	0.8786
C(15)	-0.043449	0.046516	-0.934060	0.3512
C(16)	-0.172064	0.046256	-3.719777	0.0002
C(17)	-0.010306	0.047348	-0.217659	0.8279
C(18)	-0.070426	0.047662	-1.477613	0.1408
C(19)	0.026119	0.044978	0.580698	0.5620
C(20)	0.001092	0.002233	0.488985	0.6253

R-squared	0.261012	Mean dependent var	0.000899
Adjusted R-squared	0.205073	S.D. dependent var	0.041080
S.E. of regression	0.036626	Akaike info criterion	-3.705182
Sum squared resid	0.336707	Schwarz criterion	-3.439343
Log likelihood	522.0521	Hannan-Quinn criter.	-3.598445
F-statistic	4.665989	Durbin-Watson stat	1.859356
Prob(F-statistic)	0.000000		

Amritsar –Vietnam5

Vector Error Correction Estimates
Date: 04/26/16 Time: 20:27
Sample (adjusted): 1992M06 2015M07
Included observations: 278 after adjustments
Standard errors in ( ) & t-statistics in [ ]

Cointegrating Eq:	CointEq1	
LOGAMT(-1)	1.000000	
LOGTHAI5(-1)	-0.691488 (0.11694) [-5.91306]	
C	-3.483903	
Error Correction:	D(LOGAMT)	D(LOGTHAI5)
CointEq1	-0.039701 (0.01148) [-3.45869]	0.025517 (0.01497) [1.70478]
D(LOGAMT(-1))	0.322036 (0.05885) [5.47216]	0.056864 (0.07674) [0.74100]
D(LOGAMT(-2))	-0.090078 (0.05873) [-1.53385]	0.085697 (0.07658) [1.11907]
D(LOGTHAI5(-1))	0.022149 (0.04616) [0.47977]	0.482357 (0.06020) [8.01283]
D(LOGTHAI5(-2))	-0.036162 (0.04671) [-0.77422]	-0.051812 (0.06091) [-0.85069]
C	0.000435 (0.00230) [0.18892]	0.001620 (0.00300) [0.54003]
R-squared	0.136261	0.226356
Adj. R-squared	0.120384	0.212134
Sum sq. resids	0.398689	0.677914
S.E. equation	0.038285	0.049923
F-statistic	8.582006	15.91655
Log likelihood	515.5953	441.8086
Akaike AIC	-3.666153	-3.135314
Schwarz SC	-3.587859	-3.057020
Mean dependent	0.000587	0.002819
S.D. dependent	0.040821	0.056244
Determinant resid covariance (dof adj.)		3.63E-06
Determinant resid covariance		3.48E-06
Log likelihood		958.2710
Akaike information criterion		-6.793316
Schwarz criterion		-6.610630

ECM

Dependent Variable: D(LOGAMT)
Method: Least Squares
Date: 07/11/16 Time: 17:50

Sample (adjusted): 1992M06 2015M07
Included observations: 278 after adjustments
D(LOGAMT) = C(1)*(LOGAMT(-1) - 0.691487887568*LOGTHAI5(-1) - 3.48390275498) + C(2)*D(LOGAMT(-1)) + C(3)*D(LOGAMT(-2)) + C(4) *D(LOGTHAI5(-1)) + C(5)*D(LOGTHAI5(-2)) + C(6)

	Coefficient	*Std. Error*	*t-Statistic*	*Prob.*
C(1)	-0.039701	0.011479	-3.458685	0.0006
C(2)	0.322036	0.058850	5.472158	0.0000
C(3)	-0.090078	0.058727	-1.533854	0.1262
C(4)	0.022149	0.046165	0.479771	0.6318
C(5)	-0.036162	0.046708	-0.774218	0.4395
C(6)	0.000435	0.002300	0.188917	0.8503

R-squared	0.136261	Mean dependent var	0.000587
Adjusted R-squared	0.120384	S.D. dependent var	0.040821
S.E. of regression	0.038285	Akaike info criterion	-3.666153
Sum squared resid	0.398689	Schwarz criterion	-3.587859
Log likelihood	515.5953	Hannan-Quinn criter.	-3.634742
F-statistic	8.582006	Durbin-Watson stat	1.967294
Prob(F-statistic)	0.000000		

Delhi-Vietnam5

Vector Error Correction Estimates
Date: 04/26/16 Time: 20:34
Sample (adjusted): 1992M06 2015M07
Included observations: 278 after adjustments
Standard errors in ( ) & t-statistics in [ ]

Cointegrating Eq:	CointEq1	
LOGDEL(-1)	1.000000	
LOGTHAI5(-1)	-0.625485 (0.07181) [-8.70999]	
C	-2.867114	
Error Correction:	D(LOGDEL)	D(LOGTHAI5)
CointEq1	-0.033466 (0.02132) [-1.56986]	0.084067 (0.02394) [3.51115]
D(LOGDEL(-1))	0.002314 (0.06232) [0.03713]	0.060908 (0.06999) [0.87018]
D(LOGDEL(-2))	0.053062 (0.06130) [0.86558]	0.062309 (0.06885) [0.90498]
D(LOGTHAI5(-1))	0.162318 (0.05246)	0.472686 (0.05892)

	[3.09414]	[8.02257]
D(LOGTHAI5(-2))	-0.061099	-0.060389
	(0.05330)	(0.05987)
	[-1.14629]	[-1.00876]
C	0.002551	0.001403
	(0.00262)	(0.00294)
	[0.97376]	[0.47677]
R-squared	0.046287	0.260354
Adj. R-squared	0.028755	0.246757
Sum sq. resids	0.513800	0.648123
S.E. equation	0.043462	0.048814
F-statistic	2.640216	19.14865
Log likelihood	480.3374	448.0553
Akaike AIC	-3.412499	-3.180254
Schwarz SC	-3.334205	-3.101960
Mean dependent	0.002965	0.002819
S.D. dependent	0.044101	0.056244
Determinant resid covariance (dof adj.)		4.48E-06
Determinant resid covariance		4.29E-06
Log likelihood		928.9867
Akaike information criterion		-6.582638
Schwarz criterion		-6.399952

ECM

Dependent Variable: D(LOGDEL)
Method: Least Squares
Date: 07/11/16 Time: 17:55
Sample (adjusted): 1992M06 2015M07
Included observations: 278 after adjustments
D(LOGDEL) = C(1)*(LOGDEL(-1) - 0.625485191951*LOGTHAI5(-1) - 2.86711397004) + C(2)*D(LOGDEL(-1)) + C(3)*D(LOGDEL(-2)) + C(4) *D(LOGTHAI5(-1)) + C(5)*D(LOGTHAI5(-2)) + C(6)

	Coefficient	*Std. Error*	*t-Statistic*	*Prob.*
C(1)	-0.033466	0.021318	-1.569857	0.1176
C(2)	0.002314	0.062321	0.037130	0.9704
C(3)	0.053062	0.061303	0.865582	0.3875
C(4)	0.162318	0.052460	3.094142	0.0022
C(5)	-0.061099	0.053302	-1.146285	0.2527
C(6)	0.002551	0.002620	0.973759	0.3310

R-squared	0.046287	Mean dependent var	0.002965
Adjusted R-squared	0.028755	S.D. dependent var	0.044101
S.E. of regression	0.043462	Akaike info criterion	-3.412499
Sum squared resid	0.513800	Schwarz criterion	-3.334205
Log likelihood	480.3374	Hannan-Quinn criter.	-3.381088
F-statistic	2.640216	Durbin-Watson stat	1.989595
Prob(F-statistic)	0.023743		

Mumbai- Thailand100

Vector Error Correction Estimates
Date: 04/26/16 Time: 20:43
Sample (adjusted): 2006M06 2015M07
Included observations: 110 after adjustments
Standard errors in ( ) & t-statistics in [ ]

Cointegrating Eq:	CointEq1	
LOGMUM(-1)	1.000000	
LOGTHAI100(-1)	0.650047 (0.37708) [1.72390]	
C	-11.81829	
Error Correction:	D(LOGMUM)	D(LOGTHAI100)
CointEq1	-0.077186 (0.01988) [-3.88300]	-0.010358 (0.01402) [-0.73891]
D(LOGMUM(-1))	-0.334504 (0.09475) [-3.53028]	0.048379 (0.06682) [0.72402]
D(LOGMUM(-2))	0.156323 (0.09356) [1.67076]	0.193922 (0.06598) [2.93903]
D(LOGMUM(-3))	0.121286 (0.09729) [1.24663]	0.056568 (0.06861) [0.82448]
D(LOGMUM(-4))	0.033433 (0.09330) [0.35835]	0.032286 (0.06579) [0.49071]
D(LOGTHAI100(-1))	-0.030260 (0.14414) [-0.20993]	0.465394 (0.10165) [4.57834]
D(LOGTHAI100(-2))	-0.214023 (0.15567) [-1.37487]	0.095102 (0.10978) [0.86631]
D(LOGTHAI100(-3))	0.222846 (0.15235) [1.46277]	-0.197015 (0.10743) [-1.83381]
D(LOGTHAI100(-4))	0.029946 (0.13958) [0.21454]	0.014230 (0.09843) [0.14456]
C	0.006992 (0.00617) [1.13255]	7.38E-05 (0.00435) [0.01695]

R-squared	0.273705	0.365804
Adj. R-squared	0.208339	0.308727
Sum sq. resids	0.407728	0.202769
S.E. equation	0.063854	0.045030
F-statistic	4.187237	6.408890
Log likelihood	151.7867	190.2061
Akaike AIC	-2.577940	-3.276475
Schwarz SC	-2.332441	-3.030977
Mean dependent	0.006685	0.002449
S.D. dependent	0.071765	0.054160

Determinant resid covariance (dof adj.)	7.91E-06
Determinant resid covariance	6.54E-06
Log likelihood	344.4175
Akaike information criterion	-5.862136
Schwarz criterion	-5.322040

ECM

Dependent Variable: D(LOGMUM)
Method: Least Squares
Date: 07/11/16 Time: 17:58
Sample (adjusted): 2006M06 2015M07
Included observations: 110 after adjustments
D(LOGMUM) = C(1)*(LOGMUM(-1) + 0.650046599579*LOGTHAI100(-1) - 11.8182902296) + C(2)*D(LOGMUM(-1)) + C(3)*D(LOGMUM(-2)) + C(4)*D(LOGMUM(-3)) + C(5)*D(LOGMUM(-4)) + C(6)*D(LOGTHAI100(-1)) + C(7)*D(LOGTHAI100(-2)) + C(8)*D(LOGTHAI100(-3)) + C(9) *D(LOGTHAI100(-4)) + C(10)

	Coefficient	*Std. Error*	*t-Statistic*	*Prob.*
C(1)	-0.077186	0.019878	-3.883000	0.0002
C(2)	-0.334504	0.094753	-3.530281	0.0006
C(3)	0.156323	0.093564	1.670758	0.0979
C(4)	0.121286	0.097291	1.246634	0.2154
C(5)	0.033433	0.093299	0.358347	0.7208
C(6)	-0.030260	0.144144	-0.209929	0.8342
C(7)	-0.214023	0.155668	-1.374874	0.1722
C(8)	0.222846	0.152345	1.462767	0.1467
C(9)	0.029946	0.139582	0.214538	0.8306
C(10)	0.006992	0.006173	1.132551	0.2601

R-squared	0.273705	Mean dependent var	0.006685
Adjusted R-squared	0.208339	S.D. dependent var	0.071765
S.E. of regression	0.063854	Akaike info criterion	-2.577940
Sum squared resid	0.407728	Schwarz criterion	-2.332441
Log likelihood	151.7867	Hannan-Quinn criter.	-2.478364
F-statistic	4.187237	Durbin-Watson stat	2.042591
Prob(F-statistic)	0.000130		

Nagpur-Thailand100

Vector Error Correction Estimates
Date: 04/26/16 Time: 21:02
Sample (adjusted): 1992M06 2015M07
Included observations: 278 after adjustments
Standard errors in ( ) & t-statistics in [ ]

Cointegrating Eq:	CointEq1	
LOGNAG(-1)	1.000000	
LOGTHAI100(-1)	-0.689548 (0.09412) [-7.32634]	
C	-2.314603	
Error Correction:	D(LOGNAG)	D(LOGTHAI100)
CointEq1	-0.024111 (0.01920) [-1.25597]	0.067566 (0.01920) [3.51869]
D(LOGNAG(-1))	-0.169888 (0.06237) [-2.72398]	0.051328 (0.06238) [0.82278]
D(LOGNAG(-2))	-0.086508 (0.06234) [-1.38761]	0.059549 (0.06236) [0.95494]
D(LOGTHAI100(-1))	-0.033431 (0.05893) [-0.56726]	0.386177 (0.05895) [6.55115]
D(LOGTHAI100(-2))	-0.011543 (0.05941) [-0.19428]	0.035238 (0.05943) [0.59294]
C	0.002873 (0.00264) [1.08900]	0.000762 (0.00264) [0.28879]
R-squared	0.045427	0.204258
Adj. R-squared	0.027879	0.189630
Sum sq. resids	0.521811	0.522077
S.E. equation	0.043800	0.043811
F-statistic	2.588807	13.96384
Log likelihood	478.1870	478.1162
Akaike AIC	-3.397029	-3.396519
Schwarz SC	-3.318735	-3.318225
Mean dependent	0.002189	0.001656
S.D. dependent	0.044423	0.048668

Determinant resid covariance (dof adj.)	3.68E-06
Determinant resid covariance	3.52E-06
Log likelihood	956.3587
Akaike information criterion	-6.779559
Schwarz criterion	-6.596873

ECM

Dependent Variable: D(LOGNAG)
Method: Least Squares
Date: 07/11/16 Time: 18:32
Sample (adjusted): 1992M06 2015M07
Included observations: 278 after adjustments
D(LOGNAG) = C(1)*(LOGNAG(-1) - 0.689548051867*LOGTHAI100(-1) - 2.31460349687) + C(2)*D(LOGNAG(-1)) + C(3)*D(LOGNAG(-2)) + C(4) *D(LOGTHAI100(-1)) + C(5)*D(LOGTHAI100(-2)) + C(6)

	Coefficient	*Std. Error*	*t-Statistic*	*Prob.*
C(1)	-0.024111	0.019197	-1.255973	0.2102
C(2)	-0.169888	0.062367	-2.723985	0.0069
C(3)	-0.086508	0.062343	-1.387612	0.1664
C(4)	-0.033431	0.058933	-0.567265	0.5710
C(5)	-0.011543	0.059414	-0.194285	0.8461
C(6)	0.002873	0.002638	1.089001	0.2771

R-squared	0.045427	Mean dependent var	0.002189
Adjusted R-squared	0.027879	S.D. dependent var	0.044423
S.E. of regression	0.043800	Akaike info criterion	-3.397029
Sum squared resid	0.521811	Schwarz criterion	-3.318735
Log likelihood	478.1870	Hannan-Quinn criter.	-3.365618
F-statistic	2.588807	Durbin-Watson stat	1.921033
Prob(F-statistic)	0.026203		

Nagpur-Vietnam5

Vector Error Correction Estimates
Date: 04/26/16 Time: 21:05
Sample (adjusted): 1992M06 2015M07
Included observations: 278 after adjustments
Standard errors in ( ) & t-statistics in [ ]

Cointegrating Eq:	CointEq1	
LOGNAG(-1)	1.000000	
LOGTHAI5(-1)	-0.620580 (0.07376) [-8.41331]	
C	-2.796396	
Error Correction:	D(LOGNAG)	D(LOGTHAI5)
CointEq1	-0.014675 (0.02077) [-0.70668]	0.089376 (0.02290) [3.90248]

D(LOGNAG(-1))	-0.174564	0.052945
	(0.06309)	(0.06958)
	[-2.76703]	[0.76093]
D(LOGNAG(-2))	-0.092127	0.101829
	(0.06290)	(0.06937)
	[-1.46474]	[1.46793]
D(LOGTHAI5(-1))	-0.007944	0.467882
	(0.05291)	(0.05835)
	[-0.15016]	[8.01863]
D(LOGTHAI5(-2))	0.011021	-0.023952
	(0.05339)	(0.05889)
	[0.20641]	[-0.40674]
C	0.002818	0.001321
	(0.00265)	(0.00292)
	[1.06475]	[0.45243]
R-squared	0.040596	0.271969
Adj. R-squared	0.022960	0.258586
Sum sq. resids	0.524452	0.637945
S.E. equation	0.043910	0.048429
F-statistic	2.301848	20.32205
Log likelihood	477.4853	450.2554
Akaike AIC	-3.391981	-3.196082
Schwarz SC	-3.313687	-3.117788
Mean dependent	0.002189	0.002819
S.D. dependent	0.044423	0.056244
Determinant resid covariance (dof adj.)		4.52E-06
Determinant resid covariance		4.33E-06
Log likelihood		927.8404
Akaike information criterion		-6.574391
Schwarz criterion		-6.391705

ECM

Dependent Variable: D(LOGNAG)
Method: Least Squares
Date: 07/11/16 Time: 18:34
Sample (adjusted): 1992M06 2015M07
Included observations: 278 after adjustments
D(LOGNAG) = C(1)*(LOGNAG(-1) - 0.620579949399*LOGTHAI5(-1) - 2.79639614943) + C(2)*D(LOGNAG(-1)) + C(3)*D(LOGNAG(-2)) + C(4) *D(LOGTHAI5(-1)) + C(5)*D(LOGTHAI5(-2)) + C(6)

	Coefficient	*Std. Error*	*t-Statistic*	*Prob.*
C(1)	-0.014675	0.020766	-0.706679	0.4804
C(2)	-0.174564	0.063087	-2.767029	0.0060
C(3)	-0.092127	0.062897	-1.464738	0.1441
C(4)	-0.007944	0.052905	-0.150159	0.8808

C(5)	0.011021	0.053393	0.206407	0.8366
C(6)	0.002818	0.002647	1.064746	0.2879

R-squared	0.040596	Mean dependent var	0.002189
Adjusted R-squared	0.022960	S.D. dependent var	0.044423
S.E. of regression	0.043910	Akaike info criterion	-3.391981
Sum squared resid	0.524452	Schwarz criterion	-3.313687
Log likelihood	477.4853	Hannan-Quinn criter.	-3.360570
F-statistic	2.301848	Durbin-Watson stat	1.922614
Prob(F-statistic)	0.045142		

Appendix 6(a): Wheat—Unit Root Results

Series	*ADF Statistic*	*P value*	*Inference*
lnbenguluru	-3.72	0.02	I(1)*
	-14.96	0.00	I(0)
lndelhi	-3.09	0.11	I(1)
	-18.6	0.00	I(0)
lnhyderabad	-1.71	0.74	I(1)
	-22.26	0.00	I(0)
lnkarnal	-3.00	0.13	I(1)
	-22.02	0.00	I(0)
lnmumbai	-0.33	0.98	I(1)
	-16.09	0.00	I(0)
lnpatna	-4.35	0.00	I(0)
lnus	-2.69	0.23	I(1)
	-12.86	0.00	I(0)

Appendix 6(b): VECM Results

Benguluru –US

Vector Error Correction Estimates
Date: 04/27/16 Time: 18:44
Sample (adjusted): 1992M06 2015M07
Included observations: 278 after adjustments
Standard errors in ( ) & t-statistics in [ ]

Cointegrating Eq:	CointEq1	
LOGBENGSA(-1)	1.000000	
LOGUSSA(-1)	-0.830480	
	(0.14368)	
	[-5.78013]	
C	-1.999347	
Error Correction:	D(LOGBENGSA)	D(LOGUSSA)
CointEq1	-0.042497	0.053356
	(0.01892)	(0.01920)

	[-2.24616]	[2.77901]
D(LOGBENGSA(-1))	0.107580	-0.059059
	(0.06095)	(0.06186)
	[1.76493]	[-0.95478]
D(LOGBENGSA(-2))	0.062395	-0.084082
	(0.06068)	(0.06158)
	[1.02824]	[-1.36544]
D(LOGUSSA(-1))	0.158311	0.285032
	(0.05896)	(0.05983)
	[2.68511]	[4.76397]
D(LOGUSSA(-2))	-0.004303	-0.057336
	(0.06023)	(0.06112)
	[-0.07143]	[-0.93802]
C	0.001426	0.001152
	(0.00358)	(0.00364)
	[0.39794]	[0.31697]
R-squared	0.062202	0.098932
Adj. R-squared	0.044963	0.082368
Sum sq. resids	0.968425	0.997281
S.E. equation	0.059669	0.060551
F-statistic	3.608237	5.972795
Log likelihood	392.2342	388.1529
Akaike AIC	-2.778663	-2.749302
Schwarz SC	-2.700369	-2.671008
Mean dependent	0.001934	0.001115
S.D. dependent	0.061057	0.063211
Determinant resid covariance (dof adj.)		1.30E-05
Determinant resid covariance		1.24E-05
Log likelihood		781.4330
Akaike information criterion		-5.521101
Schwarz criterion		-5.338415

ECM

Dependent Variable: D(LOGBENGSA)
Method: Least Squares
Date: 07/11/16 Time: 20:59
Sample (adjusted): 1992M06 2015M07
Included observations: 278 after adjustments
D(LOGBENGSA) = C(1)*(LOGBENGSA(-1) - 0.830480009017*LOGUSSA(-1) - 1.99934711063) + C(2)*D(LOGBENGSA(-1)) + C(3)*D(LOGBENGSA(-2)) + C(4)*D(LOGUSSA(-1)) + C(5)*D(LOGUSSA(-2)) + C(6)

	Coefficient	*Std. Error*	*t-Statistic*	*Prob.*
C(1)	-0.042497	0.018920	-2.246164	0.0255
C(2)	0.107580	0.060954	1.764931	0.0787

C(3)	0.062395	0.060681	1.028240	0.3048
C(4)	0.158311	0.058959	2.685114	0.0077
C(5)	-0.004303	0.060234	-0.071432	0.9431
C(6)	0.001426	0.003583	0.397939	0.6910

R-squared	0.062202	Mean dependent var	0.001934
Adjusted R-squared	0.044963	S.D. dependent var	0.061057
S.E. of regression	0.059669	Akaike info criterion	-2.778663
Sum squared resid	0.968425	Schwarz criterion	-2.700369
Log likelihood	392.2342	Hannan-Quinn criter.	-2.747252
F-statistic	3.608237	Durbin-Watson stat	1.991492
Prob(F-statistic)	0.003546		

Mumbai-US

Vector Error Correction Estimates
Date: 06/06/16 Time: 19:00
Sample (adjusted): 1992M07 2015M07
Included observations: 277 after adjustments
Standard errors in ( ) & t-statistics in [ ]

Cointegrating Eq:	CointEq1	
LOGMUMSA(-1)	1.000000	
LOGUSSA(-1)	-2.283262 (0.39611) [-5.76427]	
C	5.737375	
Error Correction:	**D(LOGMUMSA)**	**D(LOGUSSA)**
CointEq1	0.013635 (0.00495) [2.75211]	0.019579 (0.00673) [2.90891]
D(LOGMUMSA(-1))	-0.369755 (0.06116) [-6.04611]	-0.028469 (0.08308) [-0.34265]
(LOGMUMSA(-2))	-0.258300 (0.06322) [-4.08541]	-0.035533 (0.08590) [-0.41368]
D(LOGMUMSA(-3))	-0.051169 (0.05983) [-0.85517]	0.013301 (0.08129) [0.16363]
D(LOGUSSA(-1))	0.165035 (0.04439) [illegible]	0.289797 (0.06031) [illegible]
D(LOGUSSA(-2))	-0.019503 (0.04675) [-0.41721]	-0.075066 (0.06351) [-1.18197]

D(LOGUSSA(-3))	0.109148	0.038717
	(0.04535)	(0.06161)
	[2.40693]	[0.62844]
C	0.005789	0.000868
	(0.00273)	(0.00371)
	[2.11874]	[0.23391]
R-squared	0.177437	0.101198
Adj. R-squared	0.156032	0.077809
Sum sq. resids	0.538664	0.994228
S.E. equation	0.044749	0.060795
F-statistic	8.289493	4.326739
Log likelihood	471.5653	386.6822
Akaike AIC	-3.347042	-2.734168
Schwarz SC	-3.242377	-2.629503
Mean dependent	0.003601	0.001027
S.D. dependent	0.048710	0.063308

Determinant resid covariance (dof adj.)	7.40E-06
Determinant resid covariance	6.98E-06
Log likelihood	858.2524
Akaike information criterion	-6.066804
Schwarz criterion	-5.831308

ECM

Dependent Variable: D(LOGMUMSA)
Method: Least Squares
Date: 07/11/16 Time: 21:02
Sample (adjusted): 1992M07 2015M07
Included observations: 277 after adjustments
D(LOGMUMSA) = C(1)*(LOGMUMSA(-1) - 2.28326237971*LOGUSSA(-1) + 5.73737494787) + C(2)*D(LOGMUMSA(-1)) + C(3)*D(LOGMUMSA(-2)) + C(4)*D(LOGMUMSA(-3)) + C(5)*D(LOGUSSA(-1)) + C(6) *D(LOGUSSA(-2)) + C(7)*D(LOGUSSA(-3)) + C(8)

	Coefficient	*Std. Error*	*t-Statistic*	*Prob.*
C(1)	0.013635	0.004954	2.752110	0.0063
C(2)	-0.369755	0.061156	-6.046112	0.0000
C(3)	-0.258300	0.063225	-4.085414	0.0001
C(4)	-0.051169	0.059835	-0.855173	0.3932
C(5)	0.165035	0.044389	3.717939	0.0002
C(6)	-0.019503	0.046747	-0.417206	0.6769
C(7)	0.109148	0.045347	2.406927	0.0168
C(8)	0.005789	0.002732	2.118743	0.0350

R-squared	0.177437	Mean dependent var	0.003601
Adjusted R-squared	0.156032	S.D. dependent var	0.048710
S.E. of regression	0.044749	Akaike info criterion	-3.347042
Sum squared resid	0.538664	Schwarz criterion	-3.242377
Log likelihood	471.5653	Hannan-Quinn criter.	-3.305046
F-statistic	8.289493	Durbin-Watson stat	1.987718
Prob(F-statistic)	0.000000		

5

Economic Liberalization and Agrarian Crisis in India

Virendra Kumar

Introduction

Though India enjoys food self-sufficiency and has witnessed increased production across crops, farmers cutting across different agro-climatic zones and linguistic states confront similar circumstances regarding farming. The latter is becoming unprofitable and unviable. Against the background of an unfinished land reform process and class divide on account of the technology-led Green Revolution in the late 1960s, the farming community, especially small and marginal farmers including tenant cultivators who do subsistence farming and do not generate a large marketable surplus, is facing increasing indebtedness and poor remuneration. In post-liberalized India a large number of these farmers in dry land regions (rain-dependent areas of Central India) have been compelled to commit suicide owing to unsustainable debt in different parts of India including rich states like Punjab and Maharashtra. Many others in well irrigated areas also are forced to engage in 'distress sale' despite bumper crops. Millions of farmers are 'giving up' farming because of uncertainty of return and joining informal workforce in cities. This has been termed the phenomena of 'vanishing villages' as not many farmers including richer ones want their sons and daughters to take up farming. Real estate corporate and industry tycoons in collusion with government officials are taking advantage of a pro-corporate land use policy to take over fertile lands at throw away prices and thus increasing pressure on the remaining agricultural land besides creating uncertainty for farmers. Many farmers' organizations and groups, have intensified their protest in recent times demanding assured and reasonable returns for farming and right over their land notwithstanding high compensation.

In this chapter an attempt has been made to analyse the broader policy changes in agriculture since India embarked upon liberalization and globalization. Instead of discussing state-specific problems in agriculture, I will discuss broader institutional and policy changes, especially the implication of withdrawal of the 'state' in areas of critical inputs, farmers' income, and how this dwindling internal support system in conjunction with external market pressures have created agrarian distress, especially for marginal farmers and landless cultivators. The corporate sector's increasing leverage vis-a-vis farmers allows it to extract a large profit and also causes a persistent crisis for peasants both in rain-fed and irrigated regions. The analysis will also explore the impact of the vagaries of nature on agriculture.

Post-Independence Agriculture Policy

The agrarian structure in India has undergone transformation since independence but some basic characteristics remain intact: high density of small and marginal farmers and landless agricultural labourers and shrinking size of landholdings; high share of rainfed areas in the country facing vagaries of monsoon; imperfect land market (lease and sale) which works against the interest of the farmers. These underlying conditions make farmers vulnerable and susceptible to distress in an environment where state policies influence prices of most of the inputs required for agriculture (Deshpande and Arora, 2010).

The Indian state adopted a combination of institutional measures to transform the agrarian economy. While laying down a broader framework of national planning for overall socio-economic development, community development programmes (CDP) and land reforms were envisaged in the agricultural sector for equitable distribution of land holdings by taking surplus land from big landlords. But the implementation of this progressive measure remains half-hearted and therefore vast numbers of small and marginal farmers together with landless peasants remained vulnerable. The failure of land reform created considerable discontent among poor peasantry and landless labourers and turned the vast majority of them into an agrarian proletariat (Desai, 1986).

With the class divide in the farming community, most of the increase in production between 1949-50 and 1964-65 happened from an increase in the area under cultivation (Vaidynathan, 2006). By the mid-1960s possibilities of expanding the cultivated area had been exhausted and issue of food availability arose. In response to this a new agriculture policy popularly described as the Green Revolution was initiated on the part of the Indian state. This marked the end of equity concerns such as land distribution but some institutional incentive structure to make farming viable and profitable was provided. The new agricultural strategy aimed at improving productivity by means of adoption of new HYVs (high-yielding variety seeds), irrigation, fertilizers and pesticides, deliberately concentrating on investments crop-wise (chiefly wheat) and region wise (the better endowed, higher productivity areas) where returns were expected to be relatively high and certain. It encouraged government assisted minor private irrigation and increased agriculture credit and fertilizer subsidy while also provided for remunerative price (minimum support price or MSP). The Commission on Agricultural Costs and Prices and Food Corporation of India were set up to carry out new pricing and marketing policies The minimum support price was devised to carry out public procurement at pre-specified cost plus remunerative prices of the agriculture produce supplied by farmers. These support prices were to be revised each year to ensure that there is a rising floor to agricultural income, which could stabilize income and guarantee farmers a return on investment that could help raise productivity (Ghosh and Chandrashekhar, 2017).

While the Green Revolution is largely known for creating food self-sufficiency through record production, regional inequality also emerges as improvement in yield growth occurred primarily in those regions where initial conditions were favourable. The strategic deployment of new technology among well endowed districts limited the spread effect for poorly endowed ones—a tendency that was enhanced by regressive distribution across states of input subsidies, plan expenditures, power capacity and institutional credit (Rao and Storm, 1998). However small farmers were handicapped by lack of resources for technological modernization. Rich farmers having land holdings of more than five acres largely cornered the bulk of subsidized institutional credits provided by commercial and cooperative banks. Omvedt (1982) held that about 15% of all rural families could be classified as rich farmers by the 1980s which comprised the traditional feudal caste of Brahmins and Rajputs as also dominant middle income caste farmers like the Patidars, Jats, Kammas, Reddys, Vokkaligas, etc.

Economic Liberalization and Withdrawal of the 'State'

The economic liberalization since 1991 aims to 'reduce the role of the state' and provide more space to the private sector. Though economic reform measures involving delicensing, reduced protection and dereservation did not touch agriculture as such, they were considered to improve the (barter) term of trade (in the prices received to prices paid by farmers). Prices paid by farmers for inputs, it was argued, would decline because of the above mentioned policy initiatives. This would translate into higher growth (Ahluwalia, 1996). Many scholars, however hold the view that improved barter term of trade cannot be determined a priori as net impact on agriculture growth could be positive, negative or zero on account of the ambiguous impact of variables like income, wealth and substitution (Desai and D'Souza, 2011).

Further trade liberalization under WTO commitments was undertaken by gradually reducing the import duties and quota as well as promoting export of farm commodities such as rice and horticulture. With free flow of imports domestic prices will move in tandem with higher international prices and this it was argued will bring a higher income for farmers. This should also mean higher agriculture growth (Gulati and Sharma, 1994). The expectation of a higher growth was also founded on the assumption that the world agricultural market was perfectly competitive, which was far from the case. Perfect competition assumes constant returns to scale, which is inconsistent with diminishing return to scale (DRS), discussed by Ricardo. It has been argued that agriculture is prone to DRS[1] (Desai and D'Souza, 20I1). Various studies have shown that when India imports farm commodities or inputs world market prices rise, but when it exports farm products, it is a disadvantaged price taker. (Datta, 2001).

Declining Public Investment in the Post-Liberalization Era

Public investment is a necessary condition to make agriculture profitable, viable and sustainable. Public investment not only lowers the transaction costs for farmers but also promotes private investment. Such public investment in physical infrastructure like irrigation, power, roads, etc. create positive incentives for the private sector to invest more in agricultural diversification, input supply, etc. (Ghosh, 2012).

Despite a positive potential multiplier impact on the overall economy, capital formation went down first in the public sector and later in the private sector in the 1990s. There were signs of revival under the UPA-1 regime (2004-05 to 2008-09) and the early years of UPA-2. Public investment saw a decline on account of the neo-liberal policies (promoted by financial institutions like IMF and WB) prescription to cut down the fiscal deficit while private investment fell on account of falling profitability. The agricultural economy witnessed both diminishing returns and cost-push decline in profitability.

Public investment in irrigation since 1990-91 has been by and large stagnant. Despite some increase in public investment since 2004-05 the area irrigated by surface sources is almost stagnant over the last two decades (Narayanmurthy, 2011). The growth in irrigated area across states and sources has shown deceleration during the post-Green Revolution period (1980-2003) as compared to the Green Revolution period (1965-66-1980-1981). The stagnation in state-supported irrigation facilities such as canals and tanks since the mid 1990s has led to an increasing reliance on groundwater irrigation especially in the rain-dependent Central Indian states of Maharashtra and Andhra Pradesh. However the cost of ground water extraction, besides being ecologically unsustainable was also expensive. Tenants and small farmers who were denied institutional credit were compelled to borrow from private moneylenders at high interest rates to finance the process of ground water extraction.

Reforms in Credit Policy: Changes in Priority Sector Lending (PSL)

In the post-liberalization era, the definition of priorty sector lending by banks procedure has been widened. They can meet their specified PSL target by investing in the rural infrastructure development fund (RIDF) and serving more resourceful farmers in semi-urban areas. Various government reports including Reserve Bank of India (RBI) findings suggest that actual credit flow has consistently exceeded the target set by the government for both commercial banks and regional rural banks as also cooperatives. Apart from this, other measures of financial inclusion such as the Kisan credit card, interest subvention scheme and debt swap scheme were also undertaken with the professed intention to facilitate easy availability and access of institutional credit to needy farmers. Various state governments have also come out with loan waiver schemes to the tune of thousands of crores in recent times because of farmers' protests and agitation which if left unaddressed could harm their future electoral prospects.

While such measures provide an immediate solution to those rich and middle farmers who have relatively large landholdings (above five hectares) and are a 'surplus producing class ', small and marginal farmers who are also tenant cultivators do not get any relief. The actual tenant cultivators do not get leased land with registered papers and therefore land owners with registration (*patta*) get subsidized credit as also loan waivers and interest subvention benefits. Moreover most of them borrow from private moneylenders at exorbitant rates because banks demand some collateral which they are unable to provide.

During 1991-2002 the share of marginal farmers in the total area operated has increased and their share in total credit has declined while the share of large farmers in total credit has gone up. Some scholars argue that not only rich and capitalist farmers (who use bio-chemical inputs and machines like tractors, harvesters, pump-sets, etc.) but also middle peasants have shifted to cash crops with help from bank credits.

Domestic Market Reforms

The government sought to amend the essential Commodities Act, 1952 governing trade and movement of farm products, etc. leading to market fragmentation. It aimed to remove restrictions relating to storage, trade of farm products like rice,wheat, coarse grains, etc. to give impetus to private trade and investment. Besides license requirements and plant scale restrictions were also abolished to promote food and agro-business industries. Restrictions were also removed on risk management financial instruments such as future trading on several commodities such as rice, wheat, pulses, etc. (Gulati and Fan, 2007). The government also passed the Model Agriculture Produce Marketing Committee (APMC) Act in 2003 allowing farmers to directly sell their produce to buyers bypassing middlemen and commission agents. States were required to amend their respective APMC laws to enable farmers to sell directly to private buyers without routing the produce through government-controlled *mandis* (marketplace). Recently the National Democratic Alliance government has set up a national agriculture market called e-NAM. It is a single online trading platform to connect more than five hundred *mandis* to allow farmers the freedom to sell their crops. Though the government claims impressive figures in terms of volume of transactions there remain some crucial issues to be resolved. How can it be ensured that produce sold adheres to basic standards if the traders who want to buy are distantly located? Besides, the data of business transacted in *mandis* are being uploaded on the e-Nam site, showing it as having taken place through a portal (Panwar, 2017). Other reforms include introduction of contract farming(CF) wherein private corporate agro-firms would invest in the production of non-cereal crops like onions, potatoes, tobacco, etc. through a contract system on the land of existing farmers.

Reforms in Subsidy Policy: WTO Commitments

India's commitment to World Trade Organization (WTO) rules and framework has had serious implications for subsidies meant to help farmers. As subsidy on inputs (fertilizers, pesticides, power) and minimum support prices beyond 10% of total value of agriculture output (per annum) come under reduction commitment as per WTO rules. The Indian government is under pressure to reduce these supportive measures to a significant extent, though it has not yet fully succumbed to the pressure mounted by the developed world.[2]

Neoliberal scholars argue that subsidies are unproductive and also that it crowds out productive investment by diverting resources. Subsidies to inputs such as power, it is argued, results in a price of power that does not reflect their scarcity value and hence are prone to overuse resulting in environment degradation (Gulati and Sharma, 1995). The underlying logic of input subsidy is to make farming remunerative and profitable by keeping the cost of production within manageable limits. The subsidy also helps to check the growth of food prices and compensate for the risk associated with new technology. Withdrawal of subsidy, it is argued, would adversely impact profitability and viability which in turn depends critically on the ratio between input prices and output prices. Some economists held that the maintenance of the relative price consequent to a one rupee cut in fertilizer subsidy would require a transfer of Rs. 10 to the farmer either from government or from the consumers. Moreover the withdrawal of subsidies and the consequent rise in input prices and the cost of cultivation would adversely impact over 60% of small and marginal farmers and tenant cultivators who produce largely for household consumption.

Withdrawal of Subsidy on Fertilizers, Seeds and Pesticides

Till 1992 the maximum retail prices of various fertilizers were determined by the government. From 2010 prices of phosphate (P) and potash (K) fertilizers have been decontrolled following which they have become costlier by 30-40%. With the government planning to decontrol urea (nitrogen) there would be further cost pressure on the farming community. Similarly, pesticide and diesel prices have been decontrolled leading to a higher cost of production for all crops.

The domestic seed policy has been liberalized with considerable incentives offered to private players to enter into seed production. 100% foreign equity was allowed in the seed industry and seed imports were allowed under the open general license (OGL). Many multinational companies like Monsanto, Cargil, etc. have entered the Indian seed market especially in high value commercial crops and GM (genetically modified) crops. Moreover they are taking advantage of a supportive patent regime enacted by the Indian state, thereby destroying the farmers' right to conserve seed and crop diversity. This is a very disturbing development in post-liberalization India. M.S. Swaminathan has recommended having a seed bank for protecting the traditional knowledge of farmers against corporate predation.

The prices of pesticides have also been decontrolled as the government has withdrawn the concerned subsidy gradually. With seeds being controlled by corporate enterprises pesticide markets have also seen the same fate resulting in large price increases in pesticides. An increasing use of pesticides has also led to a situation where new kinds of pests, other than the targeted pest, have evolved on the same crop requiring a larger volume of pesticide to be used. All this has magnified the cost of cultivation apart from seriously damaging the quality of the soil which in turn adversely affects the productivity of agricultural land. Poor extension services because of which farmers end up taking ill-advised decisions regarding crop selection, amount of fertilizers and pesticides used, etc. resulting in crop failure. In the 1990s and 2000s a decline in public investment in extension services has been manifested in an under-staffing in the extension department.

Farmer Distress in the Cotton Belt in Central India (Dry Land Areas)

With the macro policy framework favouring a more open market economy and a limited role for government intervention in order to promote agricultural growth, peasants at micro level except big farmers have experienced unfavourable conditions. Despite some minor increases in public investment and consequent improvement in terms of trade for agriculture during the United Progressive Alliance (UPA) government's tenure, farmers especially those growing commercial crops have experienced extreme distress.

In the post-liberalization era farmers in central India have increasingly moved towards high value cash crops like cotton, tobacco, vinegar, soybean, etc. Cotton growers in water-stressed and less irrigated sub-regions in Maharashtra, Andhra Pradesh, Karnataka, Madhya Pradesh and Chattisgarh have been found to be in an extremely distressed situation and are compelled to commit suicide. Studies establish that farmers' suicides in this region are very high. Over the sixteen-year period between 1997 and 2012, a total of 1,65,640 farmers took the extreme step to end their life in this region (Sainath and Nagraj, 2014).

Various studies take mounting indebtedness as the central causative factor behind the increasing number of suicides though a one to one correlation cannot be established with full certainty (Mishra, 2008)). The grim agrarian distress is a direct product of the neoliberal policies of import liberalization and a shrinking space for state intervention in credit, seed, irrigation. etc. With a reduction of subsidies on fertilizers, pesticides, etc. along with corporate monopoly over cotton seeds, the cost of cultivation has risen for cotton growers. Farmers are compelled to buy cotton seeds only from multinational corporations such as Monsanto who charge prices which are very high. These high prices of cotton seeds increase costs of farmers as compared to a situation when they were free to conserve their seeds. Further these seeds become vulnerable to non-target pests as target pets evolve resistance (Shiva, 2002). The small farmers and tenant cultivators, unable to meet the strict documentary collateral requirement of formal banking, turn to private moneylenders-cum-input suppliers who charge very high interest rates. Eventually the farmers get trapped in debt (Sridhar, 2006).

Since 1994 cotton was made easily importable by lowering import duties. This made domestic cotton prices susceptible to price fluctuations/shocks from the world market. Moreover, USA and China provide a huge subsidy to their cotton farmers to increase their production. Then they dump the excess supply in the international market (including India) at very low prices. The low output prices of cotton because of free import made it difficult for farmers to recover their cost of production let alone repay their loans. Thus volatile global prices of cotton together with higher prices of private irrigation and seeds provided by private companies have made cotton cultivation unprofitable and unviable for small and marginal farmers.

Various other research studies, however, do not see the open economy as the driving cause behind increasing farmer distress. Vaidynathan (2006) argues that while there has been a removal of quantitative restrictions on import of crops/livestock products, the overall increase in volume of foreign trade is too small relative to the country's overall crop output to significantly affect domestic production and pattern of resource use. He maintains that the farmers are driven to take the extreme step not only because of high and imprudent borrowing but also because of the failure of their expectation of high yields and good prices after high investment but concurs that institutional barriers such as the quality of the public support system for farmers, governance and economic policies has become the most serious impediment to agricultural growth. Various states have failed to provide/regulate basic requirements for export-oriented capitalist farming adopted by big farmers leading to severe stress on the local resources, a falling return cost ratio and adverse term of trade (Narayanmurthy, 2006).

Farmer Resentment Over Low Return Despite Abundant Production

Farmers from well irrigated regions from different states reaped a bumper harvest of wheat, pulses, onions, soyabeans, etc. in recent years but were unable to get remunerative prices. In government-owned *mandis* prices were so low that it could not even cover the cost of cultivation. Nominal increases in minimum support prices across the crops despite a huge jump in the cost of cultivation is the running thread that connects farmers' distress and their cultivation of different crops depending upon agro-climatic conditions across India.

Box 1: Minimum Support Price for Major Crops

	During UPA regime		During NDA period	
Commodity	Average increase in MSP between 2007-08 and 2013-14 in percentage	Average annual incremental increase in ₹/quintal	Average increase in MSP between 2014-15 and 2015-16 in percentage	Average annual incremental increase in ₹/quintal
Paddy	11.21	95	3.68	50
Jowar **hybrid**	15.61	129	2.61	35
Ragi	14.84	129	6.45	75
Tur dal	18.28	393	6.32	163
Maize	11.59	99	1.15	8
Moong dal	16.48	400	5.43	175
Urad	15.86	371	6.32	163
Groundnut	16.30	350	0.75	15
Sunflower	15.15	313	1.33	50
Sesamum	16.03	417	2.17	100
Cotton **medium staple fibre**	11.33	271	1.33	50

Source: Computed from Commissions for Agricultural Costs and Prices Data

Annual increases in MSP have been smaller than earlier with support prices not keeping pace with rising costs. Since support prices, at which the government offers to procure as much as farmers want to sell, influence the level of market prices, the latter too have been depressed (Chandrasekhar and Ghosh, 2017).

Farmers are forced to sell their produce at rates lower than MSP on account of delay in purchase and multiple conditions placed by purchasing agencies (Rajalakshmi, 2017). This sale below MSP amounts to distress selling partly as they could not store the crop for long because of lack of storage facility and partly because they need cash for the next phase of cultivation. This infrastructure lag and absence of procurement by state agencies compel farmers to accept the prices offered by private commission agents. The rates invariably fail to cover production costs. However the consumer is charged up to three or four times the rate offered to farmers. For a certain variety of basmati rice for which consumers pay Rs. 100 a kg (Rs. 10,000 a quintal) the farmers receive Rs. 1,500-Rs. 2,000 a quintal. The intermediaries-cum-traders with covert support from the political class is believed to have been appropriating the surplus contained in this large price differential. Recently the government has initiated some studies on the role of intermediaries between farmers and consumers.

The method of arriving at MSP is full of inadequacies. Rent on leased land is underestimated. Inclusion of interest rate paid to moneylenders is not included. Family labour is considered at minimum daily wage labour rate while farmer multi-skilled role in planning management crop science and marketing is not valued properly. Moreover the cost of cultivation varies but MSP is fixed based on weighted average of state-wise cost of cultivation. Further it does not include the 50% profit margin above cost of production as recommended by the M.S. Swaminathan national commission on farmers so as to improve profitability[3]. It is argued that because of fiscal and budgetary constraints in a liberalized economy like India, government has not been able to implement the aforementioned recommendation (Chandrashekhar, 2017).

The liberalization of trade in agricultural commodities has linked domestic prices to international prices. As a result of the lowering of import tariffs, agriculturalists are facing rising costs and competition from low cost import across the crops (Ghosh and

Chandrashekhar, 2017). This results in a precarious situation for farmers. When there is a bumper harvest low prices hit their net income depending on how global prices move while in the case of the poor harvest they are not compensated by increase in crop prices. Thus farmers lose out as a result of declining market prices (as opposed to procurement prices) in good harvest years but also do not gain in terms of higher prices (even if they are affected by lower output) in bad monsoon years. Moreover support prices do not cover all the crops and all poor farmers (Ghosh and Chandrashekhar, 2017).

Some economists, however, do not share the aforementioned reasoning regarding import liberalization and its consequences for domestic prices and farmers' incomes. India has preferred 'strategic opening' rather than complete free trade in response to the varying global price situation (Chand and Bazar, 2012). Indian policy initiatives have sought to protect consumer interest largely by controlling inflation while tinkering with MSP. During 2001 when global agricultural prices were low, the Government of India imposed a high import duty to prevent cheap import and encouraged export. MSP was also raised by a small amount. These measures were meant to protect producers' (farmers') interests. When global prices witnessed a sharp increase during 2007-09, India reversed its earlier policy and allowed imports while exports were restricted. This was done to prevent a steep hike in the domestic price for consumers due to transmission of the global price increases. MSP was increased during these years to minimize the gap between global prices and domestic prices (Chand and Bazar, 2012). While the debate continues in academic circles as to whether total openness or strategic opening is preferable, it is the case that the macroeconomic and institutional framework in the post-liberalization era has deliberately focused on controlling inflation while farmers' income and remuneration have not acquired a due role in the policy agenda. Media debates expect 'populist' announcements on loan waiver and other schemes during elections. Corporate profits are skyrocketing partly due to the routing of investment through the 'tax haven' apart from various tax benefits and exemptions in budgets.

The farming community's income, except 10-15% rich farmers, has remained more or less stagnant despite the fact over 60% of the people of India are engaged in agricultural and allied activities and ensure food security for all. As per official national account statistics, income per head of the agriculture dependent population increased by 16% over the three periods 2014-15 to 2016-17. Over the same period inflation based on the consumer price index for rural India rose by 16.3%. This indicates that the inflation adjusted incomes of agriculture dependent population has stagnated. This also explains why farmers taking working capital/consumption loans as well as loans for investment in agricultural production are unable to pay off their debts (Chandrasekhar and Ghosh, 2017). While farm incomes have not shown much upward movement in tandem with the rising cost of living, corporate and real estate developers are acquiring agricultural land at low prices.

Corporate Takeover of Agricultural Land

Many rich farmers in Karnataka and elsewhere have entered into contracts with private agri-business companies which seemingly guarantee an assured return. These farmers prefer to buy food and produce cash crops such as flowers, grapes, mulberries, etc. for the domestic/international market as they fetch higher prices. Owing to liberalization and globalization a division has emerged between big farmers and small and marginal farmers. These rich farmers having benefited from agribusiness do not agitate against multinational corporations such as Cargil, Monsanto, etc. whose actions threaten biodiversity and the autonomy of farmers over traditional knowledge.

Real estate developers are also acquiring fertile agricultural land in their pursuit to extract higher profits through real estate development due to urbanization. This together with various government projects like highway development, setting up of power plants, etc. have further led to shrinking of cultivatable land, though in many cases they are offered high prices especially in the suburban periphery, 'consent' is elicited through allurement and other coercive means. Farmers' organizations in Maharashtra,

Andhra Pradesh and elsewhere have been protesting against land acquisition for special economic zones (SEZ) and other corporate projects over the past few years but without much success. The recent intensified protests and agitations across the country, triggered by the death of six protesting farmers by police firing in Madhya Pradesh, have compelled various state governments to announce ad hoc farm loan waivers for some indebted farmers and assurances of better minimum support price.

'Jobless' Growth Since Economic Reforms and Inadequate Non-Farm Alternatives

The inadequate generation of proper remunerative employment in other sectors of the economy have been distressing features of the growth process in the post-liberalization era. This has meant that farmers do not have a genuine choice of engaging in other productive work even as cultivation becomes less profitable (Ghosh, 2015). The manufacturing and service sectors absorb only a fraction of the 1.2 crore people who join the potential workforce every year. A large number of ex-farmers have joined the informal construction sector. The availability of alternative non-farm opportunities could cushion the adverse impact of agrarian distress. It has been seen that even though the agrarian crisis is acute in some regions, farmers' suicides are not observed there because of availability of off farm and rural non-farm employment options (Nagraj et al., 2014).

Conclusion

Economic liberalization and consequent opening of the Indian market has created a context where sections of farmers have increasingly moved to cultivate high value non-cereal crops. While they have reaped benefits sometimes on account of higher global prices they have also suffered huge losses owing to the inherent volatility of the functioning of the market economy in terms of fluctuating demand and prices. A majority of small farmers who are engaged in subsistence farming are also not able to enjoy a decent standard of living compared with other groups. This is happening because of the increasing cost of production and diminishing returns in agriculture. This huge mismatch owing to the functioning of markets turns into distress, crisis and hopelessness when the institutional mechanism of state support dwindles and makes farming more expensive. An increasing number of farmers' suicides is symptomatic of a larger agrarian crisis where farming is neither viable nor profitable and this has forced millions to abandon farming and work as informal sector workers in urban areas. The increasing urbanization has also led the corporate sector to buy fertile land for real state development thereby reducing cultivable land—a disturbing trend not just for food security but also ecological sustainability in the long run. In the 21st century economic growth will be sustainable only if it is socially inclusive and ecologically viable. The persistent agrarian crisis in India calls for the setting up of a holistic framework to address the stagnant income and vulnerability of farmers to market forces and ecological challenges. The various existing government schemes including the price stabilization fund has been both inadequate and poorly implemented. Farmers' incomes need to be at the centre of policy formulation and execution. If successful it would generate demand for the good and services of the other sectors of the economy and usher in an era of equitable growth and distribution.

NOTES

1. Ricardo 's law of diminishing returns to scale implies that a change in production is obtained at diminishing returns to the cost of all inputs. Such returns cannot be overcome if there is a severe constraint on the availability of land.
2. Report of the Expert Group on Agricultural Indebtedness chaired by R. Radhakrishna (2007).
3. Amber box subsidies are directly related to production promotion and this must be reduced by the member countries to the prescribed level. Blue Box subsidies are a certain direct payment made to farmers by the government in the form of assistance programmes to encourage agriculture development. Many countries want to set limits on it. Green box subsidies include all those government expenses which are not directed at particular products and related to the current level of production or prices. It includes: public storage

for food security, pest, and disease control, research and extension, some direct payment to farmers that do not stimulate production like crop and income insurance and environment protection.

4. The UPA regime took important policy initiatives to promote agriculture but farmers' indebtedness and suicides remained a recurring feature.

   Credit to agriculture increased manifold; agriculture research and extension (to ensure farmer' access to current and relevant knowledge for production) were given a boost through more public spending and the rural employment guarantee act (MGNREGA) provided the rural poor a secure base of income that helped rural economy through enhanced demand. Also farmers were benefited from a positive movement in world prices and favourable terms of trade assisted relative improvement in farm income. (Ghosh 2015) These measures resulted in significant increases in volume of production of both food grains and non-food crops. The value added in agriculture also improved substantially driven by both higher output and relative price changes. Capital formation during the UPA regime increased substantially driven in the later part of the decade by private investment that responded to higher crop prices and more opportunities for crop diversification as well as improved extension services. But the recent period has witnessed a sharp fall in capital investment in agriculture. In fact deceleration in agricultural performance had set in during the last two years of the UPA government. Small and marginal farmers, however, especially in dryland areas did suffer hardships as this agriculture boom did not translate into better material conditions. (ibid)

5. Report of national consultation on policy perspective and state response to agrarian crisis and farmer distress, organized by the National Institute of Rural Development and Panchayati Raj, Centre for Sustainable Agriculture, Hyderabad. Available at http://aidindia.org accessed on December 20, 2017.

REFERENCES

Ahluwalia, Montek S. (1996). "New Economic Policy and Agriculture: Some Reflections", *IndianJ Journal of Agriculture Economics,* Vol. 51, No. 3.

Chand, R. and Bazar, S. (2012). 'Agricultural Trade Liberalization policies in India: Balancing Producer and Consumer Interest' in *Twenty Years of India's Liberalization,* Centre for WTO Studies, UN, NewYork.

Chandrashekhar, C. and Ghosh, Jayati (2017). Viability of Indian Agriculture, Available at www.hindubusinessline accessed on December 20, 2017.

Chandrashekhar (2017). In a Policy Trap, *Frontline.*

Datta, Samar K. (2001). 'Problems and Prospects of India's Rice Trade in WTO Regime' In *CMA, IIM-A, Implication of WTO Agreements for Indian Agriculture*, Oxford and IBH, New Delhi.

Desai, A.R. (1986). *Agrarian Struggles in India After Independence*, Oxford University Press, New Delhi.

Desai, M. Bhupat, D'Souza, Mellor, and John W. (2011). "Agricultural Policy Strategy, Instruments and Implementation", *Economic and Political Weekly*, Vol. 46, No. 53.

Deshpande R.S. and Arora, Saroj (2010). *Agrarian Crisis: Farmer Suicides,* Sage Publications, New Delhi.

Ghosh, Jayati (2012). 'Development', In *International Relations*, Siddharth Mallarappu and B.S. Chimni (eds.), Pearson Publications, New Dellhi.

——— 2015. 'Agriculture in Crisis', *Frontline*, 32(7).

Gulati, Ashok and Fan, Shenggon (2007). *Dragon and Elephant: Agriculture and Rural Reform in China and India,* Oxford University Press, New Delhi.

Gulati, Ashok and Sharma, Anil (1994). "Agriculture Under GATT: What it Holds for India", *Economic and Political Weekly*, Vol. 29, No. 29.

Mishra, Srijit (2008). "Risks, Farmer Suicides and Agrarian Crisis in India: Is There a Way Out?", *Indian Journal of Agricultural Economics,* Vol. 63, No. 1.

Nagraj, K., Sainath, P., Rukmani, R. and Gopinath, R. (2014). Farmer Suicides in India: Magnitude, Trends and Spatial Pattern, *Review of Agrarian Studies*, Vol. 4(2), pp. 53-83.

Narayanmurthy, A. (2011). "Development and Irrigation in India: Temporal Trend and Regional Pattern, Irrigation and Drainage", *Indian Journal of Agricultural Economics,* Vol. 66, No. 4.

——— 2006. "State of India's Farmers", *Economic and Political Weekly,* Vol. 15, No. 47.

Omvedt, Gail (1982). *Land, Caste and Politics in Indian States*, University of Delhi, New Delhi.

Pai, Sudha (2010). 'Farmers' Movements', in *The Oxford Companion of Indian Politics*, P.B. Mehta and N.G. Jayal (eds.), Oxford University Press, New Delhi.

Panwar, Sudhir (2017). A Wake Up Call, *Frontline*, 34(13).

Rajalaxmi, T.K. (2017). Bumper Problem, *Frontline*, 34(13).

Rao, J. Mohan and Storm, Servass (1998). 'Distribution and Growth in Indian Agriculture', in *The Indian Economy; Major Debates Since Independence*, Terrence J. Byres (ed.), New Delhi.

Shiva, Vandana and Jalees, Kunwar (2002). *Farmers Suicides in India*, Research Foundation for Science, Technology and Ecology, New Delhi.

Sridhar, V. (2006). "Why Do Farmers Commit Suicides?" *Economic and Political Weekly*, Vol. 41, No. 16, pp. 1559-1565.

Vaidynathan. A. (2006). *Agrarian Crisis: Roots, Causes and Remedies*, www.hindu.com/opinion accessed on December 15, 2017.

6

Social Identity as a Determinant of Differential Outcomes to Education: Reflections from a Survey of Delhi's Informal Labour Markets

Simin Akhter Naqvi

Education, Employment and Adverse Incorporation

Conceptualizing Social Exclusion imperatively requires us to understand the economic and political conditions of Capitalist Europe in the early phases of Europe's industrial development, where early notions of Social Exclusion emerged. Following Byrne (2005), early approaches to Social Exclusion include the Classical Liberal position with a focus on possessive individualism and negative liberties, the traditional conservative approach that focuses on integration of individuals into a traditionally legitimized and coherent social order and the radical transformational social position that sought to eliminate inequality and exploitation through the transformation of capitalism to socialism. The poor are seen as the redundant reproducing masses by the possessive individualists, in trying to explain poverty through the emergence of specialization and consequent social differentiation, conceiving the economy and the markets as networks of voluntary exchange between autonomous individuals for mutual gain and benefit, overlooking the contradiction of basing the premise of 'free markets' on the notion of negative liberty while the inherent need of the capitalist system for surplus labour, denying labour the liberty to disassociate with capital. These early approaches however, and rightly so, highlight the need to understand the concept of residuums and 'underclasses' as a structural concept, located in the functioning economy and polity. Early deliberations on the subject also overlooked the need to look at 'Citizenship' as a real historical and social practice as opposed to a vague philosophical abstraction. The domination of political decisions by corporate interests in post-democratic societies and the need to achieve political disassociation from the limited interests of private capital in mass democracies also needs to be discussed in the context.

Looking at modern notions of exclusion as discussed by Sen (2000), Seers (1969), Lenoir (1975), Nevile (2007) and others, one finds exclusion as understood in these later academic writings to broadly overlap poverty when defined as multi-dimensional deprivation, yet going beyond the latter in terms of the former's relational and instrumental aspects. While Sen (2000) looks at it in terms of capability deprivation and denial of basic economic freedoms, Seers says some of the most important questions to be asked in terms of a nation's development include what is happening to poverty and inequality and who is being left out of these processes of growth and development.

In a discussion on Sen's understanding of Social Exclusion, Nevile (2007) presents a detailed discussion on how the concept of 'social exclusion' is a 'relatively recent import' into development theory. It is also argued that the concept has limited use in the field and understanding of development studies, highlighting that chronic poverty may actually have more to do with 'adverse incorporation', which captures the state of affairs more pragmatically and realistically as opposed to 'exclusion'. Nevile (2007) also highlights the importance of understanding the links between development and deprivation, and argues that though exclusion may be one of the many ways of understanding the dynamics of deprivation, it is certainly not indispensable or exhaustive as a means to this end. Nevile (2007) also quotes Sen (2000) and states that the latter himself warns students of development studies of the dangers of trying to explain all deprivation through exclusion. Like exclusion, says the author, unfavourable inclusion too, has relational and instrumental aspects and at times may offer a better explanation of deprivation than exclusion (say, for instance, in the case of workers working on exploitative informal contracts). Nevile (2007) also highlights the need to differentiate between 'active' and 'passive' instances of unfavourable inclusion as not all policy-decisions and designs may be 'designed' to result in 'exclusion' or 'deprivation'. Further, it is claimed that for a community/social-group, a history of active exclusion may result in subsequent passive exclusion and/or informal social relations characterized by unfavourable inclusion may cause formal exclusion of these social-groups from other socio-political domains, which is why one needs to understand the concepts of Active/Passive, Formal/Informal exclusion together and in totality.

In careful observation of wider social practice one thus finds that the 'excluded' population may not summarily or even necessarily be 'excluded' or kept out of these apparently monolithic and homogeneous structures comprising private markets and socio-political institutions; rather compelled to stay at the bottom of this highly segmented and differentially-responsive structures. In India's Labour Markets, for instance, one finds Dalits concentrated in low-paying, casual and menial work at the bottom end of the wage-spectrum, women receiving lower wages for the same work and exhibiting much smaller workforce participation compared to men, Muslims concentrated in self-employment and facing discriminatory odds of hiring and tribals and other marginalized populations having very limited or no access to formal labour-markets.

In terms of its conceptual vantage, this chapter loosely agrees with Nevile's criticism of Sen's included/excluded dichotomy and treads the line that the utility of this approach in explaining the cause of persisting poverty needs to be questioned. It may well be emphasized that one needs to understand the distributional attributes of a market/social process before recommending integration of the 'excluded' into this mainstream as a solution to their deprivation; and that there is much need for incorporating a more sophisticated understanding of the causes of deprivation into policy-discourse, looking beyond the monolith of exclusion.

Following Shariff (1995), "When we take a look at the distribution of employed persons by category of work it is interesting to note that over 53 and 60% of male and female Muslims, respectively, in urban areas and 59 and 68% of males and females, respectively, in rural areas are 'self-employed', This percentage is substantially lower for both Hindu and Christian males and females in urban areas. On the contrary, Hindus' and Christians' share in 'regular-workers' category is substantially higher for both males and females in urban areas. Muslims' employment in regular wage/salaried jobs is marginal. This presents a very dismal picture, especially for Muslim females since their Workforce Participation Rates (WPR) are very low to start with and only an insignificant proportion of them are in regularly paid jobs. One possible reason for this may be the lack of secular education among Indian Muslim females". Collating the observation with Basant's (2012) findings, using estimates drawn from the NSSO survey report 2009-10, one finds out that "Literacy rates are much lower in rural areas as compared to urban areas but both for males and females, the rates have improved in the last decade, especially after 2004-05. Also, the patterns and trends are more or less the same as the aggregate trends described above, except that literacy rates have not improved very significantly for rural women belonging to Muslim-OBC households; in urban areas the rates of literacy are higher but the improvements have not been that dramatic. Moreover, while for urban females belonging to the Muslim community (both OBC and general) show the same pattern as the one described above, Muslim men living in urban areas are worse-off than all other SRCs, Muslim OBCs reporting the lowest literacy rates" and "Dropout rates are also among the highest for Muslims and this seems to go up significantly after middle school. Higher secondary attainment levels are also among the lowest for Muslims and in relative terms, inter-SRC differences rise at the school leaving stage. This contributes to large deficits in higher education; graduate attainment rates (GARs) are also among the lowest and not converging with the average. The major problem appears to lie at the school level; once that hurdle of eligibility is crossed, differences in GARs across SRCs narrow down substantially and are often not very different. As with other areas of education, participation of Muslims in technical and engineering education is also among the lowest." Clearly, deprivation of and lack of participation in education, particularly at the school level, has worked to limit the community's workforce participation and work-outcomes, especially in formal wage-employment.

However, as Kabeer (2000) points out social exclusion is not a monolithic deprivation of some enabling attribute rather a complex product of institutional processes, group dynamics and social practices. Social policy, to deal with exclusion, accordingly needs a multi-pronged intervention in the functioning of each one of these forces and requires us to study in detail the role of the state and its institutions in limiting these forces, or conversely in reproduction and reinforcement of the same in case of the state failing its duties. Constructive and affirmative social-policy intervention also requires us to analyse and evaluate the various 'cultural' forms of exclusion, including the use of myth and metaphor to the disadvantage of any community or ethnic group in literature, public discourse and in the writing of history, and in the day-to-day execution of cultural prejudices and stereotypes by members of the society, media and administration at large.

Looking at the recently released religion-wise population data (The Census 2011 data on Population by Religious Communities, released by the Registrar General and Census Commissioner of India, August 2015), one finds a "declining trend in the population growth rate in the country. While decadal growth rates are declining among all religious communities, the decline has been sharper among Muslims than among Hindus over the last three decades. In fact, the decadal growth rate among Muslims during 2001-11 is the lowest ever". Further, "the share of Hindus in the population declined marginally from 80.5% in 2001 to 79.8% in 2011. In 2001, Muslims constituted 13.4% of the country's population; this rose marginally to 14.2%, making the Hindu population to increase by 13.9 crores during 2001-11; and the Muslim population to increase by 3.4 crores." The largely underplayed factor, however is the 'Sex-Ratio', where sex ratio among Muslims as per Census 2011 was 951 (better than the 939 among Hindus) and was found to have improved significantly over the decade (from 936 in 2001 to 951 in 2011, compared to a smaller improvement among Hindus; from 931 in 2001 to 939 in 2011). The point to be understood here, is that while the Muslim community in India is a large and growing SRC, which itself partially justifies the need and scope of this study, what needs to be read between the lines, though is that there is evidence of significant progressive change in the internal demographics of the community, despite which the majority within Muslims continue to remain concentrated at the margins of society, in low-paying professions and dead-end jobs, mostly within the informal and unorganized sector. Deprivation of education also appears to be central to the skewed labour-market outcomes for the community and its role as an 'enabling attribute', needs to be explored in both the organized and unorganized sectors in the economy. Also, whether provisioning of public education and health is concentrated in the non-Muslim dominated districts needs to be established.

Looking at deprivation of education by socio-religious categories, even as recently as 2010-11, 35% of Dalits, 46% of Adivasis and 33% of Muslims had never enrolled in schools as opposed to an average of only 17% for upper-caste Hindus (Basant, 2012). In terms of access to schooling, the Lok-Sabha Secretariat report on Minority Education for 2007-08 reveals that access to primary schooling within a reasonable distance (i.e. within 1 kilometre for primary and within 3 kilometres for upper primary) is reasonably low for minorities, particularly in rural areas, with only 88% of Muslim children reporting access at the primary level and 57% at the upper-primary level.

Dalits are also found to fare poorly at 90% for primary and 52% for upper primary and Christians at 73% and 48% respectively; as opposed to significantly higher upper primary access for upper-caste Hindus at 64% (and a higher access at the primary level at 94%). "Muslims are also found to fare pathetically in terms of matriculation rates with a percentage participation of 11% which is nearly half that of the national average and about a third of that for upper-caste Hindus" (ibid). Further, "while India has attained universal primary school enrolment according to official data, the percentage of girls who had never attended school was just above 25% among Muslims, Dalits and Tribals. Among Muslims officially recognized as lagging behind (classified as "Other Backward Class Muslims"), the rate was even higher, at 31 and 20% for girls and boys respectively. Incidence of malnutrition among children below five was estimated at 48% among Dalits, 55 among Tribals and 42% among Muslims, against the 26% target. This was in 2006, and the government has since stopped collecting disaggregated data." (OXFAM, 2013).

Quoting Shariff (1995): "When we take a look at the distribution of employed persons by category of work it is interesting to note that over 53 and 60% of male and female Muslims, respectively, in urban areas and 59 and 68% of males and females, respectively, in rural areas are 'self-employed'. This percentage is substantially lower for both Hindu and Christian males and females in urban areas. On the contrary, Hindus' and Christians' share in 'regular-workers' category is substantially higher for both males and females in urban areas. Muslims' employment in regular wage/salaried jobs is marginal. This presents a very dismal picture, especially for Muslim females since their WPRs are very low to start with and only an insignificant proportion of them are in regularly paid jobs. One possible reason for this may be the lack of secular education among Indian Muslim females".

Collating the observation with Basant's findings (2012), using estimates drawn from the NSSO Survey Report 2009-10, one finds that Literacy rates are much lower in rural areas as compared to urban areas but both for males and females, the rates have improved in the last decade, especially after 2004-05. Also, the patterns and trends are more or less the same as the aggregate trends described above, except that literacy rates have not improved very significantly for rural women belonging to Muslim-OBC households; in urban areas the rates of literacy are higher but the improvements have not been that dramatic.

Moreover, while urban females belonging to the Muslim community (both OBC and general) show the same pattern as the one described above, Muslim men living in urban areas are worse off than all other SRCs, Muslim OBCs reporting the lowest literacy rates. Dropout rates are also among the highest for Muslims and this seems to go up significantly after middle school. Higher secondary attainment levels are also among the lowest for Muslims and in relative terms, inter-SRC differences rise at the school leaving stage. This contributes to large deficits in higher education; graduate attainment rates (GARs) are also among the lowest and not converging with the average. The major problem appears to lie at the school level; once that hurdle of eligibility is crossed, differences in GARs across SRCs narrow down substantially and are often not very different. As with other areas of education, participation of Muslims in technical and engineering education is also found to be among the lowest. Clearly, deprivation of and lack of participation in education, particularly at the school level, has worked to limit workforce participation and work outcomes, especially in formal wage-employment for the deprived communities.

Within the labour-markets, again, strong evidence of segmentation and discrimination on religious and caste lines can be seen. Over-qualified Dalit and Muslim youth are routinely found to be employed in low-paying jobs. At the same level of qualification, Muslims are found concentrated at lower wages and in self-employment. Also, within private formal labour-markets, controlling for capabilities, one finds much fewer Muslims and Dalits in managerial or superior positions, with an IIDS study on urban labour-markets reporting the odds of Dalits and Muslims with the same level of 'capabilities' as upper-caste Hindus, landing the same job at only 0.67 and 0.33 respectively (Thorat et al., 2009).

Theoretically, exclusion in/deprivation of education is an important determinant of exclusion/adverse inclusion in Labour markets. Communities/individuals deprived of education and access to skill-forming training processes cannot make it to the upper end of the income/employment spectrum. In the absence of substantial inheritance and/or family tradition, it gets very difficult for the uneducated to run even small businesses that require any amount of paper-work, registration, record-keeping or account maintenance. As a result, even those who possess local and traditional skills like weaving, embroidery, wood-craft, bamboo-weaving, stone-carving, etc. have to access markets through middle-men and/or are compelled to operate as hawkers/ vendors/contracted/sub-contracted artisans in the unregistered sector in the absence of formal education, with considerably reduced profit-margins and growth-prospects. Inter-generationally, lack of education coupled with poverty tends to limit the access of the next generation to education and other skill-forming processes. Continuing and extreme poverty in agriculture compels indigenous populations to migrate to cities and work as casual labour, causing them to lose traditional skills acquired over generations. Those who continue to work in villages have exposure only to local markets with a lower price and profit structure.

Deprivation of education also makes it less profitable for the poor/traditionally employed to migrate, given their limited ability to cope with the generally more information/ knowledge intense social/economic structures of cities. Within urban labour-markets, the uneducated are adverse-included rather than excluded, for it is precisely this section of the labour-force that serves as a surplus reserve casual workforce in the urban unorganized sector. A systematic lack of access to education (coupled with limited poverty-alleviation measures and sustenance provisions for school-going children) for communities thus leads to sustained exclusion of these people from education and subjects them to limited employability and socio-economic mobility over generations subjecting them to the compulsion of entering labour-markets at subordinate positions marked by highly compressible ex-ante wage-claims and no job security; which in turn makes it 'rational' for these populations to not invest in the education/training of their children, in a vicious and circular manner.

While reporting low educational attainment by Muslims or Dalits it also needs to be said that reasons for low attainment lie not only in poor availability or active denial of education, the decisions also rest with the parents who are the decision-making agency for their children; however, these micro decisions have both macro motivations and macro impacts on the society as a whole and are therefore important to understand in a framework of rationality.

If parents (that is the decision-makers) feel/ perceive that there would be insufficient labour market returns from investing in their children's education they will decide not to educate their children (and this might as well be a completely rational decision given their information set). Similarly, general perceptions/knowledge of a lack of availability of institutional finance and formal work opportunities, coupled with conditions of extreme poverty and a general lack of socio-economic opportunity and lack of employable skills, conditions these individual decision-makers to stay on in self-employment and not 'try too hard' to have their children acquire non-traditional skills by going to schools and/or other vocational training centres.

One also needs to point out here that wherever socio-cultural integration has taken place, whether through access to social media and public information or through informal social networks, it has resulted in economic mobility and increased access to income-earning opportunities for the marginalized, as can be seen in the sections that follow.

Positive impact of citizen activism and affirmative NGO action on both, capability formation and access to work opportunities, has also been observed and reported but the scale of that kind of intervention mostly remains experimental and has been found to cover only a very small section of the overall population.

A Macro-Economic Model of Wage Difference and Differential Returns to Education

In this model, the difference between marginalized wages (Wm) and non-marginalized wages (Wnm) is explained as a function of differences in capability attributes, social capital/network externalities, living spaces, identity barriers to market entry and inter-generational social mobility ($\alpha_{nm} > \alpha_m$).

The four basic hypotheses underlying the model are:

H_{01}: Marginalized wages are a floor for non-marginalized wages.

H_{02}: Access to social capital/network externalities significantly impacts odds of being employed.

H_{03}: Socio-religious identity and gender significantly impacts market entry and wages.

H_{04}: Socio-religious identity, gender, land-ownership and asset-formation significantly impact inter-generational economic mobility.

Further, in the model, wage expectation by self ($Wexp_{nm,}^{self}$) is explained to be a function of ($W_m - W_{nm}$), wage offered(Woff), and wage in time period t +1 is $W^{t+1}_m = a + bW^t_m$, i.e. it is a function of community-specific inter-generational job mobility b times wage at time t plus the general systemic wage change a, or the intergenerational change in wage between t, t+1 is some function of the coefficient of economic mobility, narrowly defined here in terms of job and/or wage-bracket mobility for any given community.

Total static wage share $WS = WS_m + WS_{nm}$

Static wage share ratio $\dfrac{WSm}{WS} = c + d(W_m - W_{nm})$

Difference between marginalized and non-marginalized wages is $W_m - W_{nm} = \beta\delta$

Where δ is a function of ratios of marginalized and non-marginalized educational levels, productivity levels and inter-generational economic mobility,

$$\delta = \theta\frac{enm}{em} + \Psi\frac{pnm}{pm} + \alpha\frac{mnm}{mm} \tag{1}$$

and educational levels at time t +1 depend on wages earned at time t (last generation) for both, marginalized and non-marginalized communities,

$$e_{nm} = \chi_{nm} + \varphi_{nm} W^{t}_{nm} \tag{2}$$

$$e_{m} = \chi_{m} + \varphi_{m} W^{t}_{m} \tag{3}$$

productivity levels for both, marginalized and non-marginalized communities depend on own-community's wages as well as other community's wages in two ways, first, wage-increase leads to increase in AD and demand-driven technical change; second, cost-productivity rises to combat wage-increase, i.e.

$$p_{nm} = \tau_{nm} + \omega W_{nm} + \varepsilon W_{m} \tag{4}$$

$$p_{m} = \tau_{m} + \omega W_{m} + \varepsilon W_{nm} \tag{5}$$

Finally, static community-wise wage levels depend on educational levels, labour productivity and inter-generational mobility (which in turn is a function of socio-religious and gender identities and network externalities), i.e.

$$W_{nm} = \theta^{nm.enm} + \Psi nm \, . \, pnm + \alpha \, nm \tag{6}$$

$$W_{m} = \theta^{m.em} + \Psi m \, . \, pm + \alpha m \tag{7}$$

Results from a Survey of Informal Workers in Delhi-NCR

A pilot survey of 240 workers employed in the informal sector in Delhi, mostly in construction, domestic work, vending/hawking, plumbing, carpentry, tailoring, motor mechanic 'sweat-shops', cleaning, driving and cooking was carried out as part of a larger research between July 2016 and February 2017. Findings reveal significant gender wage gaps between men and women, and between non-Dalit and Dalit workers, with women consistently earning only about 66% of counterpart male earnings, despite minimum wage legislations; given the same hours of work and previous work experience. A significant concentration of Muslims in low-wage segments and in self-employment is reported, though the qualitative binary for religious category 'Muslim' did not turn out to be significant controlling for capabilities. Dalit female respondents were found to be concentrated either in construction or in non-cooking segments of domestic work, with significantly lower wages reported for both categories, 'Dalit' and 'Women'. Gender and Caste are found to significantly affect both wages and location of the respondent within the labour-market. [Ref. Table 1, Appendix]

Results from the survey also reveal concentration of members of certain communities in specific occupations; with by far stereotypical perceptions of employers about these workers and their communities. About 180 of the 240 individuals working as cooks, agency-placed full-time house-maids, part-time domestic-help, drivers, car-cleaners, mechanics, gardeners, plumbers, electricians, carpenters, tailors and sanitation-workers surveyed were found to be concentrated in traditional occupations. 100% of the sanitation workers were found to be from 'Balmiki' and 'Bhangi' sub-castes from Haryana. Muslims were by far missing from the professions of drivers and cooks, with most employers reporting they were 'not comfortable' employing Muslims as drivers and cooks, some refusing to elaborate why, others straightforwardly saying they did not 'trust' people from the Muslim community enough to drive their children and women around. Considerations of 'purity' and 'pollution' were cited as the main reason for not employing Dalit and Muslim women as cooks. The self-employing professions of carpenters, tailors and mechanics were found to be dominated by members of the Muslim community; though within 'Tailors' high-end tailoring boutiques were found to be owned by women from the Hindu majority community, while the tailors doing small-time mending jobs or working for these boutique-owners were also from the Muslim community. Within the category 'carpenters', Muslim workers had a higher chance of being employed for a given project if either/ both of the contractor and the contracting employer were from the Muslim community.

In a binary-logit regression on the 'probability of being employed' in all the three relatively high-paying professions 'drivers', 'cooks' and 'agency-placed full-time house-maids' within the domestic help segment, all three category variables, 'caste', 'community' and 'gender' were found to be significant at the 5%

level, with 'Dalits' nearly absent from all three professions. Only 6 out of the 45 Muslim women working as part-time domestic help, were employed as 'cooks', only 2 out of the 'agency-placed full-time house-maids' were found to be Muslim; both employed by Muslim households and 36 out of 45 respondents working as carpenters and tailors, were found to be working for either Muslim Contractors and/or Muslim employers [Ref. Table 2, Appendix]. Further, while all 116 of the male respondents said they were 'equally comfortable' working for 'own community' and 'other community' employers, 90 out of the 124 women interviewed, said they were/would be more comfortable working for employers belonging to their 'own community', and all 58 women working in the domestic help segment reported that they felt more comfortable reporting to a woman in the employing household as opposed to a male member of the same household.

About 210 out of the 240 respondents reported that they came to know about the current job-opportunity from a family member/neighbour and reported that access to informal community-networks, defined along caste and religious lines, increased their chances of landing a job and finding an accommodation. Most 'work-groups' commanded by local labour-contractors were also found to be caste-based, while a few were also region-based and thus had people of more than one caste/community from a region in the work group, indicating that while both, the vertical and horizontal social arrangements in the system of work through contractors, is not entirely caste or community based, it is still heavily dominated and determined by caste identification and communal/ethnic association.

In terms of asset-formation, only 20 out of the 124 women interviewed said they had a house, bank savings or other substantial assets in their name. While most women reported to have some jewellery (gold and silver) and cash stacks as 'personal assets/security', all of them said, they needed their husbands/son's permission and consent before they could spend or sell these assets for any purpose. Most women also reported that the cycles/motorcycles/mobile phones that their parents had given to their husbands as dowry were 'personal assets' of their husbands while television sets/coolers/gas stoves, etc. that they brought along as dowry, were 'household assets'. Women who owned houses, bank savings and LIC policies reported a higher say in household matters and were usually older women, who had been working for more than 20 years. Daughters of working mothers were found to be more likely to work, and daughters of women with a qualification of 8th (middle school) and above, were almost entirely found to be studying beyond middle school.

Access to education was also found to be skewed along caste and gender lines, with Dalits and lower-caste (mostly migrant landless) Muslims, at the lower end of the distribution and women of all communities, suffering a disadvantage in both access and attainment rates compared to men. Average male and female wages differed significantly, [see Table 3] both with and without controlling for capabilities. Gender, asset-ownership and caste, turned out to be significant determinants of wages and financial autonomy in household decision-making and though the dummy for religion 'Muslim' did not turn out to be statistically significant, probability of being educated and employed was found to be skewed along caste, gender and communal lines.

The findings thus comprise the following; controlling for capabilities (i.e. education and/or work-experience) both gender-wage gaps and inter-community gaps in average-wages are common-place. Caste and gommunity add additional dimensions of disadvantage in terms of job-exclusion and limited possibility of job mobility for Dalits, Muslims and women, with Dalits concentrated in the occupations of sanitation-work and part-time house-maids, Muslims predominantly concentrated in self-employment, women excluded from the occupations, 'derivers', 'car cleaners', 'mechanics', 'carpenters' and 'gardeners', and upper-caste Hindu men' most likely to be employed at the upper-end as drivers/contractors (for carpentering or agency-hiring). Though no considerable gaps were found to exist between men and women and between 'upper caste Hindu' and 'lower caste Hindu' or 'Muslim' men/women in the sample in terms of wages, controlling for occupation, all three categories, Dalits/lower caste, Muslims and women are found to be concentrated at the lower end of the spectrum for both education and income/wages. Ownership of assets and educational attainment of women tends to positively impact the financial autonomy of the respondent, and the odds of daughters' access to education and work, thus bearing a positive influence on inter-generational mobility.

Institutional Bottlenecks and Policy Imperatives

Exploitation, ex-ante wage-compression and exclusion of Dalits, Muslims and women in the informal labour markets has clear material bases and is being persistently perpetuated by a continuous interaction of the multiple agencies of exclusionary and exploitative systems of (adverse) inclusion based on gender, community, ethnicity and caste among others. The same needs to be acknowledged and identified in the proper light if labour-market dynamics have to be understood in the light of the day, giving due recognition to gendered asymmetries. Debasing 'within the household inequality' from its essentially 'class-systemic' origins will only negate a long process of understanding of how the emergence of an industrial middle class in India led to the creation of the typical 'proletarian-family' and idealization of the 'housekeeping proletarian wife'; not thwarting the existing patriarchal order, rather, reinforcing it all the more dramatically.

Gender, religion and caste are all significant variables in the equation, and their effects are not simply interceptal, rather inter-active; something that needs to be incorporated in the mainstream discourse on understanding the structure and functioning of Indian labour-markets. Wide inequalities in access to and attainment of education prevail between various socio-religious categories in India, in turn, causing segmentation, wage-differentiation and exclusion within labour-markets. Muslims and Dalits are found to be the worst sufferers of the discriminatory social forces operating along 'caste' and 'communal' lines, along with 'women', who suffer gendered inequality in access to education and discriminatory wage gaps.

Exclusion and differentiation of women from disadvantaged socio-religious categories in education and employment works to the compounded disadvantage of these women as deprivation groups; making them 'deprived within the deprived'. Since this disadvantage is very likely to persist and cascade over generations in the absence of mobility-ensuring measures; deprivation of access to attribute-enhancing resources (including education) will cause 'persisting' inter-generational poverty for these social groups since poverty has a debilitating effect on capability formation (Sen, 2010).

Since private markets have failed to even out the capability and wage gaps these groups face, there is a strong need for affirmative intervention from the state. There is thus, an urgent and pressing need for the policy-makers to develop a 'Religion-Community-Gender' approach in understanding deprivation and exclusion in labour-markets. 'Dalit', 'Muslim' and 'Tribal' Women need to be identified as specific disadvantaged groups and social policy needs to be reformed accordingly; but most importantly, mainstream academic discourse needs to open up its frontiers to include the social realities of discrimination, exclusion and segmentation in education and employment to make our understanding of the 'virtual spaces' that we know as 'markets', more realistic and meaningful.

Since private markets have emerged as apparently 'modern' social spaces, engaging in factory-production, urbanization of living spaces and proliferation of private 'English' medium education and media, without any significant social reorganization along class-lines, they have failed to thwart patriarchy, casteist and communal tendencies and constructs. The social landscape of the informal economy is essentially describable only in terms of overlapping and often clashing caste, communal, gender, ethnic/tribal identities, with the class categories of 'landless' and 'oppressed' 'have-nots', vastly populated by Dalits, Tribals, 'lower caste' Muslims and women from these communities, who happen to face the double disadvantage of gender and socio-religious identity, and are thus deprived within the deprived and at the bottom of the social pyramid. Policies for affirmative action and social justice need to recognize this and include Dalit/Muslim/ Tribal Women as a sub-category among the deprived and a priority-group for targeted support.

Since women-headed households tend to support higher educational rates of daughters and higher odds of workforce participation, women-oriented direct policy interventions can be argued for. Women-based community action programmes and livelihood schemes are also found to have generated more substantial 'empowerment' of women, both in terms of access to opportunity and income-generation, as reported by most migrants and workers covered by some of these schemes, and are thus recommended as a preferable model of targeted intervention.

Given the generally unarguably low levels of educational attainment and skill-formation among most informal sector workers, skill building programmes and professional and vocational training support can go a long way in alleviating the condition of these workers through capability formation.

Finally, given the burgeoning size of the informal economy, and thus the very limited scope of labour-regulation, more direct living-spaces based intervention is being argued for. Public health and educational provisioning in the mostly under-serviced, unauthorized and unhygienic living spaces of the urban poor needs to be made on a massive scale and urgently, particularly in view of the massive loss of jobs and economic slowdown post-demonetization, which has effectively taken away income-based access to health and education from the poor, throwing them off the social-welfare net and onto a continuum of disadvantaged, both immediately and inter-generationally.

REFERENCES

Asian Development Bank (2011). "Key Indicators for Asia and the Pacific 2011", August 2011, retrieved from http://www.adb.org/

Bardhan, P. (1994). *The Political Economy of Development in India*, 4th ed, Oxford University Press, New Delhi.

Bardhan, P. (1992). 'A Political-Economy Perspective on Development,' *The Indian Economy: Problems and Prospects*, Bimal Jalan, ed., Penguin Books, New Delhi.

Byrne, D. (2005). *Social Exclusion (Issues in Society)*, McGraw-Hill Education, UK.

Demerath, K., Loren, R. and others (2006). "Interrogating Caste and Religion in India's Emerging Middle Class", *Economic & Political Weekly*, September 2, 2006, Vol. XLI, No. 25.

Deshpande, A. (2011). *The Grammar of Caste*, Oxford University Press, New Delhi.

Gill, K. (2012). "Promoting Inclusiveness: A Framework for Assessing India's Flagship Social-Welfare Programmes", *UNICEF Social Policy Working Paper Series 2*.

Hariss-White, B. (2003). *India Working: Essays on Society and Economy*, Cambridge, Cambridge University Press.

Kabeer, N. (2000). "Social Exclusion, Poverty and Discrimination: Towards an Analytical Framework", *IDS Bulletin*, Vol. 31, No. 4.

Kannan, K.P. and Raveendran, G. (2011). "India's Common People: The Regional Profile", *Economic and Political Weekly*, September 17-24, 2011, Vol. XLVI, No. 38.

Khanna, S. (2012). "Gender Wage Discrimination in India: Glass Ceiling or Sticky Floor?" Centre of Development Economics Working Paper, http://www.cdedse.org/pdf/work214.pdf accessed on January 12, 2018.

Kulkarni, P.M. (2007). 'Human Development Differentials among social Groups' in *State, Markets and Inequalities*, Shariff, A. and Krishnaraj, M. (eds.). Orient Longman, New Delhi.

Kundu, A., Shariff, A. and Ghosh, P.K. (2007). 'Indexing Human Development in India: Indicators, Scaling and Composition' in *State, Markets and Inequalities*, Shariff, A. and Krishnaraj, M. (eds.). Orient Longman, New Delhi.

Madheswaran, S. and Khasnobis, B.G. (2007). "Gender Discrimination in the Labour Market: Evidence from the NSS", WIDER Research Project on Gender Wage Gap and its Impact on Poverty: Evidence from India. SOAS.

Nagindrappa, M. and Radhika, M.K. (2013). 'Women's Exploitation in Modern Indian Society', *International Journal of Scientific and Research Publications*, Vol. 3, Issue 2, February 2013.

Gimenez, M. (1987). 'Marxist and Non-Marxist Elements in Engels' in *Engels Revisited: Views on the Oppression of Women*, Sayers, Evans and Redclift (eds.).

Nevile, A. (2007). "Amartya Sen and Social Exclusion", *Development in Practice*, Vol. 17, No. 2.

Razzack, A. and Gumber, A. (2007). "A Case for Empowerment of Muslims" in *State, Markets and Inequalities*, Shariff, A. and Krishnaraj,

M. (eds.). Orient Longman, New Delhi.

Razzack, Azra (2006). "Being an Indian Muslim: No Cause for Celebration", Commentary, retrieved from http://www.cpiml.org/liberation/year_2006/December/indian_muslim.html.

Rehaman, Mujib (2016). *Communalism in Post-Colonial India*, Routledge, New Delhi.

Reilly, B. and Dutta, P.V. (2005). "The Gender Pay Gap and Trade Liberalization: Evidence for India", *Poverty Research Unit at Sussex Working Paper*, No. 3.

Shariff, A. (1995). "Socio-Economic and Demographic Differentials Between Hindus and Muslims in India" *Economic and Political Weekly*, Vol. 30, No. 46 (November 18, 1995), pp. 2947-2953.

Sankaran, Kamala (2013): "Domestic Work, Unpaid Work and Wage Rates", *Economic & Political Weekly*, Vol. 48, No. 43.

Sen, A. (1980). "Description as Choice", *Oxford Economic Papers*, Vol. 32.

Sen, A. (1983). "Poor, Relatively Speaking", *Oxford Economic Papers*, Vol. 35.

Sen, A. (1985). "Well-Being, Agency and Freedom. The Dewey Lectures 1984", *The Journal of Philosophy*, Vol. LXXXII, No. 4, April.

Sen, A. (1990). "Justice: Means vs Freedoms", *Philosophy and Public Affairs*, Vol. 19, No. 2, Spring.

Sen, A. (1992). *Inequality Re-Examined*, Harvard University Press, Cambridge MA.

Sen, A. (1993). 'Capability and Well-Being', in *The Quality of Life*, Nussbaum, M. and Sen, A., (eds.)., Clarendon Press, UK.

Sen, A. (1996). "Freedom, Capabilities and Public Action: A Response", *Notizie di Politeia*, Vol. 12, No. 43/44.

Sen, A. (1999). *Development as Freedom*, Oxford University Press.

Sen, A. (2000). "Social Exclusion: Concept, Application, and Scrutiny", Social Development Paper, Asian Development Bank.

Sheth, D.L. (1999). "Secularization of Caste and the Making of New Middle Class", *Economic and Political Weekly*, August 21-28, 1999, Vol. XXXIV, Nos. 34-35.

Soyler, T. (2010). 'Re-Thinking "Community" in Religion and Development as a Milieu' in *Religion, Community and Development: Changing Contours of Politics and Policy in India*, Mahajan, G. and Jodhka, S.S. (eds.). Routledge, Abingdon and New Delhi,

Unni, J. (2007). 'Earnings and Education Among Social Groups' in *State, Markets and Inequalities*, Shariff, A. and Krishnaraj, M. (eds.). Orient Longman, New Delhi.

Upadhyay, Prakash, S. and Robinson, R. (2012): "Revisiting Communalism and Fundamentalism in India", *Economic & Political Weekly*, September 8, 2012, Vol. XLVII, No. 36.

Reports Consulted

GOI (2011) 'India Human Development Report: Towards Social Inclusion', Institute of Applied Manpower Research, Planning Commission, Government of India.

GOI (2011-12) *Economic Survey, 2011-12*. Ministry of Finance, GOI

GOI (2014-15) *Economic Survey, 2014-15*. Ministry of Finance, GOI

GOI (2015-16) *Economic Survey, 2015-16*. Ministry of Finance, GOI

GOI (2016-17) *Economic Survey, 2016-17*. Ministry of Finance, GOI

Hasan, Zoya and Mushirul Hasan (eds. (2013)). *India Social Development Report 2012: Minorities at the Margins*, Council for Social Development.

Mander, H. (2016) *Indian Exclusion Report (IXR)*, Centre for Equity Studies (CES), New Delhi.

Mishra, Ranganath (ed.) (2007). *Report of the National Commission for Religious and Linguistic Minorities*, GOI.

Sachar, R., (ed.) (2006). *Report of the High Level Committee on Social, Economic and Educational Status of the Muslim Community of India*. GOI.

Sengupta, A. (ed.) (2008). *Report on Conditions of Work and Promotion of Livelihoods in the Unorganised Sector*. National Commission for Enterprises in the Unorganised Sector. GOI. Academic Foundation.

World Bank (2011). *Poverty and Social Exclusion in India*, World Bank, Oxford.

Statistical Appendix

Table 1: Regressing Wages on Demographic Characteristics of Respondents

Dependent Variable: Wages
Method: Least Squares
Sample (Unadjusted): 1 240
Included Observations: 224 After Adjustments

Variable	*Coefficient*	t-Statistic	*Prob.*
====			
C	-29.2392	-1.211335	0.2575
age	1.071375	0.919260	0.1790
edq	20.787944	1.160619	0.3656
hrswrk	10.101535	2.397241	0.0096

workex	5.189731	1.760084	0.2205
gender	-20.375680	-2.155930	0.0404
caste	-45.458169	-2.124663	0.0022
Muslim	-10.245365	-1.346722	0.4123
R-squared	0.621075	F-statistic	9.917790
Log likelihood	-31.49302	Prob(F)	0.000823

Where dependent variable wages represents daily-wage of the respondent, age is age of respondent, edq, educational qualification, hrswrk, hours-worked per day, work-ex, work-experience of the respondent in the trade, gender, the binary qualitative for gender (1 Female, 0 Male), Caste, the binary qualitative variable for Caste (1 Lower-Castes, 0 Upper Caste) and Muslim, the qualitative binary for religious community 'Muslim' (1 Muslim, 0 non-Muslim)

Table 2: Probability of Being Employed

*Probability of Being Employed as**	*Socio-Religious Category*			
	Upper Caste Hindu	*Dalit Hindu*	*Muslim*	*Women All Women Dalit Women Muslim Women*
Driver/Cook/ Agency Employed Maid	74%	10%	6	30% + 3% 0.5%
Others (Including Cleaners, part-time house-maid, gardener, plumber, electrician)	5-15 % for various occupations	32%	10-18% (for various occupations)	42% 23% 46%
Sanitation worker/ Garbage collection worker	0	52%	42%	28% + 44% 23%
Construction worker	14%	32%	24%	33% 30% 26%
Self-employed (mechanics, carpenters, tailors, hawkers, vendors)	5-10% (for various occupations)	12-16% (for various occupations)	66-72% (for various occupations)	18-22% (for various occupations)

[*Based on reported % of total in every category of work, +none as drivers]

Table 3: Computation of Inter-Category Wage-Differentials

Component and equation	Value
Mean Non-Muslim wage	225
Mean Male wage	240
Mean female wage	158
Mean Dalit female wage	110
Mean Dalit wage	120
Mean Muslim wage	150
Mean Dalit and Muslim wages evaluated at non-Dalit pay structure	145 (Dalit) 195 (Muslim)
Difference in Dalit and Muslim wages due to wage-bias	25 (17.24% of mean Dalit wage) 45 (30% of mean Muslim wage)
Percentage difference in wages due to difference in wage generating characteristics	63% (Dalits) 67% (Muslims)

+Computation of Inter-Category Wage-Differentials

The Oaxaca's decomposition method hypothesizes the discrimination coefficient to be

$$D = \frac{\left(\frac{Wnm}{Wm}\right) - \left(\frac{Wnm}{Wm}\right)}{\left(\frac{Wnm}{Wm}\right)} \quad \ldots \text{(i) Where,}$$

$\left(\frac{Wn_m}{Wm}\right)$ is the observed ratio of non-Muslim to Muslim wages,

$\left(\frac{Wn_m}{Wm}\right)$ is the wage ratio that would prevail in absence of discrimination

It is assumed that in absence of discrimination non-Muslim wages (W_{nm}) would prevail.

7

Comparison of Learning Outcomes in Private and Government Schools (A Pilot Study)

Leema Mohan Paliwal and Poonam Kalra

Introduction

The importance of basic literacy and education in ensuring economic as well as societal well-being cannot be overemphasized. Amartya Sen has repeatedly lamented on the state of primary education in India.

> India does have many achievements in the success of a relatively small group of privileged people well trained in higher education and specialised expertise. Yet our educational system remains deeply unjust. Among other bad consequences, the low coverage and low quality of school education in India extracts a heavy price in the pattern of our economic development, Amartya Sen, *Hindu*, 2011.

Mincer (1974) is one of the first papers that brought to the forefront the importance of education in harnessing earning premiums[1]. Most policy makers in developing countries see education as a necessary requirement to ensure lower levels of poverty, by ensuring higher earnings. However education also contributes in other ways to the well-being of individuals and the society. Education leads to greater labour productivity and labour mobility. Also there are positive interlink ages between health and education. One can also expect a higher level of democracy with primary education. To sum up, education enables people to escape poverty by building "capabilities" (Sen, 1999).

Despite the accepted relevance of education in the development experience of a country, the state of education especially primary education leaves a lot to be desired. School enrolment; primary (% net) in India was last measured at 93.34 in 2011, according to the World Bank[2]. This is a heartening figure, but the drop- out rates continue to be high.

Moreover the quality of education is questionable to say the least. According to Pratham's Annual Status of Education 2016 Report, only 42.5% of Std 3 children can read at least a Std 1 level at the all India level, and the proportion of children who can read at Std 2 level is 25.2%. (Wadhwa, ASER 2016).

One of the well researched areas in the context of primary education has been the relative effectiveness of private versus government schools in educating children. In fact the whole debate about the relative effectiveness of school type on educational outcomes/achievements of students at different stages of schooling emerged after the Coleman's Report (1966) was presented. The report found that while private school-going children performed better in standardized tests than others, this difference was not significant after controlling for socio-economic background and parental characteristics. While these results were later reaffirmed by many studies in the developed countries, the impact of schools for developing countries was likely to be different. Thus similar studies in developing countries showed that school characteristics do matter affecting scores even after controlling for parental characteristics. Studies pertaining to India have also found a similar impact. Notable amongst these are Govinda and Varghese (1993), Kingdon (1996), Muralidharan and Kremer (2006), Tooley and Dixon (2005). Given, in India, schools are not secular in terms of the economic background from which children come, a private school is more than management and funding, it subsumes parental background as well.

This scenario where children of a particular socio-economic background go to private schools was altered, to some extent, by proper implementation of the RTE Act, at least in Delhi starting with 2011 nursery admissions. The Act mandates that private schools, which have been built on land provided by the government at subsidized rates, allocate 25% of seats in nursery classes to children coming from economically weaker sections (EWS). The allocation of these seats is based on a lottery replicating an experimental design. If private schools really are more effective, then test scores of children who won a lottery to get admission in a private school will on an average be higher than of those who did not win and are going to a government (public) school. There is however a catch: it is also possible that the very act of private school enrolment may spur a child to try harder and parents to focus more on academics. Hence, any observed increase in academic achievement could be due to factors that have nothing to do with school level inputs.

The ultimate objective of our study is to evaluate the impact of this legislation. In a build up to this final objective, we are first attempting to ascertain the role of school type on educational outcomes. In pursuit of this secondary study, we conducted a pilot to identify any robust results and/or major failures of the design of the exercise. Thus this paper is a report of the major findings of the pilot. The following section offers a brief survey of literature. The data and the methodology used are given in Section III. The empirical results are presented in Section IV. Section V concludes.

Literature Review

"Does the school institution influence students' achievement levels after accounting for their family background?" (Fuller, 1987). This question has received enormous attention. Researchers have tried to identify the type of school resources which influence learning outcomes. Studies have also been conducted to check if these resources are more likely to be found in private schools than otherwise. The impact variable which is the educational outcome is often measured by conducting a standardized test, science exam, numeracy or literacy test. There could also be a reading test as well.

School characteristics have been captured by different variables. An important review (Fuller, 1987) of 60 studies, looking at the importance of school characteristics in the context of developing countries, found that desks, chairs, electricity/fans, blackboard, flip charts, toilet and drinking water facilities, library facilities and scientific laboratories, instructional media and nutritional and feeding programmes have been used to determine school facilities. These studies also included teachers' characteristics like teachers' education, experience, their nature of appointment: permanent or contractual, etc. While teaching quality cannot be directly observed but length of experience and training are likely to have a strong positive impact on quality. Teaching practices like homework frequency and length of preparation time by teachers have also been studied and found to be statistically significant in most of the studies.

Studies reported in Glewwe et al. (2011) reviewing close to 79 studies found that having a fully functioning school—one with better quality roofs, walls or floors, with desks, tables and chairs, and with a school library—is conducive to student learning. Another consistent result was that having teachers with greater knowledge of the subjects they teach, having a longer school day improved scores. Fehrler et al. (2009) found in a study of 13 Sub-Saharan countries in Africa robust positive correlations of achievement test scores and the possession of textbooks and negative correlations with teaching in shifts. The most striking result in their study was the weak correlation of achievement test scores and teacher education and professional training.

All these studies controlled for parental/household and child characteristics. Amongst the parent characteristics, the mother's age, the highest schooling obtained (i.e. highest grade completed) by the mother and also a test of whether the mother was able to read were included .In another study (Desai et al., 2009) the highest education level attained by any of the household adults, log of family income, a standard of living index consisting of ownership of various consumer durables (TV, refrigerator, telephone, car, cot, etc.) and quality of housing (toilet, piped water, etc.), household size, number of children under the age of 15, place of residence and state of residence were used to characterize households. Caste, ethnicity and religion have also been included as controls as they are seen to be linked to private school enrolment, particularly enrolment in madrasas or convents, as well as having an independent impact on educational outcomes. In a similar study conducted for Pakistan by Arif and Saqib (2003), the child's pre-school attendance was included. Child or pupil characteristics used as controls include gender, age, age in Class 1, height to weight ratios to capture nutritional status. Another study by Kiran Javaid et al. (2012) used Annual Status of Education Report (ASER) for the years 2010 and 2011 for Pakistan using the OLS technique and Oaxaca decomposition found that private school students perform 0.12 standard deviations better than public school students (in OLS) and around 5% of the variation in the scores between public and private schools is explained by endowment differences between the two while 95% owing to the private school effect or some unobservable aspects like innate abilities(decomposition analysis).

A few studies related to factors affecting educational outcomes in India have similarly been conducted. Those pertaining specifically to private-government difference are Govinda and Varghese (1993), Desai et al. (2009), Goyal (2009), Murlidharan and Kremer, (2006) Tooley and Dixon (2005) and French and Kingdon (2010) .

Govinda and Varghese (1993) studying districts of Madhya Pradesh, after controlling for parental characteristics found that learning outcomes of government school-going children were below others. Kingdon (1996) in a study in urban UP finds that even after controlling for student background and selection effects, private schools were significantly more effective in teaching mathematics and language. French and Kingdon (2010) use ASER data from 2005 to 2007 in OLS, panel data and Altonjiet et al. (2005) methods to evaluate the differential cognitive skills of students in private schools and in government schools for India. They find a *"..consistent evidence of a private schooling advantage throughout the methodologies"* (French and Kingdon, 2010).

Tooley and Dixon (2003) using data from a Hyderabad slum

found that mean scores of students in private schools were 22%-23% higher compared to government schools. In an important study, Desai et al. (2009) use ordinary least squares, the Heckman control function method (Heckman and Navarro-Lozano, 2004), family fixed effects model to evaluate the academic performance of students in private schools and public schools. They found that reading and arithmetic skills of students of private schools are significantly better than those going to government schools after correcting for other factors and this is especially true for disadvantaged groups.

In another study, Goyal (2009) uses the strategy evolved by Altonji, Elder and Taber (2005). She finds that there is a positive and significant impact of private schooling on learning outcomes for schools in Odisha. Kremer and Murlidharan (2006) use a nationally represented survey of rural private and public primary schools in India and find that students from private schools have higher standardized test scores and higher attendance rates as compared to public school students after controlling for observable family characteristics, private tuitions and other school characteristics. In a similar exercise we investigate if school type matters for learning outcomes.

Data and Methodology

In our attempt at studying the importance of private versus government schools in the learning outcomes of primary school students, we collected information from 55 students studying in Classes I to IV. The data was collected from a J.J. Colony at Wazirpur, Delhi. Information was collected on child characteristics like gender, age, age in Class 1, birth order, height, using private tuition, nature of school (government, private, government aided, mosque schools). Information was also collected on family characteristics including religion, ages of father and mother, occupation of parents, education of parents, household assets, whether the family is living in a rented accommodation or not, number of rooms, ownership of bicycles, motor bikes or cars, coolers, air conditioners, water purifiers, tiles, geysers, etc.

Since the objective of the study was to analyse the difference between the learning outcomes of children going to private and government schools, a dummy would have been sufficient. But like many other studies, to further control for the possibility of endogeniety, we have controlled for other school characteristics. These include teacher regularity, homework from school, oral and written testing, parent-teacher meetings, school infrastructure in the form of library, sports room, windows, flipcharts etc. Since this area is largely inhabited by Tamil families, many parents send their children to the Delhi Tamil Education Association (DTEA) school. We decided to treat them separately and created a dummy to examine its impact. Furthermore, a school run by a mosque nearby was also a popular option among the Muslim families. This was also treated separately with a dummy. The questionnaire used is given in Appendix 1. To measure learning outcomes a test on English and Mathematics (based on the ASER format) was given to the children. The mode of assessment and the tests are listed in Appendix 2.

There were certain variables related to the child which we considered to be indispensable for the study and included in all the models. These are gender, age, age in Class 1. Similarly some family characteristics were never dropped from any model. These are mother's characteristics (her education level or the number of languages she can read), religion, economic resources (through a combination of various assets), rented or owned house.

A simple OLS model was run on a combination of variables but it showed the presence of heteroscedasticity using the White's and Breush-Pagan Tests. Thus a heteroscedasticity corrected model was used throughout the estimation exercise.

In our study we followed the general to specific approach and selected models based on theory, significance of the regressors, adjusted R^2 as well as the Akaike Information Criterion and the Schwarz Bayesian Criterion. We also tested the residuals for normality to ensure that the errors are as per the assumptions of the Ordinary Least squares model.

Results

Several alternative models covering school, child and family characteristics were estimated. Some of the significant ones are reported in Appendix 3A and 3B.

Results for Mathematics

We report here the results of the best fitting model for mathematics scores as Table 1.

In our regression involving educational outcomes in mathematics, the regressors include gender of the student, age and age in class 1 for the student, dummies for nature of school. We have three dummies for school type with the government schools as the base category. The other variables include position of the child, number of siblings, whether the child takes private tuitions, whether the family lives in their own house, religion of the family, a household asset index[3], mother's education, whether the school has oral assessment or not. The results of the exercise are presented according to school characteristics, child characteristics and family characteristics.

School Characteristics

The key variables of this study were the coefficients of the dummies for the type of schools. Results show that there is no statistically significant difference in math scores for children going to private schools and government schools. This is a strong result given the general perception about the efficiency of private schools. However, students going to the mosque school are doing significantly better than the students going to government schools after controlling for other factors. The size of the differential coefficient is also large—about 2. (Given that we were not able to visit the schools, our understanding of this observation is incomplete). On testing for difference between the coefficients of the mosque school dummy and private school dummy we found the difference statistically significant. The same is true for the difference between the mosque school and DTEA schools.

We also tried to incorporate teachers' characteristics by asking questions on whether the teacher was regular or not, whether homework was given and whether oral tests were conducted. For maths scores oral work turned out to be significant.

To control for other school characteristics we gathered data on school infrastructure like library facility and its access, sports room and equipment, toilets and water facilities, flip charts, tables and chairs, white boards, broken windows and physical punishment. Many of these could not be included in the study because either there were many missing observations (as children were too young to tell us about libraries, broken windows etc.) or no variability was found in some (for example, all children said that their schools have chairs and tables, toilets and water).

Table 1: Dependent Variable: Mathigh

	Coefficient	*Std. Error*	*t-ratio*	*p-value*	
const	3.88141	1.37658	2.8196	0.0089	***
gender	0.354696	0.2501	1.4182	0.1676	
age	0.631751	0.167116	3.7803	0.0008	***
Dpvt	“0.441931	0.444586	“0.9940	0.3290	
DDTA	“0.620815	0.650509	“0.9544	0.3484	
Dmasjid	1.64161	0.508263	3.2298	0.0032	***
position	“0.272806	0.239397	“1.1396	0.2645	
noofsiblings	“0.0140764	0.240875	“0.0584	0.9538	
tution	1.42811	0.303993	4.6978	<0.0001	***
ageinclassI	“1.34791	0.308552	“4.3685	0.0002	***
religion	0.856912	0.605416	1.4154	0.1684	
oral	1.99756	0.413274	4.8335	<0.0001	***
hhasset	0.449486	0.153726	2.9239	0.0069	***
rentown	“1.84173	0.475135	“3.8762	0.0006	***
Motheredu	0.165702	0.0526034	3.1500	0.0040	***

Statistics based on the weighted data:

Sum squared resid	44.40473	S.E. of regression	1.282427
R-squared	0.842894	Adjusted R-squared	0.761431
F(14, 27)	10.34701	P-value(F)	1.78e-07
Log likelihood	“60.76462	Akaike criterion	151.5292
Schwarz criterion	177.5943	Hannan-Quinn	161.0831

Child Characteristics

The results show that the age of the child enters with a positive coefficient that is significant indicating that the older the child the better the test score. Position of the child is also significant with the coefficient being negative.The interpretation is that the older the child, the better the academic performance. Clearly our data supports the view that first born or more generally the older the child, the better the performance. This may be because parents are able to focus to a larger extent on the first born both in terms of time as well as resources. Number of siblings turned out to be insignificant.

Age in Class 1 enters the regression with a negative sign and is significant. We infer that when a child is sent to school earlier, she performs better. This has to be understood in the context of the area we visited. It might be that parents who admit their children to school at the correct age are more concerned about academics compared to parents who delay admissions.

Private tuition is highly significant and the coefficient is positive implying that the children who opt for private tuition tend to score more than students who do not. We were told that these tuition centres have many students in a group but it seems children learn more in such centres. It is interesting to note that gender is actually insignificant so our data does not support the common perception that boys do differently than girls in mathematics.

Family Characteristics

The noteworthy result here is the robust positive significance of mother's education in the child's performance. Rent or ownership of house and the household asset variable are important, whichever the specification, it is difficult to rationalize the negative coefficient for ownership of house. Religion was not a significant variable in most of the estimated models.

To summarize, the mathematics scores do not differ due to school type. This result is unlike what other Indian studies, reported in the review, have found. Other robust results are found for age, age in Class 1, gender, tuition, mother's education, oral assessment and household assets.

Results for English

We report here the results of the best fitting model for English scores as Table 2.

Our analysis of test scores in English included gender, age, age in Class 1 of the child; availing of private tuition, religion, teacher regularity, household assets, family size, education of mother as regressors. Three dummies for school type as explained above were added. The results of the exercise are presented according to school characteristics, child characteristics and family characteristics.

School Characteristics

The results of English regressions show marked differences as far as the role of the schools is concerned. Children going to private schools score more in English reading compared to their counterparts in government schools after controlling for child and family characteristics. This result confirms other studies reported above. The scores of DTEA students are also significantly greater than the government school students.

Another significant variable was teacher regularity. To obtain information on this variable we had asked the children what they ended up doing in classes when a teacher is absent. We considered teachers are regular if the children responded by saying that some other teacher comes and teaches and not regular if they say that we are made to sit idle.

Table 2: Dependent Variable: Maximum Score in English

	Coefficient	*Std. Error*	*t-ratio*	*p-value*	
Const	“0.154343	0.840459	“0.1836	0.8555	
Gender	0.00155266	0.191675	0.0081	0.9936	
Age	0.304494	0.104129	2.9242	0.0065	***
Dpvt	1.01938	0.253235	4.0254	0.0004	***
DDTEA	1.29056	0.298331	4.3259	0.0002	***
Dmosque	“0.00459126	0.215732	“0.0213	0.9832	
Tution	0.577792	0.20612	2.8032	0.0088	***
ageinclassI	“0.506714	0.160911	“3.1490	0.0037	***

Religion	“0.361191	0.228791	“1.5787	0.1249	
teachregular	0.816363	0.238681	3.4203	0.0018	***
Hhasset	“0.284165	0.154954	“1.8339	0.0766	*
Familysize	0.224676	0.075096	2.9919	0.0055	***
Motheredu	0.126192	0.0254991	4.9489	<0.0001	***

Statistics based on the weighted data:

Sum squared resid	79.49281	S.E. of regression	1.627808
R-squared	0.929810	Adjusted R-squared	0.901734
F(12, 30)	33.11758	P-value(F)	5.46e-14
Log-likelihood	“74.22539	Akaike criterion	174.4508
Schwarz criterion	197.3464	Hannan-Quinn	182.8940

Child Characteristics

As far as child characteristics are concerned we get results that are similar to the results for mathematics with age, age in Class 1, being highly significant. Private tuitions are significant and positive. Gender of the child continues to be insignificant.

Family Characteristics

Here again mother's education is highly significant and plays a positive role in the learning outcomes for the students. Family size enters the regression with a positive and significant coefficient implying that children from larger families tend to do better than those from smaller families. This may be due to benefits of siblings living and learning together. Religion continues to be insignificant.

Household's assets are significant with a negative sign implying children of relatively affluent families do worse in the English reading test. We find it difficult to be explained.

To sum up, the nature of schools make a difference in the learning outcomes for students for English, with students going to private schools doing better.

Conclusion

The results obtained from this study are robust when it comes to the role of the mother's education and the teacher's efforts in influencing the learning outcomes of pupils, irrespective of the type of school they study in. We also find the largest/baseline impact of private schools on English reading is positive. These results and their robustness give us confidence to upscale this pilot and incorporate not only more observations but also better estimation techniques which have been employed by researchers for larger studies.

REFERENCES

Arif, G.M. and N.U. Saquib (2003). "Production of Cognitive and Life Skills in Public, Private and NGO Schools in Pakistan", *The Pakistan Development Review*, Vol. 42, No. 1.

Desai, S.A., R. Dubey, Vanneman, and R. Banerji (2009). "Private Schooling in India: A New Educational Landscape", *India Policy Forum*, Vol. 5.

Dreze J. and G. Kingdon (1999). "School Participation in Rural India" *DEDPS* No. 18.

Fehrler, S., K. Michaelowa and A. Wechtler (2009). "The Effectiveness of Inputs in Primary Education: Insights from Recent Student surveys for Sub-Saharan Africa", University of Zurich, Zurich Open Repository and Archive.

French, R. and G. Kingdon (2010). "The Relative Effectiveness of Private and Government Schools in Rural India: Evidence from ASER Data." *DoQSS Working Paper*, No. 10-03

Fuller, B. (1987). What School Factors Raise Achievement in the Third World? *Review of Educational Research*, Vol. 57, No. 3.

Glewwe P.W., E.A. Hanushek, S.D. Humpage, and R. Ravina (2011). "School Resources and Educational Outcomes in Developing Countries : A Review of Literature from 1990-2010", *NBER Working Paper* 17544.

Goyal, S. (2009). "Inside the House of Learning: the Relative Performance of Public and Private Schools in Orissa", *Education Economics*, Vol. 17, No. 3.

Javaid, K., T. Musaddiq and A. Sultan (2012). Prying the Private School Effect: An Empirical Analysis of Learning Outcomes of Public and Private Schools in Pakistan. Lahore: University of Management Sciences (LUMS), Department of Economics.

Kingdon, G.G., (1996). "The Quality and Efficiency of Private and Public Education: A Case-Study of Urban India", *Oxford Bulletin of Economics and Statistics*, Vol. 58, Issue 1, pp. 57-82.

Mincer, J.A. (1974). *Schooling Experience and Earnings*, National Bureau of Economic Research.

Tooley and Dixon (2005). "A Study of Private Schools Serving the Poor in Low-Income Countries", Cato Institute, Washington, D.C.

Wadhwa, W. (2016). School Matters, *ASER 2016.*

.APPENDIX 1

Questionnaire

1. Child's name
2. Child's age
3. Gender
4. Name and nature of school
5. Position of child in family
6. Other children, their age and nature of schooling
7. Does the child take tuition Y/N
8. Height
9. Age of entering Class I
10. Mother's age
11. Mother's education
12. Mother's occupation
13. Father's age
14. Father's occupation
15. Father's education
16. Family's religion
17. Can mother read in Hindi/English/any other
18. Maximum adult education in the family
19. Total time spent by adults on studies: Average per day
20. Family size
21. Do you know any government worker
22. Do you know any medical personnel
23. Do you subscribe to any newspaper
24. No. of books at home
25. Frequency of parent-teacher meetings per month
26. Per month expenditure on education (transport/stationery)
27. Do you have a bike/car
28. Do you have tiles in the kitchen Y/N
29. How do you heat water for bathing in winters; geyser/rod/gas
30. How far is the toilet from home?
31. No. of rooms in the house
32. Rental or self-owned house
33. Do you have an A/c / cooler/water purifier
34. Computer in home/office/cyber cafe
35. Do you give your child any work during vacation (extra work) Y/N
36. Do you have a caste certificate
37. Do you have an income certificate
38. Do you have a BPL card

39. Is this a female-headed household
40. No. of students in a class in the child's class
41. Is the teacher regular at school
42. Does the teacher give homework
43. Is assessment oral/written
44. Does the school provide meals
45. Total school enrolment
46. Does the teacher make the child work in groups
47. Does the teacher give examples
48. Student attendance
49. Does the teacher give punishment (physical)
50. Medium of instruction
51. Does the teacher give instructions in Hindi too
52. Does the classroom have desks/tables/chairs for every student
53. Computers in school: Y/N Allowed to use? Y/N
54. Electricity in school
55. Blackboard/white boards/flip charts/smart boards/colourful welcoming
56. Library and access
57. Are the window panes of your classroom broken
58. Which day of the week do you have a games/PT period?
59. Does the school have a playground
60. Do the toilets have water
61. Drinking water
62. Sports room or equipment

APPENDIX 2(A) TESTS

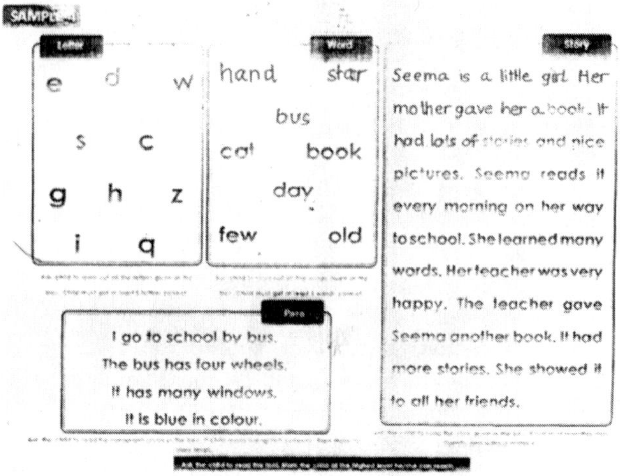

A weary traveller once bought seven cakes. Tired and hungry, he **gobbled up the first three. But this hurried eating did not make his hunger any less. So he decided to eat another cake. Thereafter, he quickly ate a fifth and a sixth cake. He was no longer mad with hunger. Yet, he was glad he had one cake left. Next, he started on the seventh cake. This time, he ate more slowly. And, as he finished the last mouthful of the last cake, he felt very pleased and satisfied. Then he began to feel very sad. It had taken him so long to satisfy his hunger.** The man said: **"What a fool I've been. I should have eaten the seventh cake first! Then, my hunger would have gone away at once. Besides, I could have saved the rest of the cakes." Listening to the man babbling, everyone laughed at him.**

$$

बहुत दिनों से बारिश हो रही थी। गाँव में सभी जगह गंदा पानी भर गया था। सभी बारिश के रुकने की राह देख रहे थे। अचानक एक दिन बारिश रुक गई। सूरज निकल आया। सब लोग खुश हो गये। आसमान में चिड़ियाँ उड़ने लगीं। लोग अपने कपड़े सुखाने लगे। बच्चे भी घरों से बाहर निकलकर खेलने लगे।

राधा के पास एक तोता
उसकी चोंच लाल है।
वह बहुत बोलता है।
सब को हँसाता है।

म र थ
ह श
ल ब न
क घ

गाना खु
मोती
पैर झो
आलू धू
किला
आग मो

2 6 9
8 0 5
3 7

6 + 3 = ___ 4 + 2 = ___ 3 + 4 = ___
8 + 1 = ___ 5 + 2 = ___ 9 + 3 = ___

36 45
73 82
99 69 57
19

15, ___, 17 20, ___, 22
19, ___, 21 44, ___, 46
89, ___, 91

48 + 28 = ___ 15 + 37 = ___ 19 + 24 = ___
79 + 11 = ___ 45 + 39 = ___ 66 + 19 = ___

23 × 3 = ___ 17 × 2 = ___ 15 × 4 = ___
28 × 5 = ___ 82 × 2 = ___ 43 × 3 = ___

51 − 35 = ___ 67 − 48 = ___ 84 − 49 = ___
73 − 36 = ___ 56 − 37 = ___ 31 − 13 = ___

7)91(6)76(
5)43(9)82(
8)63(11)41(

Appendix 2(b): Mode of Assessment

Testing Scheme	*Score*	*Testing Scheme*	*Score*
English		**Mathematics**	
Reading letters	1	Recognition of single digits	1
Reading words	2	Recognition of double digits	2
Reading short paragraph	3	Simple addition	3
Reading short story	4	Addition with carry over	4
		Subtraction with borrowing	5
		Multiplication	6
		Division	7

Appendix 3A: Heteroskedasticity-Corrected Estimates

Dependent Variable: Mathhigh

	-1	-2	-3	-4	-5	-6
const	3.856**	4.662**	3.457*	4.002**	3.245**	3.881**
	-1.765	-2.258	-2.017	-1.726	-1.581	-1.377
	[0.0378]	[0.0491]	[0.0976]	[0.0282]	[0.0496]	[0.0089]
gender	0.1774	0.1194	0.2571	0.1251	0.4333	0.3547
	-0.3373	-0.39	-0.3426	-0.3142	-0.2916	-0.2501
	[0.6033]	[0.7619]	[0.4592]	[0.6936]	[0.1485]	[0.1676]
age	0.6555**	0.5340**	0.5027**	0.6260**	0.4612**	0.6318**
	-0.2236	-0.2207	-0.2351	-0.2297	-0.1839	-0.1671
	[0.0068]	[0.0228]	[0.0414]	[0.0111]	[0.0182]	[0.0008]
Dpvt	-0.468	-0.3843	-0.5065	-0.5732	-0.6594	-0.4419
	-0.6043	-0.6028	-0.6455	-0.583	-0.5398	-0.4446
	[0.4454]	[0.5293]	[0.4392]	[0.3342]	[0.2321]	[0.3290]
DDTA	-0.6367	-0.6486	-0.04875	-0.6134	-0.2587	-0.6208
	-0.8182	-0.8222	-0.9912	-0.8036	-0.9314	-0.6505
	[0.4432]	[0.4374]	[0.9611]	[0.4519]	[0.7832]	[0.3484]
Dmasjid	1.732**	1.669**	1.645**	1.752**	1.469**	1.642**
	-0.485	-0.434	-0.4886	-0.4493	-0.5145	-0.5083
	[0.0014]	[0.0007]	[0.0022]	[0.0006]	[0.0080]	[0.0032]
position	-0.4259	-0.4839	-0.4013	-0.376	-0.2941	-0.2728
	-0.3245	-0.4091	-0.2705	-0.2681	-0.181	-0.2394
	[0.2004]	[0.2475]	[0.1491]	[0.1721]	[0.1154]	[0.2645]
noofsiblings	-0.1061	-0.02289				-0.01408
	-0.2899	-0.3208				-0.2409
	[0.7174]	[0.9437]				[0.9538]

tution	1.389**	1.496**	1.477**	1.449**	1.443**	1.428**
	-0.407	-0.4743	-0.4509	-0.4144	-0.3106	-0.304
	[0.0020]	[0.0040]	[0.0028]	[0.0016]	[0.0001]	[0.0001]
AgeinclassI	-1.217**	-1.264**	-1.009**	-1.161**	-0.9513**	-1.348**
	-0.3412	-0.3892	-0.3697	-0.3358	-0.338	-0.3086
	[0.0014]	[0.0032]	[0.0109]	[0.0018]	[0.0088]	[0.0002]
religion	0.8712	1.394	1.129	0.8957	0.9516	0.8569
	-0.7144	-0.8578	-0.7733	-0.7407	-0.6674	-0.6054
	[0.2332]	[0.1162]	[0.1554]	[0.2371]	[0.1650]	[0.1684]
oral	2.287**	2.054**	2.068**	2.376**	1.806**	1.998**
	-0.4899	-0.5414	-0.5187	-0.5091	-0.4357	-0.4133
	[0.0001]	[0.0008]	[0.0004]	[0.0001]	[0.0003]	[0.0000]
hhasset	0.2681	0.2119	0.2498	0.2372	0.4233**	0.4495**
	-0.19	-0.1949	-0.2057	-0.1968	-0.1947	-0.1537
	[0.1696]	[0.2870]	[0.2348]	[0.2387]	[0.0383]	[0.0069]
rentown	-2.053**	-2.024**	-2.218**	-2.141**	-2.178**	-1.842**
	-0.5192	-0.5727	-0.5835	-0.5193	-0.5584	-0.4751
	[0.0005]	[0.0016]	[0.0007]	[0.0003]	[0.0005]	[0.0006]
mother-canread	0.5418*	0.7042**	0.4451	0.4595		
	-0.3158	-0.3182	-0.3335	-0.3242		
	[0.0977]	[0.0359]	[0.1927]	[0.1678]		
Teach-regular		-0.1151				
		-0.76				
		[0.8808]				
Familysize				-0.1045		
				-0.1588		
				[0.5161]		
Motheredu					0.1348**	0.1657**
					-0.05858	-0.0526
					[0.0290]	[0.0040]
n	42	42	42	42	42	42
Adj. R^2	0.6975	0.7821	0.6119	0.6728	0.6663	0.7614
lnL	-63.94	-62.88	-67.47	-63.2	-67.62	-60.76

Appendix 3B: Heteroskedasticity-Corrected Estimates

Dependent Variable: Enghigh

	-1	-2	-3	-4	-5	-6
Const	-0.6511	0.8621	-0.2969	-0.4157	-0.5858	-0.1543
	(-0.6523)	-0.8379	(-0.3262)	(-0.4754)	(-0.6793)	(-0.1836)
	[0.5195]	[0.4092]	[0.7467]	[0.6381]	[0.5023]	[0.8555]
gender	-0.2614	0.07025	0.001126	0.1154	-0.08292	0.001553
	(-1.098)	-0.2486	-0.004435	-0.5556	(-0.3777)	-0.0081
	[0.2817]	[0.8055]	[0.9965]	[0.5828]	[0.7084]	[0.9936]
age	0.1564	0.1188	0.05059	0.2572**	0.3131**	0.3045**
	-0.9922	-0.7478	-0.4097	-2.56	-2.561	-2.924
	[0.3296]	[0.4608]	[0.6851]	[0.0159]	[0.0159]	[0.0065]
Dpvt	1.332**	0.6552*	0.6346*	0.9597**	1.007**	1.019**
	-3.979	-1.917	-1.758	-3.488	-3.836	-4.025
	[0.0004]	[0.0655]	[0.0896]	[0.0016]	[0.0006]	[0.0004]
DDTA	1.089**	1.286**	1.306**	1.251**	1.396**	1.291**
	-3.193	-2.252	-2.764	-3.978	-4.028	-4.326
	[0.0035]	[0.0324]	[0.0100]	[0.0004]	[0.0004]	[0.0002]
Dmasjid	-0.03065	-0.03663	0.02861	-0.0101	0.04516	-0.004591
	(-0.06900)	(-0.09717)	-0.0802	(-0.03593)	-0.1607	(-0.02128)
	[0.9455]	[0.9233]	[0.9366]	[0.9716]	[0.8735]	[0.9832]
noofsiblings	0.2323**	0.03967				
	-2.156	-0.3669				
	[0.0398]	[0.7164]				
tution	0.5473	0.3762	0.3485	0.6076**	0.5995**	0.5778**
	-1.625	-1.578	-1.278	-2.847	-2.458	-2.803
	[0.1153]	[0.1258]	[0.2116]	[0.0080]	[0.0202]	[0.0088]
ageinclassI	-0.05171	-0.2096	-0.1012	-0.4526**	-0.3948*	-0.5067**
	(-0.2223)	(-0.8960)	(-0.5297)	(-2.696)	(-2.023)	(-3.149)
	[0.8257]	[0.3779]	[0.6005]	[0.0116]	[0.0523]	[0.0037]
Motheredu	0.04283			0.1296**	0.1110**	0.1262**
	-1.146			-4.843	-3.67	-4.949
	[0.2616]			[0.0000]	[0.0010]	[0.0000]
religion	-0.6566	-0.6462*	-0.5863*	-0.303	-0.3866	-0.3612
	(-1.601)	(-1.960)	(-1.789)	(-1.186)	(-1.357)	(-1.579)
	[0.1206]	[0.0600]	[0.0844]	[0.2452]	[0.1852]	[0.1249]
Teachregular	1.532**	1.184**	1.142**	0.8600**	0.8639**	0.8164**
	-3.649	-3.214	-3.891	-3.325	-3.316	-3.42
	[0.0011]	[0.0033]	[0.0006]	[0.0024]	[0.0025]	[0.0018]

oral	-0.2646	0.2547	0.037			
	(-0.8327)	-0.658	-0.1079			
	[0.4121]	[0.5159]	[0.9148]			
hhasset	-0.06104	0.007832	-0.05555	-0.3046*	-0.276	-0.2842*
	(-0.3373)	-0.04516	(-0.2802)	(-1.879)	(-1.573)	(-1.834)
	[0.7384]	[0.9643]	[0.7814]	[0.0704]	[0.1265]	[0.0766]
mother-		0.09633	0.3152*			
canread		-0.5454	-1.895			
		[0.5898]	[0.0685]			
Familysize			0.2111**	0.2595**	0.2038**	0.2247**
			-2.682	-3.444	-2.367	-2.992
			[0.0121]	[0.0018]	[0.0248]	[0.0055]
hw				-0.01968		
				(-0.07755)		
				[0.9387]		
rentown					-0.1812	
					(-0.6491)	
					[0.5214]	
n	42	42	42	43	43	43
Adj. R^2	0.8079	0.7376	0.6776	0.7848	0.7712	0.9017
lnL	-86.39	-73.09	-65.34	-73.18	-76.69	-74.23

t-statistics in parentheses
p-values in brackets
* indicates significance at the 10% level
** indicates significance at the 5% level

NOTES

1. Rates of return on schooling with each additional year of schooling leading to a premium in earnings.
3. Household assets are based on two assets: owning a vehicle and owning a water purifier with a weight of l to the former and 2 to the latter.

8

Public Policy in Higher Education: Is Neoliberal the Way to Go? A Study of the Turkish Experience

Monami Sinha

Introduction

GATS is a multilateral agreement under the WTO which was negotiated at the Uruguay round and came into existence in 1995. According to the GATS document, the objective of GATS is to create a set of rules and regulations and reliable system for trade in services and to promote trade liberalization. GATS relates to all services with some exceptions like publicly provided services and welfare schemes of the government which are provided under non-market conditions. The GATS consists of three parts: i) the general rules and principles, ii) the schedule of commitments which is a list of service sectors that the country commits to giving access to foreign entities and iii) an annexe where for each commitment, limitations are specified. The country specifies in the schedules the sectors they want to commit and the annexe specifies the extent of commitment and limitations. GATS in education aims at deregulating trade in education. India had submitted "offers" in higher education in the Doha round. If the offers are not withdrawn and the Doha round gets completed successfully, the offers will automatically become commitments. The GATS has many dangerous clauses. I will discuss two clauses here.

A general framework of obligations that applies to all member countries of WTO includes two principles of "Most Favoured

Nations (MFN) Treatment" and "National Treatment".

As per Article II, subsection 1 of GATS on "Most Favoured Nations": "Each member shall accord immediately and unconditionally to services and service suppliers of any other member treatment no less favourable than that it accords to like services and service suppliers of any other country," which means there should be no discrimination between the members of the agreement. All member countries have to be treated equally."

As per Article XVII, subsection 1 of GATS on "National Treatment": "Each member shall accord to services and service suppliers of any other member, in respect of all measures affecting the supply of services, treatment no less favourable than that it accords to its own like services and service suppliers," which means once a service provider from a member country enters another member country under specific commitments, it cannot be discriminated from other domestic service providers in the other country. All service providers will have to be treated at par vis-a-vis tax exemptions, land, water subsidies, etc.

Justifications and Counterview: Indian Case

The justifications provided by the government for this decision are as follows. The government, according to a consultation paper on higher education and GATS, prepared by the Ministry of Commerce, wants to relax the assumption that education is a merit good, or a public good. One of the many reasons cited for considering education as a private good is that several countries consider it a private good. According to the document, higher education should not be a public good because the private benefits from higher education far outweigh the positive externalities associated with higher education and thereby far outweighs the public benefits. The document also says that higher education can be made excludable by charging a fee and is not non-rivalrous because after a point, there may be too many students per teacher and further increasing the number of students may diminish consumption of education services by existing students. The document can be found at the Department of Commerce site http:/

/commerce.nic.in/trade/Consultation_paper_on_Education_GATS.pdf. I challenge some of these justifications which I have quoted from the document and show why I think they should be challenged.

"Education is not a public good and the merit good assumption should be relaxed."

Public goods have two characteristics, non-excludability and non-rivalrousness. Non-excludability means that no one can be excluded from the consumption of such a good and non-rivalrousness means that consumption of the said good by one person does not reduce the benefits derived by all other consumers of that good. According to the document, education can easily fall into the category of private goods. The excludability of education can easily be dispensed or done away with, by charging a fee and after a point when a certain student-teacher ratio is met, adding more students diminishes the consumption of education of the existing students, thereby compromising the non-rivalrousness of education. In that sense education is not a public good. The document asserts that if the merit good assumption about education is relaxed then private provision of education is completely justified.

Education can certainly be converted into a private good, it is already being done by all the private institutions which charge a high fee and exclude students who cannot afford it. Do not invest in education and the teacher-student ratio falls, so that every additional student affects the quality of education available for existent students and the good becomes rivalrous, which is already happening in the public institutions in our country. The relaxation of the merit good assumption however goes against the basic tenets of economics. Externalities arise when a person or people or a firm might be directly affected by the actions of other agents in the economy that is there might be external effects of the actions of economic agents. Externalities might be positive or negative. It is widely accepted that education has huge positive externalities which are neither excludable nor rivalrous. Studies have shown that an educated population is a happier, healthier population. The entire economy functions on Human Capital. Human capital is the stock of knowledge, habits, social and personality attributes, including creativity, embodied in the ability to perform labour so as to produce economic value. Adam Smith said the following about Human Capital:

> of the acquired and useful abilities of all the inhabitants or members of the society. The acquisition of such talents, by the maintenance of the acquirer during his education, study, or apprenticeship, always costs a real expense, which is a capital fixed and realized, as it were, in his person. Those talents, as they make a part of his fortune, so do they likewise that of the society to which he belongs.

The essential way to build Human Capital is through education. Therefore, education is most definitely a merit good and relaxing the assumption is plain ridiculous.

The government has to ensure efficient, socially optimal consumption of the merit good. Let us take the example of a good like polio vaccination. An individual will consume quantities taking cost and personal benefit into account, however the government aims for a polio-free population and the socially optimal quantity might be more than individual demand. Similarly when an individual consumer demands education, she only takes into account her own benefits vis-a-vis costs. Her choice does not account for the positive externalities which will arise out of her consumption of education. Therefore a good like education cannot be chosen in the correct quantity in the traditional liberal framework. Interference in consumer preferences is required since education will not be demanded in a socially optimal amount and typically the quantity demanded will be less than the socially optimal quantity. This will lead to "market failure", i.e. the presence of these "externalities" which the market will not account for. Therefore the government has to intervene for efficient provision of education. Intervention to encourage consumption requires the government to subsidize education which is exactly what the GATS agreement will prevent the government from doing through its various provisions and clauses.

"Public spending on higher education is justified on the

grounds that it generates positive externalities since it is a merit good. Equally, there is an argument that public spending on higher education should be discouraged since private benefits far outweigh social benefits. Hence, private funding of higher education is not only more efficient but more equitable."

The document argues that subsidization of higher education only benefits the rich and private provision will be a more equitable option. This assertion is absolutely in contravention with what study after study has proved. Right from individual benefits like better social outcome, higher economic status, and greater life expectancy to social benefits like a higher voting percentage, a more informed citizen, the betterment of the entire economy with the presence of skilled workers, a happier population, the social benefits are huge. The public benefits of higher education are present all around; the entire economy is driven by skill and education. Most of our managers, CEOs, ministers, bureaucrats, entrepreneurs, doctors and teachers are people who have been trained in the public education system and have given back manifold to society. Even educated homemakers play a pivotal role by rearing the next generation, guiding them and helping them in career choices. In general, educated parents are better placed to raise and guide children and help them with their studies. The very ministers who are designing this GATS debacle have most likely been educated in the public education system. Therefore the claim that private benefits outweigh public benefits is an atrocious claim.

An interesting point is that the exact issue has been raised by the Government of Turkey to sign GATS. The language, curiously enough, is the same: "Discussions forming a basis for transformation at higher education level, and the emphasis that the higher education is a "semi-public" service which has a higher private return than societal return have been the justifications for the decline of public funding reserved for higher education" (Aslan, G., Kuçuker, E. and Adıgüzel, E. (2012)).

The justifications are so similar, that you would think it comes from some common source, from some higher authority which means that the sovereign decision-making of our country is being compromised.

"Higher education has low price elasticity; cost recovery through higher fees will not reduce enrolments."

Low price elasticity of demand means a demand which does not vary too much with changes in price. This assertion is true in the short run, especially for a country like India, where middle class and poor parents go to the extent of selling property to educate their children. However charging high fees and non-subsidized education will exclude the poor students from accessing higher education. Several studies have shown that demand for higher education might not be insulated from higher fees in the long run. Craig Gallet (2007) surveyed 60 studies on income elasticity of demand for education and found that for tuition elasticities, short run estimates are more inelastic than long run estimates, which means that we can expect to see a decrease in enrolment in the long run.

Laura Zimmerman (2012) tries to understand gender discrimination in the intra-household allocation of education expenditures and finds evidence of discrimination against girls. Lancaster, Maitra and Ray (2008) study the presence of gender bias in household expenditure patterns and find significant gender bias in education. They find that this gender bias is stronger in economically backward regions of the country.

Based on these studies we can safely conclude that contrary to what the consultation paper on GATS asserts, more costly higher education will adversely affect enrolment, particularly of students from lower socio-economic backgrounds and girls. And it is obvious isn't it? If a poor household is faced with high costs of education, will they not withdraw their children from college, or if, given the high cost of education and resources of a household, the household is faced with a choice of educating either the girl or the boy, who do you think they will choose to send for higher education?

"As the recent discussion in the context of reservations in higher education institutions has shown, raising the seats in institutions of higher learning by about 50% would require about Rs. 20-25000 crores. Since this excessive amount cannot be provided by the public exchequer at one go, "NIEPA has recommended that institutions of higher education should make efforts to raise their own resources by raising the fee levels, encouraging private donations and by generating revenues through consultancy and other activities."

We have already observed funds being cut in education this last year. UGC's move to dispense with the Non-NET scholarships is a move to cut funding in higher education. It led to the occupy UGC movement. Similarly, the Indian Institutes of Technology (IITs) can apply for government money subject to the following condition—the research has to have "clearly defined outcome" and 25% of the expenses have to be borne by an industry partner. A clearly defined outcome means, the result of research should be market-oriented and should have relevance for industry and manufacturing, which means that fundamental research is out, research for the sake of scholarship and knowledge will not be funded and only applied research and research that benefits industry will be allowed. Public-funded laboratories have received a directive from the Ministry of Science and Technology to seek funding support from private entities. The Council of Scientific and Industrial Research (CSIR) conducts major scientific and technological research in India. Cutting funds in scientific research will be detrimental to the technological growth and know-how of the country.

The Union Budget for 2015-16 has reduced funds for higher education by Rs. 3,900 crores in its revised budget estimates for the financial year 2014-15. The plan allocation has been cut from Rs. 16,900 crores to 13,000 crores. The government has also revised allocation for the Rashtriya Uchchatar Shiksha Abhiyan (RUSA)—which is a Centrally Sponsored Scheme (CSS), launched in 2013 that aims at providing strategic funding to eligible state higher educational institutions—to Rs. 397 crores as against Rs. 2,200 crores in the original budget.

So basically the Ministry of Commerce is claiming that they

just do not have enough money to fund higher education. However, let us look at the other picture: This year's budget write-off in customs duty on gold, diamonds and jewellery is Rs. 75,592 crore. In the first year of the Modi government, the corporate tax write-off was Rs. 62,399 crores and as P. Sainath (2015) says, "it means on income tax alone, the corporate world in 2014-15 received write-offs of Rs. 171 crores every 24 hours or over seven crore every 60 minutes. Add to that the Rs. 1.84 lakh-crores in excise duty waived and Rs 3.01 lakh-crores knocked off in customs duty."

So it does not seem as if the government is short of funds at all. It is a matter of priorities where the interest of the people is being sacrificed at the altar of corporate profits.

By signing GATS, education will become a tradable service. Public institutions will be forced to go commercial and operate for profit. Once public funding is withdrawn, students from a lower socio-economic background, girls, will be excluded from the higher education system. Reservations will have to be withdrawn. Even the few students, who could dream of breaking out of the marginalized social strata they were born into, can dream no more. Not only poor students, even students from the middle socio-economic class will be able to afford the quality of education we, the previous generations got at the public universities of this country.

GATS in Higher Education: Terms and Conditions

The full form of GATS is General Agreement on Trade in Services. It is a set of multilateral rules concerning trade in services. The GATS was negotiated in the Uruguay round and came into effect in 1995. GATS is under the aegis of the WTO. The GATS consists of three parts: (i) The framework of general principles and rules. (ii) National Schedules which is a list of the country's specific commitments on the extent on access to their domestic market by foreign providers. (iii) Annexes which specify limitations for each sector.

According to GATS, there are four modes of supply of the traded service. The first is the cross-border supply where the service crosses the border and the consumer does not have to cross the border. Distance learning, e-learning and virtual universities come under this mode. The second mode is the consumption of the service abroad and this involves the consumer crossing borders. For example, students who go abroad to study. The third mode is commercial presence, i.e. the service provider sets up shop in another country. The commercial facilities established by the service provider, render services, in this case education. This mode includes franchising, a local branch, an affiliated campus, etc. The fourth mode is the presence of natural persons, teachers and facilitators travelling to another country to provide education. In this mode professors, teachers and researchers can travel abroad for teaching assignments.

GATS in higher education pertains to post-secondary technical education, vocational services and other higher education services leading to university degrees.

Four unconditional obligation clauses exist under GATS. (i) The most favoured nation clause (ii) transparencies (iii) dispute settlement (iv) monopolies.

The Most Favoured Nation (MFN) clause requires the country to treat all its trading partners equally. For instance, if a country allows a service provider from a particular country to set up a campus to provide education services, then the country will have to allow service providers from all WTO member countries to set up a campus. Basically equal opportunities for commercial ventures in education have to be provided to all WT members, without favouring any nation over another. This clause may apply even if the country has made no specific commitment to provide foreign access to their market.

The transparency clause requires signatories to act in good faith, maintain transparent relations with other WTO members and the secretariat. Accurate trade-related information and access to information is the basic principle of this clause. All regulations and measures within the scope of GATS have to be published and communicated. This clause requires member countries to publish all measures undertaken by the country which might have an effect on the GATS agreement or on the trade in the services to which the country is a signatory. If publication is not possible, such information will be made publicly available. The members are also legally bound to inform the Council for Trade in services about the introduction of any new laws or change in existing laws which significantly affect trade in the services which the country has committed. The member countries also have to respond promptly to all information requests by any other member.

The Dispute Settlement clause specifies a series of consultations to settle disputes and there are ways to settle "violation claims", enforce discipline and compliance through dispute settlement procedures.

The "Monopolies" clause requires member nations to ensure that certain suppliers are not given preference and that the suppliers within the nation do not violate the Most Favoured Nation clause and do not enjoy monopoly position.

There are a number of conditional agreements like market access and national treatment. Market access means the extent to which the foreign provider can access the market of the member country. The member countries decide on the market access for the committed sector.

National treatment requires equal treatment for domestic and foreign providers. Once a country has committed a service, in this case education and allowed foreign providers of education into their borders, then all providers have to be treated equally, there can be no discrimination between foreign and domestic providers.

There are other obligations if you are a GATS signatory like Progressive liberalization and bottom up and top down approach. Progressive liberalization means that with each round of negotiations, the sector has to be further liberalized, trade restrictions have to be removed and further market access has to be given. The bottom up and top down approach means that though each country decides on the extent of commitment in each sector, there will always be a pressure from the top to increase the commitments and remove trade barriers.

Critical Analysis of the GATS Agreement

Many concerns have been raised regarding the above clauses,

especially the "National Treatment" clause. Though GATS says that publicly provided services are exempted from this clause, but there is ambiguity. For instance, a government college which collects a nominal fee from the students will be considered a private college. The fact that the nominal fee that is collected, goes back into the student's welfare fund and is used for the students, and that the funding for the college comes primarily from the government will not be taken into consideration. Once the college is viewed as private, the funding that the college gets from the government will be viewed as discriminatory, and the government will have to provide all colleges, private or public with the same funds, facilities, support or withdraw support from the Government College. Since most of publicly provided higher education in India is not provided as a pure public good, this clause can lead to treating all public institutions as private and scrapping of all subsidies scholarships and funding. The national treatment clause requires all foreign players to be treated at par with domestic institutions. Though the agreement says that it applies to all educational services except those "services provided in the exercise of governmental authority". This clause is ambiguous because according to GATS, "in exercise of government authority" implies all the educational services which are provided on a non-commercial basis and are "not in competition" with other service providers. What exactly do they mean by non-commercial or not in competition? If, for instance, a public institute of higher education charges a nominal fee the proceeds of which go towards student welfare, will that be considered as commercial? If that is the case then the governmental institutes might not actually be exempt from the "National Treatment" clause which will then require the removal of all subsidies, all funding, and all special facilities for such institutes or provide the same treatment to all players—private, public, foreign or domestic. If the public educational institutes are given those facilities, it could be viewed as discriminatory and violation of the GATS agreement. Also there are quite a few institutions which get substantial funding from the private sector as well as receive government funding and how such institutions will be treated remains a mystery. In all probability, signing the GATS agreement and this clause would essentially lead to rolling back of all subsidies and all funding to public institutes of higher learning and would result in dismantling of the public education system in higher education. Also doesn't the mere existence of public-funded higher education institutes imply that they will be "in competition" with the private/foreign players? Therefore the exemption on the basis of "not in competition" does not make sense, on the contrary a public-funded educational institute, if allowed to exist in its subsidized form will always provide competition for private players and in fact will be preferred over private players by students, because of the substantially lower fees.

The "Most Favoured Nation" clause stipulates that all nations be treated at par, whether the nation is developed, developing or underdeveloped. If the "education market" is opened then it should be opened to the same extent for all nations. This clause will primarily benefit the developed nations and will make it impossible for developing or underdeveloped nations to enter into agreements and mutually beneficial understanding and cooperation.

The "Transparency" clause requires institutions to report on every bit of policy making, every file, every bureaucratic decision that the institutions make. This might be a way to determine what the government intends to do in subsequent rounds of negotiations and whether these decisions are being taken in favour of further trade liberalization. Also transparency might require the government to finalize decisions only after prior consultation with WTO and foreign players completely compromising on sovereign decision-making powers. The WTO in effect wants to have a say in the government legislation-making process and also formulate legislation for their own benefit and for furthering of their own trade interests.

Though GATS seems like a voluntary agreement where the countries decide which sector to commit and to what extent to commit though preparation of national schedules, however the progressive liberalization clause makes the "voluntary" claims of the GATS agreement suspect. The objective of GATS is liberalization of trade in services. One of the justifications cited in favour of GATS in education is that education is a "billion dollar industry". WTO seeks to internationally liberalize trade in education and to perceive education as a service rather than a "merit good" or a "public good". It seeks to dispense or do away with visa restrictions and taxation of foreign educational institutes and minimize accreditation problems that these institutes face in foreign lands with different educational standards and curriculum. This points to the involuntary aspects of the agreement wherein, the state will be forced to provide accreditation to institutes even when they might not be up to the mark, might not adhere to the local educational standards, might be sub-standard or might have a curriculum which is not in sync with the recognized domestic higher education programmes. This might compromise quality assurance. Also once GATS is signed the progressive liberalization clause would require the country to extend GATS to more and more sectors and also expand the extent of liberalization in the existing committed sectors. In every subsequent round of negotiations the countries will be expected to add sectors to the schedules of commitments and also remove restrictions in the existing sectors. Therefore the so-called voluntary nature of the GATS agreement is suspect and the agreement will hamper the sovereign decision-making of the nation.

The Turkey Experience

Turkey signed the GATS agreement in 1995. In Turkey with the higher education draft law, private universities have been established. With this draft law, it became possible for Turkish universities to establish higher education institutions abroad and for foreign universities to start higher education campuses in Turkey. Turkey opened education to the market economy and allowed national and international capital in higher education. There was also a general understanding that now universities needed to get their own funding from different sources and that there would be a decrease in public resources allotted to universities.

Table 1: Annual Distribution of Income Sources of State Universities (%)

Years	*Budget*	*University*	*Student*
1990	79	19	2
1995	69	27	4
2000	57	38	5
2005	57	38	5

Source: YÖK, The Current State of the Turkish Higher Education, Ankara, 2005, p.132.

Since 1980, higher education students have been stipulated by law to contribute towards the cost of education they received. This contribution is known as contribution margin and is a percentage of the cost. We observe from Table 1 that the contribution of students towards the cost of education has been increasing since GATS accession in 1995.

Table 2: Higher Education Budget and MEB Investment Expenditure

Year	*% share of Higher Education Budget in Total Education Budget*	*in GDP*	*in Consolidated Budget*	*% share of MEB Budget in Total Education Budget*	*in Cons. Budget Invts*	*in GDP*
1997	39.5	0.69	3.18	15.01	-	-
2000	31.5	0.63	2.25	19.9	28.35	0.4
2005	35.1	0.8	3.34	8.27	12.13	0.19
2010	33.1	0.85	3.26	6.32	8.06	0.16
2012	32.5	0.89	3.63	6.64	8.09	0.18

Source: *MEB Formal Education Statistics*, 2013.

There has been a consistent decrease in public resources allocated to higher education. The investment budgets of the Turkish Government and the Ministry of Education as a per cent of the total education budget have seen a steady decline from 39.5% in 1997 to 32.5% in 2012. Also the higher education budget as a percentage of GDP has grown from .69% to .89% in the same period, whereas the number of students enrolled in higher education increased by 27 percent. Also the Ministry of Education budget fell in the total education budget. In 1997, the MEB budget in the total education budget was 15.01% in 1997, this decreased to 6.64% in 2012. The trends show that steadily the government was moving out of public-funded higher education. Turkey is very similar to India in the sense that there is very high public demand for education. Hence many private players view it as a profitable business. In Turkey a shrinking number of students have access to public-funded education. The students from a higher socio-economic background have access to private education, while more and more students from the lower socio-economic background are being thrown out of the education system. Some poor students are accessing education through loans, selling property and giving up on basic needs. This is very similar to the situation that prevails in India already, even before accession to GATS. We can see from Table 2, the de-emphasis of the Ministry of Education funding in education. It can be seen that the MEB budget decreased significantly between 1997 and 2012. In this period the number of students enrolled increased, however the state was moving out of higher education.

Table 3: Percentage Increase in No. of Universities and Student Enrolments

Period	*Public Institutions*	*Students*	*Private Institutions*	*Students*
1986 - 1987	27	356,967	1	386
2012-2013	105	2,718,838	72	228,824
% Increase	2.9	6.6	71	591.8

Source: Higher Education Statistics, www.osym.gov.tr

From Table 3 we observe that the number of private universities has been growing at a much faster rate. The increase in the number of universities was 1.9 times, while the number of enrolments increased by 2.6 times, the rate at which the number of public universities are growing, has not been able to keep up with the student enrolments in these universities, thereby putting pressure on infrastructure and compromising on the quality of education.

Table 4: Annual Distribution of Research-Development Expenditures in Turkey (%)

Years	*Public*	*Private Sector*	*Higher Education*
1990	9.8	20.4	69.8
1995	7.4	23.6	69.0
2000	6.2	33.4	60.4
2005	11.6	33.8	54.6
2010	11.4	42.5	46.0

Source: Statistics by the Turkish Statistical Institute (TÜRKSTAT), www. tuik.gov.tr

Universities have been asked to diversify incomes. Decrease in state funding towards research has led to market-oriented, commodity-oriented research. Table 4 shows this trend of decreasing research expenditures over the last decades.

Table 5. State Budget Allocation for Higher Education, by Years

Share of YÖK (%)

Year	*Total of Educational Expenditures*	*In GDP*
1981	24.0	3.1
1982	22.6	3.1
1983	24.9	3.8
1984	25.7	3.7
1985	24.4	3.0
1986	26.3	3.0
1987	25.7	2.9
1988	25.5	2.9
1989	26.2	3.2
1990	22.8	3.9
1991	23.7	4.2
1992	22.9	4.3
1993	22.5	4.1
1994	25.0	3.8
1995	25.1	3.2
1996	26.4	2.6
1997	28.4	3.1
1998	25.4	2.9
1999	22.9	2.8
2000	23.9	2.2
2001	25.2	2.8
2002	25.0	2.5
2003	24.7	2.3
2004	23.2	2.6

YÖK is Turkey's Council for higher education, much like our UGC. If we look at Table 5, we see that the share of YOK in the education budget has more or less remained the same from 1981 to 2004, with minor fluctuations. However the share of YOK in GDP has consistently decreased post-1995, which is the year of accession to GATS.

Public higher education institutions receive funding from the government. However the higher education sector has been suffering since accession to GATS due to reduced funding and limited subsidies. Also individual institutions had discretionary spending powers which are being taken away. Infrastructure spending, spending on building maintenance, funds for modernization, area allotted to these institutions, insufficient internet facilities and research funds have been insufficient and have been systematically decreased over the years. Insufficient funds have also been allocated for staff development programmes and new institutions. This consistent and prolonged lack of funds has actually hindered the process of development of higher education in Turkey. It is like a chronic illness which has gripped Turkey and has led to decreased competitiveness of higher education institutes in Turkey and led to slow adaptation to job market skill requirements. The financial decision-making of institutions have been crippled and they are now dependent on public bodies for intrinsic spending decisions. Therefore we see that Turkish Public Higher Education faces huge challenges post-GATS. Higher education has seen budgetary cuts and rolling back of subsidies. Discretionary spending powers of individual universities have been progressively slashed. The chronic under-funding in higher education over decades has been detrimental to the quality of education. This has also affected the competitiveness of public universities compared with private universities which have funds at their disposal and spend according to their infrastructural needs and evolve according to demographic and job-market needs. The gap between the number of students in the age-group ideal for higher education and the actual enrolments in universities is huge and growing, which means that university education is becoming an elusive dream for a huge percentage of youth and an increasing number of people are being kept out of the university education system due to its unaffordability. Access to higher education has become a challenge. Also because of budget cuts, the universities are understaffed, have falling teacher-student ratios and flailing infrastructure. Also contrary to the claims made by the government, that private and foreign universities will provide interdisciplinarity to programmes, will be more contemporary and integrated into the globalized system of education, with academic programmes different from Turkish traditional programmes and methods of teaching, the private and foreign universities have proven to be the same run-of-the-mill mono-disciplinary and teaching methodologies have not really been much different from the traditional teaching methods. Private universities have not been unique or superior in any sense or adapted to global markets, hence the graduates have the same lack of skills which apparently necessitated the reforms in the education sector and the GATS-ification of it. The Turkish public university system faces authoritarianism and over-regulation by the government and hiring of teachers has become a very difficult process with universities resorting to contract teaching to meet their needs. Contrary to expectations, Turkey "exports" students more than "imports". Turkey sends students and academic stuff to foreign countries, rather than having staff and students come to Turkey (Mizikaci 2005b). Recently, the HRD Minister of India, Smriti Irani said that India wants to attract foreign students to our universities. She said and quoting her: *"The PM now has given an added push through education diplomacy. I am hopeful this educational diplomacy is a part of diplomacy that will take us from strength to strength in the times to come."* The "Education Diplomacy" that the minister is talking about might be the accession to GATS. If we go by the Turkey experience, rather than attracting foreign students to our territory, we might see an increasing number of students and staff leaving the shores. In Turkey fewer students have been coming in and the number of students leaving has increased. The universities in the US and Western Europe are attracting the best students from

Turkey by offering scholarships.

According to the "Educational Expenditure Research" conducted by the Turkish Statistics Institution (TUIC) the burden of educating children is increasing on parents. The state is moving out of higher education and this lack of funding is now being compensated by the people. Just like Indians, the Turkish people value education and higher education and there is a great demand for the same. Increasingly public-funded education is not able to meet the demand. The students have to qualify for highly competitive exams to secure a place in a public university. Students from high and middle income backgrounds go to private teaching institutions to get training for qualifying for these exams and hence have a higher chance of getting through public institutions. With public education not being able to meet the demands of the people, students from poor backgrounds suffer the most by not being able to compete with students from higher socio-economic backgrounds and thereby being kept out of the higher education system, some of those students then go to private institutions with their families forgoing basic needs. Education has become a profitable business at the cost of students and their families. This commercialization has served as an elimination tool for students from non-elite backgrounds.

Research funding has been reduced and the Draft Law for education suggests that public universities should "diversify" their incomes. This means that the state can no longer support them and they have to look for means to support themselves. The means the draft law proposes are primarily an increase in tuition fees and the universities will have to market their services in the commercial market through lifelong learning education centres and other self-financing programmes offered. The other ways for commercialization are university-industry cooperation where research funding comes from the industry which partners in the research, which implies that most research will be industry specific, for the purpose of earning profits for the industry and not for the purpose of research and pursuit of knowledge itself. By 2001, 45 technology zones were created with the purpose of giving a "good" based approach to research, where knowledge is transformed into a commercial good.

Conclusion

The cut in funds post GATS is not just a Turkish phenomenon. The sub-Saharan countries which signed GATS have seen similar decreases in education expenditure. Decline in educational expenditures has also been seen in Latin American countries. Meanwhile the US, Canada and Western Europe have still not made commitments in GATS. Already, India seems to be paving the way for GATS or similar bilateral or multilateral agreements. The funds allotted to the University Grants Commission (UGC) have been reduced by a staggering 55%. The budget for UGC stood at Rs. 9315.45 crores for the year 2015-2016 and has now been brought down to Rs. 4286.94 crores for the year 2016-2017. This cut in funds is much like the funds cut to YOK in Turkey. While presenting the budget the Finance Minister of India announced the setting up of HEFA (Higher Education Financing Agency) with 1000 crores and he claimed an additional 1000 crores will come from private firms. This also seems uncannily similar to what has been happening in Turkey, with Industry-University partnerships in research and higher education. Also the 1000 crores allocation is grossly low. Deepak Nayyar said: "Allocation made for the higher education financing agency, forgive me, is peanuts. If you feed peanuts, you will get monkeys. It is not the answer." (Reported in the *India Today* magazine at https://www.indiatoday.in/pti-feed/story/rs-1000-cr-allocation-for-hefa-is-peanuts-deepak-nayyar-568112-2016-03-04).

We have already observed funds being cut in education this last year. UGC's move to do away with the Non-NET scholarships is a move to cut funding in higher education. It led to the occupy UGC movement. Similarly, the Indian Institutes of Technology (IITs) can apply for government money subject to the following condition—the research has to have a "clearly defined outcome" and 25% of the expenses have to be borne by an industry partner. A clearly defined outcome means, the results of research should be market-oriented and should have relevance for industry and manufacturing, which means that fundamental research is out, research for the sake of scholarship and knowledge will not be funded and only applied research and research that benefits industry will be allowed. Public-funded laboratories have received a directive from the Ministry of Science and Technology to seek funding support from private entities. The Council of Scientific and Industrial Research (CSIR) conducts major scientific and technological research in India. Cutting funds in scientific research will be detrimental to the technological growth and know-how of the country.

All the above developments in higher education policy indicates that India is prepared to give commitments in education to GATS or other bilateral or multilateral agreements. The neoliberalization process of higher education in India has been rolled out emphatically. However in a country like India, this might prove disastrous. More students will be excluded from the higher education system. Expensive education means a vastly uneducated population, India already struggles with illiteracy, with neoliberalization, even those few, who could enter the higher education system in spite of being from a lower socio-economic bacground will no longer be able to enter universities. India should take into account the experiences of other countries, before taking this step. Accession to GATS, multilateral, bilateral trade agreements in higher education which treat education like a commodity, a regular non-merit good for profit, a tradable service, will destroy our public higher education system.

REFERENCES

Aslan, G. (2014). "Neo-Liberal Transformation in Turkish Higher Education System: A New Story of a Turning Point: Draft Proposition on the Higher Education Law". *Journal for Critical Education Policy Studies*, Vol. 12, Issue 2, pp. 255-283.

Aslan, G., Küçüker, E. and Adýgüzel, E. (2012). 'External Education Projects in Turkey' in *Neoliberal Transformation of Education in Turkey. Political and Ideological Analysis of Educational Reforms in the Age of the AKP.*, Kemal Ýnal Güliz Akkaymak (eds.), Springer, pp. 95-107.

Blackmore, J. (2000). 'Hanging onto the Edge: An Australian Case Study of Women, Universities, and Globalization' in *Globalization and Education*, Nelly P. Stromquist and Karen Monkman (eds.), New York.

Buenfil, R.N. (2000). 'Globalization and Educational Policies in Mexico, 1988-1994: A Meeting of the Universal and the Particular' in *Globalization and Education*, Nelly P. Stromquist and Karen Monkman (eds.), New York.

Carnoy, M. (2000). 'Globalization and Educational Reform' in *Globalization and Education*, Nelly P. Stromquist and Karen Monkman (eds.), New York.

Cemell, J. (2002). "Public vs. Private Higher Education: Public Good, Equity, Access. Is Higher Education a Public Good". Paper presented at the First Global Forum on International Quality Assurance, Accreditation and the Recognition of Qualifications in Higher Education, UNESCO, Paris, October 17-18, 2002: 131-136.

Khurana, R.. (2015). "WTO-GATS and the Education Sector in India", *International Research Journal of Social Sciences*, Vol. 4, No. 5.

Cunningham, S. et al. (2000). *The Business of Borderless Education*. Department of Education, Training and Youth Affairs, Canberra, Australia.

Deodhar, Satish Y. (2001). GATS and Educational Services: Issues, India's Response in WTO Negotiations. Working Paper No. WP2001-10-03. Indian Institute of Management, Ahmedabad, Research and Publication Department.

Fasel, Saner and Saner (2003). "Negotiating Trade in Educational Services within the WTO/GATS Context", *Aussenwirtschaft, Jahrgang*, Zurich, n. 59, Vol. II, 275-308.

Gaikwad, B.R. and Solunke, R.S. (2013). "Growth of Higher Education in India", *International Research Journal of Social Science*, Vol. 2, No. 8.

Gallet, Craig (2007). "A Comparative Analysis of the Demand for Higher Education: Results from a Meta-analysis of Elasticities", *Economics Bulletin*, Vol. 9, Issue 7, pp. 1-14.

GOI (2001). Higher Education in India and GATS: An Opportunity, in Preparation for the Ongoing Services Negotiations, Doha. Department of Commerce, Trade Policy Division, Government of India.

Hill, D. (2003). "Global Neo-Liberalism, the Deformation of Education and Resistance", *The Journal for Critical Education Policy Studies*, Vol. 1, No. 1.

Ýnal, K. (2012). 'The Educational Politics of the AKP' in *The Collapse of Public Education in Neoliberal Transformation of Education in Turkey*, Ýnal, K. and Akkaymak. G. (eds.), Palgrave Macmillan, United

States.

Kelsey, J. (2003). Serving Whose Interests? A Guide to NZ Commitments Under the WTO General Agreement on Trade in Services. Action, Research and Education Network of Aotearoa (ARENA).

Khadria, B. (1999). "Offshore Universities, and the Paradox of Factor-endowment and Factor-use in Trade in Services." Paper presented at Policy Perspective Seminar on Internationalization of Higher Education, National Institute of Educational Planning and Administration, New Delhi, November 26-27.

Kolhatkar, M.R. (1999). *Prerequisites for Internationalization of Higher Education*. Paper presented at the Policy Perspective Seminar on Internationalisation of Higher Education, National Institute of Educational Planning and Administration, New Delhi. November 26-27.

Kurul, N. (2012). 'Turkey Under AKP Rule: Neoliberal Interventions into the Public Budget and Educational Finance AKP' in *The Collapse of Public Education in Neoliberal Transformation of Education in Turkey,'* Ýnal, K. and Akkaymak, G. (eds.), Palgrave Macmillan, United States.

Kwiek, M. (2001). "Globalization and Higher Education", *Higher Education in Europe,* Vol. 26, No. 1.

Kurt, L., Martin, J. and Rosemary, M., (2002). "Trade in Educational Services: Trends and Emerging Issues", *World Economy,* Vol. 25, No. 6.

Lancaster, Geoffrey, Maitra, Pushkar and Ray, Ranjan (2008) "Household Expenditure Patterns and Gender Bias: Evidence from Selected Indian States", *Oxford Development Studies,* Vol. 36, Issue 2, pp. 133-157.

Lee, Molly (2000). 'The Impacts of Globalization on Education in Malaysia' in *Globalization and Education,* Nelly P. Stromquist and Karen Monkman (eds.), New York.

Magrath, C.P. (2000). "Globalization and its Effects on Higher Education Beyond the Nation-State" *Higher Education in Europe,* Vol. 25, No. 2.

Mcburnýe, G. (2000). "Pursuing Internationalization as a Means to Advance the Academic Mission of the University: An Australian Case Study." *Higher Education in Europe,* Vol. 25, No. 1.

NIEPA (2001). Trade in Education Service Under WTO Regime: An Indian Response. National Institute of Educational Planning and Administration, New Delhi.

Nigavekar, A.S. (2001). GATS and Higher Education: What is at Stake for India? Paper circulated at a national-level meeting on Trade in Education Services under the WTO Regime, NIEPA, New Delhi.

Powar, K.B. (2003). 'Indian Higher Education in a GATS-Controlled Regime: Looking for a Pathway in the Haze of Uncertainty, Higher Education Policy and Practices' in *Higher Education Policy and Practices*, Amity Foundation for Higher Learning, New Delhi.

Planning Commission, Government of India (2007). Draft Report of Working Group on Higher Education for the XI Plan.

Rikowski, G. (2003). "Schools and the GATS Enigma". *The Journal for Critical Education Policy Studies*, Vol. 1 No. 1.

Sainath, P. (2015). *Corporate Karza Maafi Soars, But Social Spending – New Lows*. https://psainath.org/corporate-karza-maafi-soars-but-social-spending-new-lows/ accessed on October 1, 2017.

WTO (1999). An Introduction to GATS, Geneva (Doc. 1397, October 1999). WTO Secretariat, Trade in Services Division.

WTO (2001). The General Agreement on Trade in Service (GATS): Objectives, Coverage and Disciplines, Geneva (Doc. 4904, April 2001). WTO Secretariat, Trade in Services Division.

WTO (2001). Guidelines for the Scheduling of Specific Commitments Under the General Agreement on Trade in Service, adopted on March 23, 2001 (Doc. S/L/92, March 28, 2001). WTO, Council for Trade in Service.

WTO (1999). The WTO in Brief. Prepared by the WTO Secretariat. Geneva Switzerland. Available from: www.wto.org/english/thewto_e/whatis_e/whatis_e.htm

WTO (n.d): The General Agreement in Trade in Services - objectives, coverage and disciplines. Prepared by the WTO Secretariat . Available from www.wto.org/english/tratop_e/serv_e/gatsqa_e.htm Link accessed on July 1, 2017.

YÖK (2005). *Türk Yükseköðretiminin Bugünkü Durumu*. Ankara: YÖK yayýnlarý.

YÖK (2007). Türkiye'nin Yükseköðretim Stratejisi. Link:http://www.yok.gov.tr/documents/10279/30217/yok_strateji_kitabi/27077070- cb13-4870-aba1-6742db37696b (Eri°im: 10/09/2013).

Zimmermann, Laura (2012). "Reconsidering Gender Bias in Intrahousehold Allocation in India", *The Journal of Development Studies*, Vol. 48, Issue 1, pp. 151-163.

9

A Rethink on Teaching Economics in India

Ankur Bhatnagar

Introduction

Economics as a subject has taken a drubbing in recent years from its own 'tribe' and 'outsiders'. Most of this stems from its inability to solve economic problems that plague the world and/or to suggest means and ways to get out of them that are policy implementable. The lack of adequate warning for the impending 2008 crisis is the most recent cause of ire against economists. The inability of the US Fed to interpret the warning signs, and instead consider them as signs of a booming and healthy housing sector (rather than an asset bubble, which it was) proved disastrous for all economists.

At a more fundamental level, the gulf between academia and policy implementation makes Economics seem arcane and bookish to the average person, exacerbating accusations of economists being 'closed'. This charge has led to economic models to appear like magic, with no clear sight of how to deal with real world problems. The world of mathematical models, complex equations, computational expertise and economic jargon is accused of being removed from real pains inflicted by events like recession, deflation, asset bubble bursts and hyperinflation. This is partly because of the ever changing reality around us—the real world is the lab for Economics and its conditions are never constant. To deal with these ever changing conditions Economics may have to join hands with other subjects- the rise of behavioural Economics is a case in point.

The inexact nature of Economics as a social science is also part of the reason for its 'faults'. This inexactness stems from the fact that there can be no experiments in the subject with clear, cut and dried results. The laboratory for Economics is at best a randomized control group, but it is based on assumptions that may not be true in real life. Moreover, the results for a smaller group may not be scalable for the larger population in general. The link between 'micro' and 'macro' is tenuous at best.

This chapter provides a brief history of how Economics was introduced at school level in India, followed by an overview of the institutional set up that takes Economics further to graduate and levels beyond that. It moves on to list international developments in the field of education with special reference to Economics, more so after the 2008 crisis. Drawing on these developments a few suggestions are derived to make Economics teaching more updated, relevant, and applicable in general and within the Indian context.

History of Economics in the Curriculum in India

In the context of India specifically, Economics is well entrenched as a subject at school, undergraduate and postgraduate level. We begin with a brief overview of its introduction at the school level. The National Curriculum Framework of 2005 under the chairmanship of the legendary Dr. Yashpal sought to introduce social sciences at Class 6 level as a paradigm shift away from the existing system of subjects then. It was felt that existing books of the time had given inadequate importance to marginal groups and women from the social science perspective. Civics was recast as Political Science, while the perspective of marginalized groups was meant to inform all sectors of social sciences. (Yashpal, (2005)). While such initatives look appropriate on paper their implementation was a more difficult task, as it involved state level authorities in the education sector as well as monumental changes in the pedagogy of social sciences.

A Focus Group on Social Sciences was constituted by NCERT to *'act as a reference point for syllabus committees and textbook development committees'*. This group was responsible for replacing the erstwhile environmental studies subject with social sciences from Class 6 onwards. It gave adequate importance to pedagogy of the subject, focusing on discussion of values, and drawing from experience in discussion as well as project work.

The Group was successful in developing syllabi and textbooks for subjects like history and political science, though there was no pure Economics subject as such even then at Class 6 level. The textbooks developed were full of visuals drawn by illustrators to intrigue the young minds, and engage with their own experiences. Project work was also recommended along similar lines to engage with the young mind and help her to understand the textbook concepts in a realistic way. NCERT took pains to make these books available by 2009 on the Internet for wider dissemination. It also promoted discussions with State Boards of Education where NCERT was not followed. While considerable thought went into introduction of social science as a subject in detail at school level, there was no such move at this time at the undergraduate level.

Despite the efforts of NCERT for wide scale adoption of its textbooks, the choice of Economics at Class 11 level poses its own set of issues. At this level there is considerable difference in the topics taught at Classes 11 and 12 across major education boards.

Name of Agency	First Year		Second Year	
	Semester 1	Semester 2	Semester 3	Semester 4
CBSE	Statistics for Economics	Indian Economic Development	Introductory Microeconomics	Introductory Macroeconomics
ICSE	Four modules: (i) Understanding Economics, (ii) Indian economy-challenges, (iii) Money and Banking and (iv) Statistics		Four modules: (i) Microeconomic theory, (ii) National Income, (iii) International Trade adn (iv) Public Finance	
IB	Five Sections: (i) Introduction to economics; (ii) microeconomics; (iii) macroeconomics; (iv) international economics adn (v) development economics			

As we compare 3 major boards (CBSE, ICSE and IB), we note that ICSE offers the most comprehensive range of topics for Economics, encompassing an elementary introduction to the subject and specific streams within Economics relating to development, public finance, national income, money, banking and international trade. It provides 4 modules each in Classes 11 and 12. IB also touches upon some of the modules that ICSE teaches—International trade and development economics. It includes macroeconomics, which subsumes parts of banking, national income and Indian economy (which are part of ICSE), though the scope is considerably narrower than ICSE for these topics. IB teaches a total of 5 sections only. CBSE chooses the broadest possible streams within Economics. Microeconomics, Macroeconomics, Indian Economic Development and Statistics. The last one is not taught on the IB board. This clearly shows a divergence across boards at school level for Economics content. In itself such non-uniformity creates an uneven field for any student who begins her graduate studies in the subject. There has been no effort to bridge these differences, with different schools affiliated to different boards.

The National Knowledge Commission of 2009 was constituted to suggest ways to overhaul the overall higher education system, but it failed to make any significant suggestions as it did not analyse education as a process in depth. Its suggestions to replace the University Grants Commission with the National Knowledge Commission as a regulatory body remains on paper till date. It mooted the idea of greater private sector participation in higher education, which was realized only in 2014.

The Yashpal Committee of 2009 was more systematic, but its ideas were more lofty. It identified several weaknesses of the system correctly, which include 'disciplinary fragmentation and isolation, separation of instruction from exploration, proliferation of single-discipline institutes, erosion of autonomy and democratic spirit of freedom of thought, unattractiveness of careers in education to the talented youth, excessive commercialization, uneven accessibility, poor financing, governance and management, and excessive and inappropriate regulation of colleges and universities, political pressures and control from the outside' (Sunder, 2009). It addressed many problems that plague the teaching of social sciences. Its suggestions for the development of 'liberal arts' colleges still remain on paper. (Dahiya, (2009)) The Committee argued for a more holistic approach to knowledge and changes in undergraduate studies that involve more practical experince. These ideas were ahead of their time, and remain on paper only, in the backdrop of inflation, the need for expansion of infrasructure and limited funds. As a result, undergraduate colleges have stagnated in content and delivery of the subject, with a gradual development of the private sector, especially after 2014.

The lack of coordination between boards at school level and, school and college education has been detrimental to the subject at large. Stagnation in pedagogy and non introduction of newer topics in social sciences (which includes Economics) between school and college level has led to a situation where students who opt for Economics at graduate level are a hybrid group, each with a vastly different set prior knowledge of the subject. This makes the pedagogy at college level even more critical for effective dissemination of knowledge.

The Institutional Set Up for Economics

This section is devoted to a review of the current system of teaching Economics as a subject in India. Economics finds its way into the curriculum formally in Class 9 across most school boards. ICSE has two separate papers on the subject: Economics and Economics applications, while CBSE has a single paper at this level. Students can opt for Economics as a subject in Class 11, as the student chooses her stream (Science, Humanities and Commerce are three common streams) or a selection of subjects to be studied at Class 11 and 12. After Class 12, students are free to choose a graduate degree in Economics which offers a more rigorous treatment of the subject.

It is tough to put a number to the total number of institutions that offer Economics at undergraduate and postgraduate level. According to some social media sites, there are approximately 273 universities/colleges that offer a graduate degree in Economics in India. These include Central, State, Deemed, Islamic and private universities, while colleges are affiliated to any university. Another 231 institutions offer a postgraduate degree, with 165 of them having a UGC affiliation. The lion's share of these institutions is in Delhi and NCR. For a graduate degree with UGC recognition we have only 50 institutions, with the majority of these (39) of these in Delhi itself (in affiliated colleges of Delhi University). An exact number of this kind of data is difficult to collect as new courses are offered almost each year and there are many variants of such a degree. Masters in Development Economics, Quantitative Economics are at par with a basic postgraduate degree in pure Economics which is also called a Masters in Economics. It is sufficient to argue that Economics as subject is fairly well established in quantitative terms at institutional level.

For a qualitative survey of the state of Economics as a subject, note that private universities have the freedom to set their own syllabi for graduate and postgraduate courses, while the recently launched CBCS–Choice Based Credit System strives to create a holistic syllabus across state and central universities that fall under the UGC ambit. It '*provides a paradigm shift in the national education policy seeking to bridge an increasing gap between an undergraduate degree and employability*'. (Instructional template for implementing CBCS). The institutions/universities that adopt the CBCS are allowed to decide upto 30% of the courses content, and the rest is uniform across adopting institutions. The method of instruction at college level in most universities remains lecture delivery. There are provisions for projects within the graduate degree papers, in a manner that allows an assessment. However most of such projects-based papers are optional and do not form the core of the papers to be completed for an Economics degree. Private universities have full freedom to set their own syllabus, but they are a recent development. The high cost of a degree here is a major deterrent to their popularity, especially at the undergraduate level.

The quality of Indian teaching and academic content of Economics needs a clear overhaul at all levels: school and colleges. To illustrate this it should be noted that the NCERT textbook for Class 11 and 12 has not been revised in the last 11 years, despite the subject's rising popularity among future graduates and newer developments in the field. The book today was printed in 2007 and has been in reprint since then with no content revision. Consequently, there is no mention of any recent economic event in the entire Macroeconomics book, except for a theoretical discussion of 1991 reforms, which is bereft of any data to support it despite 28 years of post-reform experience. The books for Microeconomics and Macroeconomics published by NCERT are mathematically dull, lack any real life examples and consequently completely rely on rote learning of concepts, with no application based discussion or evaluation.

The higher levels of education were recast recently. The recognition of the need for a learner-centric model and uniformity across colleges and universities in India, led to introduction of choice-based credit system (CBCS) in all the undergraduate (UG) and postgraduate (PG) courses under the XI Plan of Higher Education by MHRD. As of today most universities have adopted this system. (Hasaan and Parvez, 2015). This new system is still under debate with conflicting views on its achievements and failures. A profilic evaluation of CBCS is due, but there are clear calls for improving the system for better delivery and greater learning focus, rather than evaluation focus.

New International Developments

We attempt to provide a brief overview of some of the new developments across the world that have potential impacts on teaching of Economics, and derived from this a new found relevance of the subject in policymaking and greater respect for the subject along with understanding among the non-Economics trained average person.

Rise of Behavioural Economics: The Nobel Prize for 2017 to Richard Thaler, an expert in the subject of Behavioural Economics has demonstrated the importance of connecting Economics with other subjects. The subject lies at the intersection between Economics, human psychology and neuroscience. It replaces *'self-interested, benefits maximizing, and costs minimizing individuals with stable preferences'* with individuals *'subject to insufficient knowledge, feedback, and processing capability, which often involves uncertainty and* *is affected by the context in which we make decisions'*.(Samson (n.d.)). It questions standard assumptions of rationality of individuals whose behaviour is modelled on Microeconomics routinely. The new subject has found considerable acceptance among policy makers. The Behaviourial Insights team, was set up by the UK government in 2010 to apply its principles to public policy and services.

Call for Changes in the Teaching of Economics: Many movements across the world have surfaced that call for a change in the way Economics is taught. They seek to move away from mathematical modelling in a primary way, and look at such models only to supplement the 'core' foundations of Economics.

Joe Earle, Cahal Moran and Zach Ward-Perkins, all students of Manchester University started a campaign to reform Economics education as they failed to find answers to their questions on the 2008 crisis in their theory books. In response to their perceived inadequacy of existing textbooks, they have authored *The Econocracy,* which they propose is a better way of looking at economic ideas and concepts, allowing a better post-mortem of any crisis. The book argues for the ubiquity of economic principles in everyday life. Each decision, small (to go for a movie or not)or big (which college to choose) can be couched in economic jargon like opportunity costs, and marginal benefits. This makes Economics more a part of daily life than can be imagined in the past. But economists continue to be the high priests of Economics, guarding it with sophisticated jargon and clever mathematical tricks. The book argues that Economics must be taught in simple language so that it is easily understood, rather than being treated like an arcane mix of sophisticated models and hard to understand concepts. They also rue the lack of development of critical thinking among students of Economics. Their survey of 174 Economics modules at 7 Russell Group Universities showed that the bulk of questions used to assess Economics graduates are of multiple choice variety. Such questions are based on rote learning, rather than critical thinking of issues of the economy at hand. Among the core papers in their set only 8% marks were set aside for critical evaluation or independent judgment. When such graduates are entrusted with policy making and analysis of the economy, it is hard to expect any real and effective solutions from them. They are not trained to 'think' or 'analyse' a problem or situation using the tools that Economics has to offer (Chakraborty, 2017).

In another attempt to change the way Economics is taught the RETHINKING ECONOMICS organization was born. It is an international network of academics, professionals and students that seek to take Economics to the classroom and society in more meaningful ways. It relies on events, projects and campaigns that discuss the possible changes in the future of Economics. (Rethinking Economics) They envision Economics as a subject that is:

- Open to other academic subjects (most notable being psychology and sociology), neglected and/or new perspectives and methodologies
- Relevant to the daily situations that an average person faces, within her own role and acting on her responsibilities towards society.
- Inclusive so that persons beyond academia can discuss issues that are often shaped by social participation and economic forces.

Another attempt to salvage Economics has taken the form of the CORE-ECON project (core-econ). It is a self-professed *'open access' platform for anyone who wants to understand the economics of innovation, inequality and environmental sustainability'*. It takes the form of a book that is free for everyone and professes to be relevant to the real world teaching of Economics. Its approach involves contributions from a global community of teachers and researchers, in an interactive way replete with real examples and their analysis. This allows inclusion of recent developments in economic modelling to be used to analyse past events and crises in new ways. Each chapter of the book is replete with real examples that demonstrate the concept; the mathematical modelling is relegated to the end of the exposition. Its themes include history, global economy, inequality, environment, instability and growth, innovation and politics and policy, allowing Economics to go beyond the standard texts. The group has found support among teachers of high school as well. The book allows an introduction to topics like climate change, economics of environment, food security, financial stability and inequality in a simple and effective way which is understood by high school students. The fact that it is free adds to the movement of free dissemination of knowledge.

Free Resources and Massive Online Open Courses (MOOCs). In 2001 MIT started with an Opencouseware project which made all its courses, their content, assignments, readings open to the public for free. By 2007 it had completed the online publication of the entire MIT curriculum, across 1800 courses and 33 academic disciplines. (Our History). This mission has since developed into the Opencurseware Consortium, which includes 250 universities that contribute to free academic resources. The stated aim is to *'advance formal and informal learning through the worldwide sharing and use of free, open, high-quality education materials organized as courses'* (ocw.abu.edu.ng).

In the same direction, the development of Massive Online Open courses is revolutionary as these allow learning for anyone, anytime, anywhere. The term was coined by Stephen Downes and George Siemens in 2008. Their intention was to generate the widest participation using online tools. (A brief history of MOOCs). The first such course was offered by 3 Stanford faculty in 2011; one of them Sebastien Thrun founded Udaicity in 2012 to develop and offer free courses. MIT developed edX platform in the same field. As of now (Shah, 2016) there are 58 million registered MOOC users with Coursera (23 million), edX (10 milion), Xuetang X (6 million), future Learn (5.3 million) and Udacity (4 million) being the top 5 providers. The graph below shows the steady growth in MOOC users since 2012. In terms of subjects buisness and management take the lion's share of 28.3%.

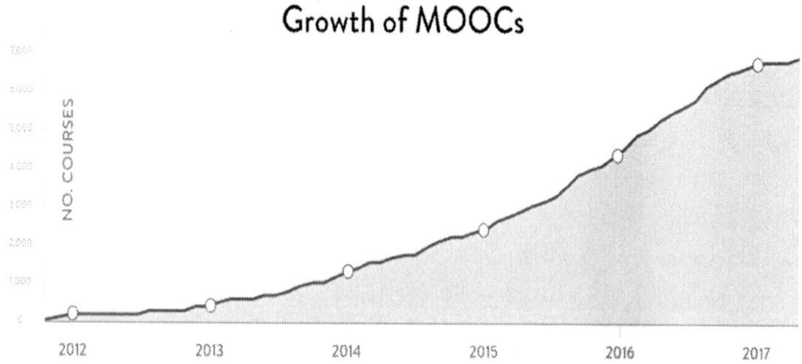

Source CLASS CENTRAL

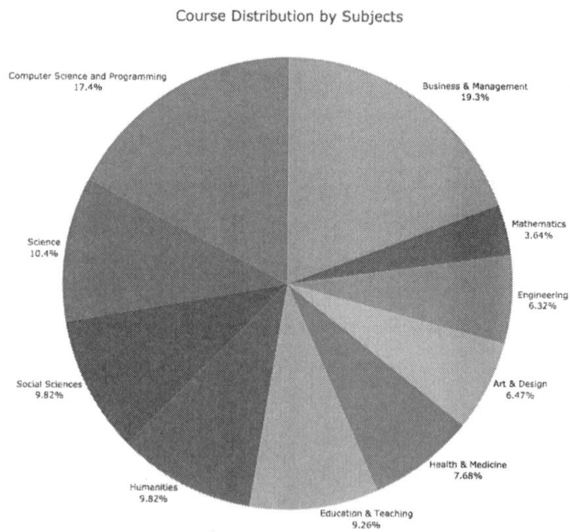

Despite such impressive numbers it is not clear how many users actually finished any course. Since each course is flexible in its timing and learning schedule, and there is no compulsory test to assess the learning outcomes, there are doubts raised on how much 'learning' has actually happened. The fact that dissemination of knowledge is encouraged is undoubtable, but its learning outcomes remain ambiguous.

The launch of Swayyam Portal India has taken this problem in its stride. The new CBCS-Choice Based Credit System in higher education in India mandates that upto 20% of course requirements can be met through online MOOCs that are part of the government's Swayyam (Study Webs of Active-learning for Young Aspiring Minds) portal. This is probably the first university system in the world that gives credits for completion of a MOOC course towards a graduate degree. It has been notified that *'an Institution can only allow up to 20% of the total courses being offered in a particular programme in a semester through the online learning courses provided through the SWAYAM platform'* (Gazette of India, Part III Section 4, 2016). It is also pertinent to note that this Indian portal is hosted by the state completely. It has been developed by the Ministry of Human Resource Development and All India Council for Technical Education (AICTE), in technical collaboration with Microsoft. Such a large scale committement to MOOCs is yet to be duplicated elsewhere in the world by any state. This has implications for teaching of Economics as well as other subjects, and will be discussed later.

The rise in MOOCs is ample evidence of a growing movement towards new ways of sharing knowledge and learning a subject. The fact that the Internet allows this at a large worldwide scale, is only incidental. The 'free' nature of the dissemination of information and knowledge signals newer ways of learning, and the concomitant newer ways of teaching.

Suggestions

We suggest a two-pronged strategy within the existing systems at school and college levels in India. At the base level, there is a need for coordination for content between senior secondary and undergraduate courses, and progressive courses thereon. This coordination is probably required for most subjects, but more so in Economics as it is clearly not a 'science' with exact formulae and iron clad rules. The disillusionment for Economics is probably due to its inexactness as a science. Natural science leads to cut and dried results, unlike Economics which deals with constantly changing conditions. There is no laboratory for Economics to carry out experiments with exact results. This inexactness of Economics as a science explains part of its inability to make predictions that are accurate enough to be avoided through policy interventions at the 'right' time. It also makes it difficult to decide whether Economics is a science at all. This difficulty is evident with some universities offering an Arts/Humanities degree to Economics students, while others prefer to call it a bachelors in science. There is still no worldwide agreement on an Economics degree being a part of Social Sciences or Humanities Departments. (Elliot, (2017))

Recognizing this inexact nature of the subject, there is an urgent need to coordinate course guidelines at school and college levels so that theoretical concepts can be developed gradually and linked with real life at progressive stages of the curriculum. There is room for a smoother transition for prospective graduates from school level economics curriculum to CBCS curriculum, to avoid confusion in the minds of students and repetition that wastes valuable time and resources for educators .The 'real' life demonstration of economic concepts each day calls for greater coordination between school boards and universities in terms of course requirements and depth of topics covered.

The second prong of the suggested strategy is based on the need to overhaul the teaching methods employed and incorporate new pedagogy for the subject after school. We have been unable to find any recent documented study that relates to India specifically. We found only one book—*Issues in Teaching of Economics in Indian Universities* (Oommen, 1987) on this theme, which was itself based on a workshop. There have been lone voices calling for a revamp of teaching specific sections such as Sukhamoy Chakravarty (1986) and Varma (2012), where the latter talks of teaching of Macroeconomics at postgraduate levels only. Most recently a workshop by a private university—Azim Premji University (De and Thomas, 2018) has been conducted on ideas for 'rethinking' teaching of Economics in India. Unfortunately there has been no such endeavour at any state-sponsored university, where the majority of students graduate from. This in itself is a telling commentary on the state of teaching of Economics in India.

Internationally, there has been a constant clamour that seeks to review and suggest changes to make Economics more relevant in the face of not just the 2008 crisis but also in line with changes in society and educational trends. There have been suggestions for Russia by Vymyatnina (2012), Angresano (1994) that include the ' development of a broader reference base in social sciences, ... and development of greater social responsibility among economists'. At another level, studies show the use of newer methods of teaching using social media (YouTube videos is an example), flipped clasroom, experimental markets, and case studies have lead to greater scores. The use of case studies has been shown to qualitatively and quantitatively improve scores. (Ray, 2018). Some other studies have demonstarted that the 'use of YouTube clips would improve students' assimilation of economic concepts by helping them realize how economics is applicable to the real world, enhancing their internalization of those notions, and recognizing the relevance of economic ideas to their lives' (Carrasco-Gallego, 2018). The use of news clippings, news stories from TV and radio are recognized as attention holding for the students, though the search for such stories can take up valuable faculty time. [Porter, (2010)] Thus, there is clear room to incorporate newer ways of teaching in today's digital world such that not only is the learning more experiential but also scoring.

In terms of developing pedagogy, 'Starting Point' is one such effort to develop Economics specific pedagogy (What is Starting Point). It is a project that is funded by the National Science Foundation, under the guidance of Mark Maier of Glendale Community College and Scott Simkins of North Carolina AT &T State University. It seeks to:

- Introduce innovative teaching strategies(from Economics and from other disciplines) to teachers of Economics with a focus on using research-based teaching/learning practices.
- Provide tools that allow integration of the above practices in classrooms. These tools take the form of background information, and ways and examples that illustrate each learning practice/strategy.
- Constant sharing of these strategies among teachers, as

well as discussions of any innovations that a teacher may have used for a particular practice.

The project seeks to develop *"a conceptual space in which communities of educators committed to inquiry and innovation come together to exchange ideas about teaching and learning and use them to meet the challenges of educating students"* (Huber and Hutchings, 2005).

This paper seeks to include the case study method as a pedagogic tool for teaching Economics at all levels. There is a strong case to develop the case study method for Economics as this method involves active learning rather than passive learning. The advantages of active learning have been recorded in quantitative terms well. (Freeman, Eddy, McDonogh, Smith, and Wenderoth, 2014). The study uses 225 reports on exam scores or failure rates for undergraduate STEM courses under, traditional lecture and active learning. It reports that 'average examination scores improved by about 6% in active learning sections, and that students in classes with traditional lecturing were 1.5 times more likely to fail than were students in classes with active learning'.

A pictorial representation for the two methods is shown below. A simple lecture transmits information and knowledge gathered by the teacher directly to the students. A case study discussion can take several routes, with the teacher acting as the facilitator and guide to maintain focus in enquiry, stimulate interactions among all, probe thinking, measure the progress and bring it to a successful closure (Economicsnetwork, 2013).

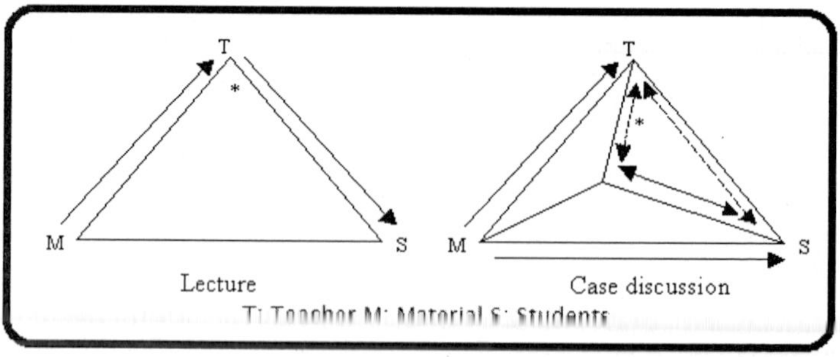

T: Teacher M: Material S: Students

Advantages of the Case Study Method

- It allows multiple assessments of the same problem, paving the way for alternative paradigms as solutions.
- It builds confidence in the participants to deal with complex issues and encourages development of 'action perspective', that goes beyond a mere theoretical solution.
- It is learning-oriented rather than memory-oriented.
- It allows application of learning and knowledge to practice, providing a vital link between theory and its real life application.

Educators also point at several requirements for a case study discussion to be useful. Some of these include a reasonable degree of homogeneity of students' abilities, availability of a pool of case studies, higher degree of collaboration among participants, acceptance of constructive criticism from participants and prior preparation for the discussion by the teacher and the students. (Economicsnetwork)

Within the two-pronged strategy discussed above, the underlying need for a review and overhaul of the content of Economics at all levels is obvious. There is a need to introduce newer content at school level, which is easily relatable to real life. For example, a simple discussion of price discrimination is unrealistic without a discussion of price gouging. The ethical aspects of discrimination/gouging lie at the heart of the debate on desirability and economic efficiency in markets that experience price discrimination of some form. Such aspects need to be discussed to make them clearer to the student, as well as linking the topic with real life welfare aspects of theory.

At the college level there is a more desperate need to allow the transition of students to greater depth of the subject. An understanding of this depth is not possible without a 360 degree view of concepts. This requires the introduction of pluralism in Economics, with adequate focus on different schools of thought. The present curriculum is heavily imbalanced in favour of Keynesian economics for macroeconomics and traditional models (rationality based) for microeconomics.

Such an overhaul of the contents of Economics is not possible without full support of the MHRD. The overhaul of course material requires a long-term and dedicated effort that involves educators and the state as partners. Newer material must take into account and allow for the tools provided by the digital revolution that has swamped the education sector. The use of online resources and methods must be woven into discussions. There is a need for educators to collaborate to develop material and case studies that provide the vital link between theoretical concepts and their real life application. It has been pointed out that that most recommended text is non-Indian for college-level teaching. This is another area that needs a revamp. The need for books that use Indian examples and provide a sound bridge between school and college level learning is imperative. Such tailor made books have the potential to allow smoother transition for students from school to college level, and fill in the blanks for lack of Indian course books on Economics.

Conclusion

The recent attacks on economists for their lack of foresight and forecast, inadequacy of modelling, arcane vocabulary and the inability to speak in the common man's language have unleashed a search for making Economics to be 'seen' as nothing but common sense. This has paved the way for introspection among a few to make Economics more real life and not as esteoric as it seems. This paper follows in these baby steps to investigate how teaching of Economics can contribute towards making it more relevant to an average person.

A brief survey of the worldwide developments in the fields of Economics (in terms of new curriculum in online forms, new pedagogy) and education in general (development of MOOCs) and similar changes within India (SWAYAM and CBCS) has be done. Such an exercise leads us to suggest an overhaul of how Economics is taught in India. These suggestions span newer content and pedagogy for Economics, and a call for institutional coordination between all the institutions responsible for content, dissemination, learning outcomes and evaluation of the subject as it is taught.

It must be acknowledged that Economics is not a science, at best it is an inexact science with one eye on the rear view mirror. All theories propounded are not only based on questionable assumptions like 'rationality', but are tested on past events. A new theory tries to explain the logic/reasoning behind any event which has already- much like a post mortem rather than preventing the event itself. The ever changing nature of situations in the real world do not allow any theory to 'fit' in perfectly with reality. The best case scenario is that the fit is 'reasonable' till a new theory comes along and gives a better fit of theoretical results to reality.

To improve this fit, Economics theorists and thinkers need to collaborate with other disciplines like Psychology, Sociology and Political Science. A simple example is the theory of political cycle, which finds its parallel in the business cycle. The role of Psychology has been talked of frequently in the wake of the rise of Behavioural Economics and its applications in real life. Such applications make the subject seem less academic and closer to reality, with easier understanding for the non-Economics listener as well. This demystification of Economics is one of the most important reasons for teaching of Economics to undergo changes. If the subject is taught in a way that encourages critical thinking instead of encouraging memorization of content, theories and implementation of models, then the gap between economic policy

REFERENCES

Anon (n.d) *A. Brief History of MOOCs.* https://www.mcgill.ca/maut/current-issues/moocs/history, accessed on December 15, 2017.

Anon (n.d) *About CORE.* http://www.core-econ.org/about/,accessed on January 4, 2018.

Anon (n.d) *About the opencourseware Consortium.* http://ocw.abu.edu.ng/about/ocw-consortium/, accessed on December 8, 2017.

Angresano, J. (1994). "The Pedagogy of Transformation: Economics Education in Central and Eastern Europe." *Higher Education in Europe,* https://doi.org/10.1080/0379772940190210.

Carrasco-Gallego, Jose A. (2018). "Introducing Economics to Millenials." *International Review of Economics Education*, September Vol. 26, 19-29.

Chakraborty, A. (2017). *The Econocracy Review.* https://www.theguardian.com/books/2017/feb/09/the-econocracy-review-joe-earle-cahal-moran-zach-ward-perkins accessed on December 12, 2017.

Dahiya, B.S. (2009) "The Yashpal Committee Report: A Review." *Mainstream*, September 12.

De, R. and Thomas, A.M. (2018). "Rethinking Undergraduate Economics Education." *Economic and Political Weekly*, Vol. 53, No. 3.

Elliot, L. (2017). "Heretics Welcome! Economics Needs a New Reformation.". https://www.theguardian.com/business/2017/dec/17/heretics-welcome-economics-needs-a-new-reformation, accessed on December 20, 2017.

Freeman, S., Eddy, S.L., McDonogh, M., Smith, M.K. and Wenderoth, M.P. (2014). "Active Learning Increases Student Performance in STEM" *PNAS*. doi: https://10.1073/pnas.1319030111.

Anon (2016). "Gazette of India, Part III Section 4." https://www.ugc.ac.in/pdfnews/4064990_UGC-(Credit-Framework-for-Online-Learning-Courses-through-SWAYAM)-Regulation,-2016.pdf accessed on Dec 10, 2017.

Hasan, Mohammed and M. Parvez (2015). "CBCS in India: Pros and Cons." *Journal of Educationand Practice*, Vol. 6, No. 25.

Anon (n.d.). "Instructional Template for Implementing CBCS." https://www.ugc.ac.in/pdfnews/4426331_Instructional-Template.pdf, accessed on January 3, 2017.

Anon (2013). "Lectures vs Case Teaching". https://www.economicsnetwork.ac.uk/handbook/casestudies/31 accessed on January 2, 2017.

Oommen, M.A. (1987). *Issues in Teaching of Economics in Indian Universities*, New Delhi: Oxford & IBH Publishing.

Anon (n.d.). *Our History.* Ocw.mit.edu: https://ocw.mit.edu/about/our-history/ accessed on December 9, 2017.

Porter, T.S. (2010). "Media for Microeconomics". *The Journal of Economics Education*, 447. https://doi.org/10.1080/00220480903280178

Ray, M. (2018). "Teaching Economics Using 'Cases'." *International Review of Economics Education*, January, Vol. 27.

Anon (n.d.). *Rethinking Economics,* http://www.rethinkeconomics.org/about/accessed on December 8, 2017.

Samson, A. (n.d). *An Introduction to Behaviourial Economics.* https://www.behavioraleconomics.com/introduction-behavioral-economics/ accessed on December 12, 2017.

Sandbu, M. (2017). *Do We a Need a New Kind of Economics?*. https://www.ft.com/content/331ff894-f876-11e6-bd4e-68d53499ed71 accessed on December 10, 2017.

Shah, D. (2016). *By the Numbers*. https://www.class-central.com/report/mooc-stats-2016/ accessed on December 16, 2017.

Shah, K.K. (2016). "Economics Curriculum", *Economic & Political Weekly*, Vol. 51 (47), No. 4.

Sunder, S. (2009). *YAshpal Committe Report on Higher Education: A Review*. http://faculty.som.yale.edu/shyamsunder/Research/India/Presentations%20and%20Working%20Papers/Review-Yash-Pal-Report-Higher%20Education26Jun2009.pdf accessed on December 12, 2017.

Anon (n.d.). *The Pedagogy of Case Studies*. http://economicsnetwork.ac.uk/handbook/casestudies/12 accessed on December 8, 2017.

Thomas, A.M. (2016). "(Un)learning Economics", *Teacher Plus*, Vol 14, No. 5.

Varma, G.V. (2012). "Some Thoughts on Macroeconomic Curriculum in India", *Economic & Political Weekly*, Vol. 47, No. 3.

Vymyatnina, Y. (2012). "Suggested Changes in Economics Education." *International Journal of Pluralism and Economics Education*, Vol. 3, No. 3.

Yashpal (2005). *National Curiculum Framework*. 2005. http://www.ncert.nic.in/rightside/links/pdf/framework/english/nf2005.pdf accessed on December 10, 2016.

10

Mainstreaming Gender in Transportation: Revisiting the Public-Private Dichotomy

Neelu Anita Tigga

Introduction

Transport can make a big difference in increasing women's productivity and promoting gender equality. For, transport enhances functioning, expands opportunities, and increases accessibility to choice of life influencing social justice (Dreze and Sen, 1995). The consideration of gender, therefore, in the transport sector is essential to ensure that transport is equitable, affordable and that it provides access to resources and opportunities required for development. Transport opens earning opportunities, access to education and healthcare services as well as infrastructure necessary for improving the welfare of individuals and households. Moreover, transport provides mobility which itself is a great freedom, for, mobility gives an exhilarating feeling of confidence, of accomplishment, a sense of expanded possibilities, aspirations, personal growth, a sense of empowerment to challenge all constraints imposed. Therefore, it is necessary that gender aspects must be considered when designing and planning for transport infrastructure and services because gender-based inequalities will slow economic growth and poverty reduction advances, especially of developing countries (WBTP, 2010).

Engendering Transportation

Traditionally, considered as a male-dominated sector, both from the employment point of view and for the values which are embedded, traditional transport planning models revealed that the gender aspect has been excluded because of certain misconceptions held by transport sector professionals, such as, gender not being a transport issue but a health, education, energy, water and sanitation issue; gender as a cultural and social issue does not come in the realm of transport to resolve; building of roads, de facto, improves the position of women and offers tremendous opportunities denied; introducing gender into project preparation are administratively cumbersome; and transport projects are assessed using economic cost-benefit analysis where there are no quantifiable benefits which can be identified with respect to women. But such misconceptions overlook the fact that access to all services are by road, either in terms of the provider or the client also, introduction of gender is no more arduous than any other requirements for project preparation and that work has been done concerning the quantification of time savings with respect to women and improved transport efficiencies (ECE/TRANS/2009/7 2008).

It is thus revealed that gender issues in transport are very complex and transport policies need to take into account gender aspects both in transport planning and operations. Considering and tackling gender aspects of transport would not only contribute to more equitable and optimal delivery of services but would also strengthen overall national economic capacity and help create favourable conditions for a more sustainable social development. However, it is interesting to note that transport is hardly mentioned in the Millennium Development Goals (MDGs), either as a cause of or as a potential solution to poverty despite the fact that transport infrastructure and services have a strong influence on employment of vulnerable groups such as women, timely and affordable delivery of basic services such as health, education, water and sanitation. Further, the United Nations Sustainable Development Goals (SDGs), adopted by all the World's

Governments at the UN in 2015 as a guide for global development until the year 2030 though consists of 17 developmental goals but transport is not yet mentioned as a potential solution to poverty or increasing women's productivity and promoting gender equality (UNDP, 2017). Similarly, looking at India's transport sector through a gender lens reveals several differences that need to be addressed.

National Urban Transport Policy - India

In the case of India we find that, overall city level transportation planning started with the framing of the National Urban Transport Policy (NUTP) in 2006. The policy objective was to bring about a more equitable allocation of road space, focusing on people and encouraging greater use of public transport. The plan policy aimed at increasing the share of public transport in cities from 22% to 60% (Planning Commission, 2013). The policy also showed a willingness to promote Non-Motorized Transport (NMT). The central government gave priority to the construction of cycle tracks and pedestrian paths in all cities under the Jawaharlal Nehru National Urban Renewal Mission (JNNURM) funding. The NUTP was revised in 2014. The vision and objective though they remained the same it did address safety for women in public transport. For the safety and security of women and commuters in general, those operating public transit in all cities should deploy only police-verified drivers and conductors in the buses. All bus stations and terminal areas should be fitted with GPS and CCTV cameras and should be connected to a centralized control room for continuous monitoring. Para transit drivers should not be given licenses unless they have police verification. Further, at micro-level, it should be ensured that the street design being adopted in the city has provision for proper lighting of the streets; avoiding dead-ends or dreary, dark spaces (NUTP, 2014; Mahadevia, 2015). Other issues that need attention relate to intensity of transport usage, trip purpose, trip patterns, distance, and frequency of travel and mode of transport. Women-specific needs include transportation, especially of primary products as head-load, access to local markets, inter- and intra-village roads/paths, pedestrian sidewalk use and security and most importantly, clean toilets and restrooms at major and mofussil bus stations (Eapen and Mehta, 2012). However, the steps taken by the government in including gender needs lay too much emphasis on safety rather than incorporating the various gender needs of women.

Interestingly, gender has begun to feature as a recognized issue in transport policy as can be seen in the various recommendations made for incorporating gender concerns in transport in the Gender Earth Summit Preparatory Conference held in Berlin in 2001 and further in the reports of the Executive Committees of the United Nations Economic Commission for Europe which met in Geneva in 2008. The recommendations emphasized the need for full integration of gender perspectives into all transport-related policy-making in all departments at all levels on a regular and proactive basis; revised definitions and understanding of mobility needs aiming to reflect women's levels and responsibilities to enable authorities to design an appropriate transport system with reduced transport burdens and transport expenditures creating equitable access and ensuring women's increased opportunities and participation; Governments were to look into the implications for pricing and safety factors negatively impacting vulnerable sections of society and define appropriate conditions if privatization was an option; governments and relevant agencies to conduct improved transport surveys, including gender relevant research and gender sensitive interviewing, analysing daily realities of female transport users, women's latent demands and their willingness to pay for sharing models at local levels, gender sensitive stakeholder consultation (ECE/TRANS/2009/7 2008; ECE/ TRANS/2009/8 2008; Earth Summit, 2002).

Gender Perspective on Transportation

The realization of mainstreaming gender has made transport policy more responsive to the needs of women and has begun to feature as a recognized issue internationally. Supported by numerous field research, case studies and analysis, has led development organizations, international development banks and the aid community in general to conceptualize new approaches to gender in transport with particular emphasis on links between transport and its contribution to increasing women's productivity and promoting social equity (ECE/TRANS/2009/7 2008). It has been found that transport models have not considered women's specific travel patterns, particularly differences in relation to trip purposes, frequency and distance of travel, mode of transportation used, and mobility constraints to access other services such as health (WBTP, 2010; UNDP, 2016). Several studies done in the United States, Sweden, Germany and other developed countries over the past two decades to determine whether men and women have similar travel patterns has shown that transport is a part of a larger structure of activities and that there are significant differences in the travel pattern of men and women, particularly among those married with children. These studies also revealed that women tend to make more trips than men, they make shorter commute trips, more non-work trips and a more likely to trip chain on the way to and from work (WBTP, 2010). Another UNDP (2016) study on Uganda highlighted the importance of infrastructure development, particularly road infrastructure and the follow-up roadside businesses as critical to eradication of poverty, eradication of hunger, creation of employment opportunities and sustainable livelihood. The study showed that most of the women owned enterprises in Uganda were small, home-based and informal in nature. Road sides were more strategic locations for their businesses for they were more visible, could sell their produce at higher rates than it would be if the produce was sold to the middlemen. Through businesses such as restaurants, women have been able to educate their children, rent houses, connect them to village financial groups and build even bigger and more sustainable businesses. However, women have raised issues of safety at the roadsides and have expressed the need for street lighting, footpaths, drainage, speed limits on roads, policing, bus shelters, emergency phones near bus stops, speed humps, pedestrian crossings, and road safety signs. Other issues include, parking space for delivery vehicles and for the customers who come to transact from such markets, motorcycle and bicycle lanes (UNDP, 2016).

Such studies reveal that traditional transport planning models have not considered women's specific travel patterns. Evidences show that women and men have different trip patterns and mobility constraints, resulting in gender differences in the mode of transport used. These differences stem from differences in the social and economic roles of men and women, with their respective household and caretaking responsibilities. Social factors such as status, residential location and type of livelihood also play a role (WBTP, 2010).

Gender-based division of labour within the family and community constitutes the major differences in the basic mobility needs of women and men. Men's stereotypical role in almost all societies as that of income-earning breadwinner, who leaves the house for work in the morning and comes back in the evening; Women, however, usually perform triple roles as income earners, home-makers, and community-managers. This results in their taking shorter, more frequent and more dispersed trips during the day. Very often they are accompanied with children and elderly, frequently carrying shopping bulky loads (Mahadevia, 2015; WBTP, 2010).

All over the world, whether developed or developing countries, car ownership is associated with success, power and social status. Even in car-owning households, it is often the men who get to drive. A study from Nairobi, Kenya revealed that while 24% of male heads of households used a car, only 9% of women heads did. A similar study made in Belo Horizonte, Brazil, showed 23% of trips to work made by men were made by car, but only 6% of the women's (Peters, 1999).

The most predominant mode of travel for low-income women in developing countries is walking and head loading. Rural women in Africa transport at least three times more ton-kilometres per year than men. For many women, cycles or animal-drawn carriages are the most accessible and affordable mode of transport besides walking. A World Bank study on Dhaka, Bangladesh revealed that 35% of women commuters relied on cycle rickshaws as their sole mode of transport. So, when the government of Bangladesh proposed to ban rickshaws from the streets of Dhaka, they were singling out not only the most environmentally-friendly mode available, but the one transport choice most essential and accessible to women gravely affecting their mobility (Peters, 1999). Further, women's access to vehicles and services is actually often more constrained by socio-cultural conventions than by physical barriers. This is particularly true for bicycles, which provide an alternative for shorter and medium length trips with multiple stops. Unfortunately, it is culturally unacceptable for women in many societies to ride bicycles (Mahadevia, 2015; Peters, 1999).

Women also tend to depend more on mass transit than men, especially women from low-income in developing countries. Unfortunately, the off-peak and peripheral public transit routes on which many women depend for their travel to shopping or social facilities have much less priority than the radical commuter corridors going straight to the city centre. Women's complex household and caretaking responsibilities usually force women to make multiple stops making getting around more costly for women since they have to pay numerous single fare tickets during such a chained trip. Women are also disproportionately affected by the privatization of public transit because bus companies operating under competitive market conditions are not very interested in serving the less lucrative routes and connections on which women depend, so this is where operators are most likely to reduce services, or cut it altogether. If service does remain, it is often at increased fare levels. In many contexts, including India, mass transit is more unreliable, more inconvenient and more inflexible than private vehicles. Personal safety and the avoidance of harassment are major concerns for women public transit users. In predominately Muslim cities such as Dhaka, it is socially difficult for women to share crowded buses with mainly male riders because of the religious dogma of the purdah, or social seclusion of women. Cultural-religious factors thus make women use special women-only services such as women-only buses or women-only passenger wagons in trains. If these services are not available, these women will not travel by public transport, and thus their mobility options are restricted. In Indian cities, constant cultural barriers and safety concerns reduce women's ability to enter the public space (Mahadevia, 2015; Peters, 1999).

Gender analysis needs to be incorporated into all transport planning, so that gender impacts are studied and considered before project implementation and international development institutions are increasingly taking note of the need to better integrate gender concerns into transport projects.

Further, in order to alleviate women's disproportionate transport burden in society, a variety of factors need to be addressed. Among the most important is access to modes of transport, the sitting and routing of facilities and infrastructures, and the timing/frequency of services. Urban projects need to ensure that off-peak hour and multi-chain trips are possible for women. Time and frequency of operation of buses and taxis should be revised and affordable services options explored. Targeted local responses that provide non-commuter or decentralized services to help women access specific destinations such as markets, educational and employment facilities, administration offices and services should be supported. Design improvements should also be added to meet women's specific needs, including lower height of entry steps into public buses or subway cars as well as the installation of handrails and ramps. Again, for women, limited network coverage and poor maintenance may result in long walks to access the main arterial roads, including trunk line and feeder buses. Buses parked on streets and at poorly planned terminals can also impede efficient transfer at terminal facilities. The lack of safe, clean, rest facilities and bathrooms at the roadside and in terminals can make commuting even worse (WBTP, 2010).

Incorporating Gender Analysis in Transport Planning

Insensitivity to gender needs is attributed to various factors such as patriarchal values, socio-cultural practices and prevailing norms. Women were expected to stay at home for they were considered unfit to take up responsibility outside the realm of the family or household. If and when women did engage with labour market or assume a public role, it was over and above fulfilling their role as nurturers, caregivers and managers of the domestic sphere, limiting their participation in productive work. This socially constructed role ascribed to women arises from social-cultural values, ideologies and institutions based on biological differentiation suited to a life of domestic and family responsibilities. Hence, it is gender that ensures the material and ideological subordination of women (Geetha, 2002; Peters, 2001). Her status is made to depend on the biological fact that she is potentially—if not in actual fact at any given time—the bearer of children, whose care at least in infancy, is usually her responsibility (Menon, 2012). This biological determinism perceives women as physically weak and unfit for heavy manual labour confining women within the house or within certain defined spaces. Denial of the opportunity to be mobile and move freely in public space result in creation of two separate spheres—sphere of non-interference "The Private" that of family and household and that of "The Public"—a sphere more justifiably accessible.

"The Private "sphere is understood to be a sphere of intimacy particularly in relations between the sexes (Okin, 1998), devoid of politics (Randal, 1982), immune from dynamics of power (Okin, 1998) and hence presumptively beyond state regulation and control (Arya, 1993; Menon, 1998). On the other hand, "The Public" is the sphere of government and state, a political arena where politics is seen inherently as a process by which members of the community—in the sense of a relatively self-sufficient group of people—decide on maters deemed to be of common, or public concern (Randal, 1982). Hence, the threefold mechanism of control through which gender hierarchy is produced. First, is ideology that men are superior to women and that women are, and should be controlled by men which is reinforced through law and customs and finally the state itself.

Elshtain (1981) has traced how state policies in successive eras have legitimately excluded women from public politics starting from Aristotle's belief that women along with slaves and children possessed only a limited capacity for good and reason so were unfit to participate in politics. Later, contrasting immorality of the public political sphere with the purity of the private insisting that the domestic haven of morality could only be preserved if women were protected from the corrupting world of public politics. Whether politics was viewed as moral or as immoral, an argument was always at hand to support women's confinement to a private world. At the same time, the government cited the privacy of the family as grounds for not interfering with a man's treatment of his wife, even when he beats or rapes her. In doing so, not only has the private-public dichotomy been used to legitimize practices oppressive to women, but it has not necessarily fitted the facts of social life (Elshtain, 1981) as is elaborated by Kate Millett in *Sexual Politics* that family and household are but "power-structured relationships, arrangements whereby one group of persons is controlled by another" (Millett, 2000). Thus, on the one hand women were deprived of public participation, on the other, private as unregulated by law implied that the state could not interfere in matters of family and household even if it was oppressive for women. In doing so, not only has the private-public dichotomy been used to legitimize practices oppressive to women, but it has not necessarily fitted the facts of social life (Elshtain, 1981) as is elaborated by Millet (2000) that family and household are but "power-structured relationships, arrangements whereby one group of persons is controlled by another" (Millett, 2000). Since the family is not immune from this power dynamics there has been a demand made by the women scholars to make "Private is Political"—is to make public in the sense of questioning life forms and values that have been oppressive to women, making them accessible to reflection and revealing their socially constructed character, and "Making Public" in the sense of making these issues subject to legislative and state action.

So, it is found that due to patriarchal attitudes, poor enforcement of law and order, lack of street planning and design and lack of appropriate public transport planning in certain communities, women are not allowed to go out in public to work or in certain cultures women are not permitted to ride bicycles and also, not to sit close to or touch male passengers. In a study of Mumbai, a relatively women-friendly city it was found that the narrative of respectability for women is woven around the urban, young, middle class, educated, able-bodied, Hindu, upper-caste, heterosexual, married or marriageable, and those who are the bearers of all moral and cultural values that define family, community and nation. Women's moving out in public spaces has to appear as purposeful, as in going to work, carrying purchases or children, or moving from one place to another. Women have to be decently dressed for it is often assumed that women invite harassment or rape due to their 'inviting' way of dressing. They are expected to wear markers of respectability such as mangalsutra (a marriage necklace), and controlled body language (Mahadevia, 2015). All these factors and lack of vehicle ownership by women and mass transit being more unreliable, inconvenient and inflexible they are forced to use special women-only services, such as women-only buses or women-only passengers' wagons in trains. However, such women-only initiatives as an option to safe public transit to combat taunting, sexual aggression and harassment are commendable steps taken by the government but are more of protectionist attempts thus, reviving public-private dichotomy. The ladies compartment in local or metro, Air India, the national carrier's announcement of setting apart six seats for women, the women's—only floor in some hotels, the reserved seats in a public bus are such but segregated all female sanctuaries (Fernandes, 2017) promising women comfortable travel, freedom from molestation and harassment. Such private spaces within a public domain are a creative cloning of women-only spaces where women are themselves without any pretence. The reasons given for the value of privacy are: development of intimate personal relations, an essential sphere where one can temporarily shed one's public roles giving the freedom to develop one's mental and creative capacities (Okin, 1998). This it-self gets revealed in reports by women passengers that they did not have to conform to the discourse of respectability attached to women's access to public space. They could talk, laugh and sit without being conscious of the male presence. Clear visibility of transformation is evident whether in their conduct, decorum and even physical looks including attire, to fit their own notions of expressivity. The private space also highlights distinct power dynamics in public transport tilted in favour of women which women protect by not allowing men to travel in it according them unprecedented authority to protest in public place (Tara, 2011).

In the gender and space discourse, the subjected position of women in public space has a lot to do with their minority status and where a space like ladies coach brings them together and provides them a sense of majority, it makes them feel empowered and renders them the capacity to protest vocally, but the same cannot be said about the general compartment (Tara, 2011). Also, claiming a "general" seat is seen not only as appropriating the male space but reservation itself is seen as "partitioning" a scarce public resource, that is, space in public transport, along lines of gender. Moreover women who might be travelling in the general compartment may feel very unwelcome in what has now been unofficially recast as the "men's coach". Thus these "people out of place" invite, participate in or are forced into gendered confrontation, contestations and reaffirmation. Also, there can be an increased risk for women who ride in mixed cars or an increased perception of risk for a woman travelling alone in women-only cars.

Moving Towards Gender-Sensitive Transportation Planning

Gender-sensitive transportation planning requires an acceptance that gender and various aspects of transport including regional/ national road systems, railways, ports and even aviation, should be gender-sensitive. Conscious inclusion of women in training and employment programmes to improve understanding of gender issues and concerns, to allow them to be articulated more appropriately in policies and projects in all transport sectors would benefit not only institutions involved but also create a more balanced work environment. Also, greater participation in decision-making bodies will allow for decisions to be based on the needs of both genders and explicit sensitivity to gender in all policies, regulations and legislative endeavours will create a more gender-sensitive environment (ECE/TRANS/2009/7 2008) instead of segregating women in separate spaces. Further, what is needed is, safety design measures that respond to women's concerns that include good lighting and landscaping at transit stops and along roadways to replace dark empty spaces with active spaces with shops and public presence; greater security personnel presence; employment of female conductors and drivers on mass transit. Some innovative programmes also include request-stops, allowing women to disembark from buses at locations closer to their final destinations during late hours, and public awareness education campaigns on safety to educate both users and drivers about respecting women. There are also security technologies such as surveillance cameras, emergency phones, panic/alarm buttons and uniformed and non-uniformed officers to patrol public buses and stops. An effort was made in this direction with a tragic death of a rape victim when the Nirbhaya Fund a corpus worth Rs. 3000 crore was announced in the Union Budget by the then Finance Minister P. Chidambram towards protecting the dignity and ensuring safety of women in India. But due to its non-utilization the Supreme Court on May 2016 issued a notice to the centre and the state governments questioning the status of a national plan for providing compensation to rape victims and witness protection programmes to prevent harassment and threats to victims seeking justice. The government in its press statement providing clarification on the issue stated that under the Nirbhaya Fund, 18 proposals amounting to Rs. 2,195.97 crores have been received of which 16 proposals amounting to Rs. 2,187.47 crores have been appraised and recommended by the Empowered Committee. Three schemes, 'One Stop Centres', 'Universalization of Women Helpline', and 'Mahila Police Volunteer' were initiated by the Ministry of Women and Child Development from the Nirbhaya

Fund. The One Stop Centres (OSC) so far have 79 operational centres and all the 186 Centres are expected to be operational by July 2017. The common Women Helpline number 181 is operational in 18 states/UTs although funds have been released by the government to 33 states/UTs. The Mahila Police Volunteer Scheme was launched in Karnal on December 14, 2016 and other states are expected to implement the scheme soon. In addition to these, there are other schemes proposed but are still to be implemented. Some such schemes are: Emergency Response Support System (ERSS) which envisages an integrated computer-aided emergency response platform to respond to distress calls and ensure speedy assistance to the distressed persons; the other being, the Ministry of Railways' Integrated Emergency Response Management System. This project which costs Rs. 500 crores has an approval to provide round the clock security to women passengers in 983 railway stations by strengthening Security Control Rooms of railways with 182 security helplines, medical facilities, RPF and police, installation of CCTV cameras. However, it is to be pointed out that most of the schemes are still at the planning stage and yet to take off. It is extremely appalling that after five years, the government is still making excuses for incompetence (Nair, 2017).

Conclusion

The role of the government has been only protectionist, denying women the claim to equality altogether and can also be seen as a throwback in the fight for women's equal access to public transportation. Moreover, the half-hearted measures prove that there is a need for an environment that acknowledges women as equal citizens-with a right to be everywhere, making a strong case for the need for continuous engagement with the gender in transport planning, acknowledging that transportation is crucial for women's empowerment, helping them both to access opportunities and challenge constraints.

REFERENCES

Arya, S. (1993). 'Patriarchy, the State and the Woman Question' in *Women's Participation in Politics*. Kaushik, Shusheela (ed.), New Delhi: Vikas Publishing House Pvt. Ltd.

Chakravarti, U. (2001). 'A Note on Patriarchy' in *Feminist Politics: Struggles and Issues*, Lokneeta, J., Arya, S. and Menon, N. (eds.), Hindi Medium Directorate.

Dreze, J. and Sen, A. (1995). *Economic Development and Social Opportunities*, New Delhi, Oxford University Press.

Eapen, Mridul and Mehta, Aasha Kapur (2012). "Gendering the Twelfth Plan: A Feminist Perspective", *Economic and Political Weekly*, Vol. XLVII, No. 17.

Earth Summit (2002). Gender Perspective for Earth Summit 2002-Energy; Transport; Information for Decision-Making. Berlin, Germany: Published by the Heinrich Böll Foundation and the Ministry of Environment, Nature Conservation and Nuclear Safety. https://www.earthsummit2002 (accessed on May 22, 2018).

UNECE (2008). *The Inland Transport Committee and Gender Issues in Transport: Report to the United Nations Economic Commission for Europe*. Executive Committee on the Implementation of the Priorities of the UNECE Reform for Strengthening Some Activities of the Committee. Seventy-First Session, Geneva.

UNECE (2008). *Review of Gender Issues in Transport*. Report to the United Nations Economic Commission for Europe Executive Committee on the Implementation of the Priorities of the UNECE Reform for Strengthening Some Activities of the Committee. Seventy-First Session, Geneva.

Elshtain, Bethke, J. (1981). *Public Man, Private Woman*, Princeton University Press.

Fernandes, Rebello, J. (2017), *Times of India*, New Delhi, Sunday, January, 22.

Fineman, Albertson, M. (2011). *The Vulnerable Subject: Anchoring Equality in the Human Condition*. New York, Routledge.

French, M. (1994). 'Power/Sex', in *Power Gender: Social Relations in Theory and Practice*, Lorraine, H. Radtke and Henderikus, J. Stam (eds.), New Delhi: Sage Publications.

Geetha, V. (2002). *Gender*. Calcutta: STREE Publications.

Geetha, V. (2007). *Patriarchy*. Calcutta: STREE Publications.

Heywood, A. (1998). *Political Ideologies: An Introduction*, Macmillan Press Ltd.

Mahadevia, D. (2015). *Promoting Low Carbon Transport in India: Gender*

Sensitive Transport Planning for Cities in India. New Delhi: Magnum Custom Publishing.

Menon, N. (1998). 'Rights, Law and Feminist Politics: Rethinking Our Practices' in *In The Name of Justice: Women and Law in Society*, Mukhopadhyay, S. (ed.), New Delhi: Manohar Publications.

Menon, N. (2012). *Seeing Like a Feminist*, Penguin/Oxford.

Millett, K. (2000). *Sexual Politics*, Urbana: University of Illinois.

Nair, S. (2017). On the Eve of Union Budget 2017, What is the Status of the Nirbhaya Fund Announced in the 2013 Budget?. https://yourstory.com/2017/01/union-budget-2017-nirbhaya-fund/ Accessed on June 25, 2017.

Okin, and Moller, S. (1998). 'Gender, the Public, and the Private', in *Feminism and Politics*, Phillips, Anne (ed.), Oxford University Press.

Peters, Deike. (1999). *Gender Issues in Transportation: A Short Introduction*. Presentation Notes for UNEP Regional Workshop "Deals on Wheels: Sustainable Transportation Initiatives in Developing Countries", San Salvador. https://www.itdp.org. (accessed on December 22, 2017).

Peters, Deike. (2001). *Gender and Transport in Less Developed Countries: A Background Paper in Preparation for CSD-9*. Background Paper for the Expert Workshop 'Gender Perspectives for Earth Summit 2002: Energy, Transport, Information for Decision-Making'. Berlin, Germany: Jointly Hosted by the Federal Ministry for the Environment, Nature Protection and Nuclear Safety and the Heinrich Böll Foundation. https://www.geschundkunstges (accessed on May 22, 2018).

Tara, Shelly. (2011). "Private Space in Public Transport: Locating Gender in the Delhi Metro", *Economic and Political Weekly*, Vol. XLVI, No. 51.

Twelfth Five Year Plan (2012-2017). Economic Sectors. 2013. Planning Commission (Government of India), Vol. II, New Delhi: Sage Publications.

United Nations Development Programmes (2017). SDGs in Action. www.undp.org., accessed on December 22, 2017.

Vickey, R. (1982). *Women and Politics*, MacMillan Press Ltd.

List of Contributors

Ankur Bhatnagar is Associate Professor, Department of Economics, Satyawati College, University of Delhi.

Leema Mohan Paliwal is Assistant Professor, Department of Economics, St. Stephen's College, University of Delhi.

Indranil Chowdhury is Assistant Professor, Department of Economics, P.G.D.A.V. College, University of Delhi.

Madhvi Moni K. is Assistant Professor, Department of Economics, Hansraj College, University of Delhi.

Monami Sinha is Assistant Professor, Department of Economics, Kamla Nehru College, University of Delhi.

Neelu Anita Tigga is Assistant Professor, Department of Political Science, Satyawati College, University of Delhi.

Poonam Kalra is Assistant Professor, Department of Economics, St. Stephen's College, University of Delhi.

Pulin B. Nayak retired as a Professor from the Delhi School of Economics.

Simin Akhter Naqvi is Assistant Professor, Department of Economics, Zakir Husain College, University of Delhi.

Surajit Mazumdar is Professor at the Centre for Economic Studies and Planning, Jawaharlal Nehru University.

Virendra Kumar is Assistant Professor, Department of Political Science, Satyawati College, University of Delhi.